Yale Publications in American Studies, 5

David Horne, Editor

Published under the direction of the American Studies Program

"Reverence we render thee, old Orienda!" cried Media, with bared brow, "original of all empires and emperors! . . ."
"Mardi's fatherland!" cried Mohi, "grandsire of the nations,—hail!"

Death's Review, drawing by Elihu Vedder. Vedder's note: "The indignation on the faces of the great army of humanity is for the ignorance in which they remain, during this brief span of conscious existence, of all that lies before and after."

MELVILLE'S ORIENDA

by Dorothee Metlitsky Finkelstein

New Haven and London: Yale University Press, 1961

© 1961 by Yale University.
Set in Baskerville type and
printed in the United States of America by
the Carl Purington Rollins Printing-Office of
the Yale University Press, New Haven, Connecticut.
All rights reserved. This book may not be
reproduced, in whole or in part, in any form
(except by reviewers for the public press),
without written permission from the publishers.

Library of Congress catalog card number: 61–6312

To Ruth

Preface

Although Melville's concern with the Orient has been best known through his use of Polynesia, there is another important side, as shown by his artistic treatment of what, in *Mardi,* he called "old Orienda"—the Near East. The scope and nature of his preoccupation with Egypt, Assyria, Babylonia, Arabia, Turkey, and Palestine are so intrinsic to his work that a full-length inquiry into it has long been needed. My purpose has been to show the depth and extent of Melville's concern with western Asia and to indicate how it affected his work.

By isolating the evidence of this interest in the Near East, it is possible to establish two components in Melville's idea of the Orient. On the one hand there is the existential, unique, and personal experience of the East, which is analyzed by James Baird in *Ishmael,* Baltimore, 1956. On the other there is a conscious, historical awareness, which was a general trend of Melville's age. It is this latter side that I intend to explore.

Melville's reading of the Bible and his religious thought have been thoroughly examined by Nathalia Wright *(Melville's Use of the Bible,* Durham, 1949) and William Braswell *(Melville's Religious Thought,* Durham, 1943). The following investigation is therefore deliberately limited to a consideration of the non-Christian elements in Melville's use of the history, creeds, and mythologies of what his century termed the Bible Lands, loosely described as the Islamic Orient. My aim has been to gather and evaluate material in Melville's reading and writings which because of its specialized "Orientalist" nature has not yet entered the main stream of scholarship, although fragments of it, free floating, have been caught here and there.

The investigation is from two directions. Part I shows that Melville shared in the general preoccupation with the Near East manifest on the American literary scene during the years when he became an author (Chapter 1), as shown by the books he is known to have read or may be assumed to have read on internal and circumstantial evidence (Chapter 2). The influence of the material examined in this part is chronologically traced in his writings.

In Part II, conversely, I have attempted to project the historical background of Melville's sources from his own writings. Chapters 4 and 5 are grouped around historical figures, central to a given area of the Near East, which consistently recur in Melville's works and were equally important to other writers of his age in Europe and America. Chapter 6 moves from the historical explorers, prophets, and conquerors of the Near East and their image in Melville to the characters, images, and symbols of Melville's own creation that suggest Near Eastern origin.

Since the progression of the book is thus from the specific and historical to the general and interpretive, the exploration of Melville's use of Near Eastern material and its sources finally leads to his idea of the Near East as a whole, which comes to a focus during his journey to Turkey, Egypt, and Palestine in 1856–57 and his personal acquaintance with their landscapes and inhabitants. I have, however, avoided repetition of what has been treated so admirably in Howard Horsford's edition of the *Journal of a Visit to Europe and the Levant* (Princeton, 1955), i.e. a discussion of Melville's literary intentions after the trip and the use of the trip in his poetry.

The great debt I owe to an imposing array of distinguished Melville scholars will be readily apparent in the

footnotes. Not so obvious is my special obligation to the
late Stanley T. Williams, Sterling Professor of American
Literature at Yale University. The list of those whose work
on Melville took its first shape as a dissertation directed by
Mr. Williams spans two decades: James Baird, Walter Bezanson, Merrell Davis, Charles Feidelson, Edward Fiess,
Elizabeth Foster, William Gilman, Ethel-Mae Haave, Harrison Hayford, Tyrus Hillway, Henry Pommer, Merton
Sealts, and Nathalia Wright. As the last one to have been
guided to Melville by Mr. Williams, I feel a particular re-
sponsibility to pay tribute to his unique importance in
Melville scholarship. This volume, too, has grown out of
a dissertation, presented to Yale University in 1957.

Throughout the preparation of the book I have been
greatly aided by Norman Holmes Pearson, who directed the
study after Mr. Williams' death. By his advice, criticism,
and encouragement Mr. Pearson, more than anyone else,
has helped the work to its final completion. I am also
grateful to David M. Potter, who first encouraged and assisted me to undertake my work at Yale.

William Coe and Sterling Fellowships from Yale University and generous assistance from the David W. Klau
Foundation enabled me to pursue the research. Publication
was assisted by grants from the Ford Foundation and from
Yale University's Fund for Young Scholars.

I am further indebted to Mrs. Eleanor Melville Metcalf,
Jay Leyda, Charles Feidelson, and Richard Sewall. Frederic
Ives Carpenter and Henry Nash Smith of the University
of California, Berkeley, have read the manuscript and given
me a number of valuable suggestions.

For many courtesies, thanks are due Donald Gallup,
Harry Harrison, and the staff of Yale University Library;
the Houghton Library of Harvard University; the New
York Public Library; and, in Albany, the New York State
Library and the Harmanus Bleecker Library. William Pe-

tersen of the University of California, Berkeley, very kindly
read the book in proof and contributed several improvements.

Two specialists in the Near Eastern field have been good
enough to read the manuscript: Franz Rosenthal of Yale
University, who reviewed the Islamic material, and my
husband J. J. Finkelstein, of the University of California,
Berkeley, who in addition to contributing from his special
province of Assyriology gave me the benefit of his critical
judgment of the entire work.

No attempt has been made to adopt a uniform and exact
transliteration of Arabic names and terms; the forms in
which they appear follow common English usage or the
sources from which they are taken.

The following short citations are used throughout:

Constable: *The Works of Herman Melville,* Standard Edition, 16 vols. ed. Raymond W. Weaver, London, Constable, 1922–24.

Horsford, *Journal: Journal of a Visit to Europe and the Levant, October 11, 1856–May 6, 1857,* ed. Howard C. Horsford, Princeton, 1955.

Letters: *The Letters of Herman Melville,* ed. Merrell R. Davis and William H. Gilman, New Haven, Yale University Press, 1960.

Leyda, *Log:* Jay Leyda, *The Melville Log: A Documentary Life of Herman Melville,* 2 vols. New York, 1951.

Sealts: Merton M. Sealts, Jr., "Melville's Reading, a Check-List of Books Owned and Borrowed," *Harvard Library Bulletin,* 2 (1948), 141–63, 378–92; 3 (1949), 119–30, 268–77, 407–21; 4 (1950), 91–109; 6 (1952), 239–47.

Stanley: Arthur Penrhyn Stanley, *Sinai and Palestine in Connection with Their History,* New York, 1863.

In all other cases the full title is given in the footnotes
whenever a reference is mentioned for the first time.

Contents

Illustrations

PART ONE: *The New Yorker as Orientalist*

"... across the great sea, however desolate & vacant it may look,
lie all Persia & the delicious lands roundabout Damascus."

MELVILLE TO SOPHIA HAWTHORNE

1. Introduction

In 1856–57 Herman Melville traveled to Europe and the eastern Mediterranean, visiting Greece, Turkey, Egypt, and Palestine. From the literary point of view the journey was an end, not a beginning: Melville was "utterly used up," as he said, when he traveled in the Near East, and in the final analysis the experience failed to stir his imagination at its profoundest beyond the entries in the *Journal of a Visit to Europe and the Levant.*

The most important artistic fruit of this Near Eastern journey was *Clarel,* "a poem and pilgrimage in the Holy Land," although in its portrayal of Near Eastern scenes as a setting for non-Christian spiritual experience *Clarel* lacks the stirring vision of the *Journal,* which transformed the mosque into an archetypal tent and the pyramids into the fortress of an archetypal deity.

The meaning of *Clarel* is focused on those dismal and monotonous deserts of Christian faith and doubt among which Melville wandered long before he set eyes on the hillocks of sand in Egypt and the bitter waters of the Dead Sea. In its essence his journey only provided the physical shock of a long-familiar and recognized spiritual reality: "On way to Bethlehem saw Jerusalem from distance—unless knew it, could not have recognized it—looked exactly like arid rocks."[1]

In spite of the restoring effect on his health, the journey to the Mediterranean and the Bible Lands did not influence Melville's idea of man and God. Yet it served as a necessary,

1. Horsford, *Journal,* p. 139.

concrete affirmation of his inner vision and gave the authority of actuality to a preoccupation with the origins and
destiny of mankind which united Melville with his contemporaries and which he had adapted to his own artistic
purposes from his earliest writings. It gave him a first-hand
knowledge of the original tools he had used for years to
hew out his oceanic image of total human reality: "Brook
Kedron—two branches—St Saba—zig-zag along Kedron,
sepulchral ravine, smoked as by fire, caves & cells—immense
depth—all rock—enigma of the depth— . . ."[2] The *Journal*
is the record of a total vision in which the contours of outer
and inner reality merge and unite.

The concept of the Orient has a unique place in this
vision. The *Journal* crystallizes what is apparent in all of
Melville's works: his awareness of the Orient is made up of
two components, which roughly separate themselves into
two distinct patterns. One complex is formed by the images
that evoke a state of primeval innocence and are usually associated with Polynesia, another by those with historical
connotations grouped around the Near East. The distinction between the two elements is best illustrated in an entry
of December 26, 1856, when Melville bade farewell to the
isles of Greece and was steaming to Egypt and the Arabs:
"Contrast between the Greek isles & those of the Polynesian
archipelago. The former have lost their virginity. The latter
are fresh as at their first creation."[3]

Melville's literary discovery of Polynesia, which launched
him as an author, has been analyzed as "existential primi-
tivism," a mode of feeling about the Orient which springs
from a sense of cultural failure in Western man. In this
view Melville's idea of Polynesia as a primitivist paradise
characterizes the entire range of his Orientalism, which, by

2. Ibid., p. 138.
3. Ibid., p. 111. Cf. "The Archipelago," *Collected Poems of Herman Melville,* ed. Howard P. Vincent (Chicago, 1947), p. 249.

definition, is the intensely personal experience of an artistic
sensibility in search of primary sacraments to replace the
loss of traditional Christian symbols.[4] Melville's concept
of Polynesia readily lends itself to an interpretation of this
kind: "J. C. should have appeared in Tahiti," he says in
the *Journal*.[5]

Yet there is another side to his Orientalism that cannot
be encompassed by an evaluation in which "emotive com-
pulsion outweighs every intellectual concern for the Orient."[6] The worn look of the Greek islands as they appeared
to Melville on his trip of 1856–57 expresses the element in
Melville's idea of the East that is bound up with a historical
consciousness. Like Greece, the seat of classical civilization,
Asia, the "original" source of mankind, is weighed down
by layer upon layer of history that have robbed it of its innocence and its power to generate new life. Asia is "sort of
used up—superannuated."[7] Before his Mediterranean journey, this feeling is clearly expressed in *Mardi* (1849): " 'Reverence we render thee, old Orienda!' cried Media, with
bared brow, 'original of all empires and emperors! . . . '
'Mardi's fatherland!' cried Mohi, 'grandsire of the nations,
—hail!' "[8] This consciousness of historical age, unlike the
freshness of "primeval" experience, is a cultural phenomenon of Melville's time.

Melville's account of Polynesia, moreover, was an intensely personal experience that established him as a fore-
runner of later writers on the South Seas. It was regarded as
a unique achievement by his contemporaries. The Near
East, on the other hand, was surrounded by a "halo of ro-

4. James Baird, *Ishmael* (Baltimore, 1956), p. 4.

5. Horsford, *Journal*, p. 263. Cf. *Clarel* (Constable), 2, 232: "Tahiti
should have been the place / For Christ in advent."

6. Baird, pp. 70–71.

7. Horsford, *Journal*, p. 75.

8. *Mardi* (Constable), 2, 270–71.

mance" long before Melville appeared on the literary scene. *Sartain's Magazine,* in a review of *Mardi* in August 1849, combined the two Easts: "We should not be at all surprised to see Polynesia, with its myriad islands and its bewitching climate, becoming to romance what the fabled East has been for more than thirty centuries. Magnetism and steam, the railroad and the newspaper, are fast stripping the East of its solemn mystery. Romance, as well as empire, it seems must travel westward. There is indeed no end to the illusions with which an active fancy may invest that vast Continent of Islands that lies outstretched in the great Pacific Ocean. Such is the feeling which rises spontaneously as we close Mr. Melville's book."

In her psychological studies of the imagination Maud Bodkin has shown that the roots of Western Orientalism are deeply embedded in the unconscious. In the nineteenth century an accumulated store of dreams, an archetypal longing for "a vision unique" was "magnetized" by the very name of the East: "It is such an illusion of the very life of life awaiting one at some point within the unknown that has lured travellers forth to distant lands."[9] Melville's individual search led him to the islands of Polynesia which, a generation later, were sought out for the same reason by Robert Louis Stevenson and Gauguin. But the collective Western dream of "the fabled East" for the most part of the nineteenth century was focused on the Near East, not Oceania, and was profoundly affected by purely intellectual considerations—political, historical, and archaeological.

Throughout Melville's time the attention of the Western world was riveted on the Near East by the "Eastern Question" involving a whole complex of international problems arising from the weakness of the Ottoman Empire and the rivalry of the European powers for the control of Oriental

9. Maud Bodkin, *Archetypal Patterns in Poetry* (New York, 1958), p. 102.

trade routes. His awareness of these problems is clearly apparent in his work.

A systematic pursuit of the age, in which Melville participated, was the study of ancient history and "sacred geography" as a means to clarify the historical problem of Christianity and to establish "the intersympathy of creeds." The return to the "original" source of religion was a general vogue which, on the most obvious level, manifested itself in the continuous stream of Western travelers to the Holy Land and the neighboring countries—a movement which Melville joined at its peak.

Most important for him were the archaeological discoveries. Belzoni's explorations in Egypt, Champollion's decipherment of the hieroglyphs, Layard's sensational excavations in Mesopotamia are all concentrated within the first half of the nineteenth century, the crucial period in Melville's development. They aroused as much general curiosity as have, in the first half of the twentieth century, the tomb of Tutankhamen and the discovery of the Dead Sea Scrolls. Melville was using Babylonian and Assyrian imagery at a time when Layard's *Nineveh and Its Remains* was a bestseller in England.[10]

The intense interest in ancient religions, which centered on Zoroastrianism and Sufism, was also a sign of the times and affected the most prominent writers, including, in America, not only Melville but Emerson and Hawthorne. While the Persian fire-worshipers owed their nineteenth-century prominence to the study of comparative religions, the Sufi mystics were discovered through the Persian poets and were therefore more closely bound up with purely literary activity. It is significant that the first popular English anthology of translations from Persian poets, *The Rose*

10. Layard's *Nineveh* was in close competition with a popular cookbook. See Sir Austen Henry Layard, *Autobiography and Letters* (2 vols. London, 1903), 2, 191.

Garden of Persia, published in 1845, was edited by Louisa
Stuart Costello, a miniature painter who "was one of the
most voluminous and popular writers of her day."[11]

The Near Eastern material that Melville used was drawn
from a reservoir of information provided not only for specialists but for the common reader on both sides of the
Atlantic. Like other writers of his time, Melville often used
it for pure decoration, cultivating allusiveness for its own
sake. Unique as his symbolistic imagination and existential
experience of the past were, he was at one with his culture in
sharing the contemporary taste for "old romance" and the
"picturesque." The "picturesqueness" of the Near East
with its "challenge of contrasts," which he recorded in his
Journal, was a significant attribute in his Orientalism long
before it affected him bodily in the streets of Constantinople and Cairo. It permeated his earliest compositions,
"Fragments from a Writing Desk," which he wrote at the
age of twenty as a fashionable literary exercise.

There was more to the nineteenth-century "illusions"
about the Near East, however, than the romantic and the
picturesque. The age was marked by an awakening historical consciousness that imparted to Western feelings about
the Orient a solid intellectual shape and form. The foremost biblical scholar of the time, the American Edward
Robinson, while discussing Layard's Babylonian discoveries
in the New York *Literary World,* praised the age in which
he was writing for "the awakened activity, coupled with
the enlarged facilities" which had resulted in "our present
exact and full acquaintance with the regions and monuments of Greece and Egypt, of Asia Minor and the Holy
Land."[12] This awakened activity, the gradual resurrection

11. *DNB, 12,* 277. Louisa Costello (1799–1870) was also the author
of *Specimens of the Early Poetry of France,* published in 1835 and
dedicated to Thomas Moore.

12. *Literary World, 4* (March 1849), 242.

of the principal ancient nations of Asia, is woven into the texture of Melville's work in both technique and theme. As a governing principle in his writing, the sense of history, which includes an awareness of ritual and belief, is secondary only to his consciousness of man's tragic destiny in his quest for truth.

The historical sense has been defined as involving "a perception not only of the pastness of the past, but of its presence."[13] Melville's sense of the immediacy of the past was not only a point of view which pervaded his theme but a symbolic method which transmuted archaeological and historical data into a "polysensuum" of timeless human experience. "With all the past and present pouring in [him]," as he put it, his historical awareness compelled him to write not merely with his own generation in his bones but with a feeling that the whole of the history of mankind from its beginnings to nineteenth-century America had a simultaneous existence and composed a simultaneous order. Melville's historical sense, inseparable from his method, distinguishes him as a writer. But the use he made of historical material is limited in scope. This may seem strange in view of our knowledge that Melville "swam through libraries" and in view of the surprisingly large number of historical references in every piece he wrote. Like many of his contemporaries, he liked to parade his learning, but as a writer he was not concerned with the depth, range, or accuracy of the knowledge which he picked up at random. His use of historical material was determined by what was easily available, and by the "hidden significances" that certain data happened to lend to a character or experience which he wanted to convey as an "original" whole.

Both the insistence with which he drew upon whatever knowledge came to him in his diversified reading and the

13. T. S. Eliot, "Tradition and the Individual Talent," in *Selected Essays* (new ed. New York, Harcourt, Brace, 1950), p. 4.

almost obsessive recurrence of certain historical images throughout his works reflect the principle underlying his artistic method—the constant reiteration of basic characters and themes. This insistence limited his scope but served psychological and artistic purposes. Psychologically, it provided a series of typical emblems which reflected the author's personal sensibility. As a literary device, it created a distinctive pattern of allusions which, constantly recurring, outline "the figure in the carpet" of Melville's symbolism.

The allusions to the Near East stand out in this landscape of Melville's imagery. On the historical level they have a double significance. They reflect the historical past but also the progress of the nineteenth-century discovery of the Near Eastern past: the archaeological explorations which rediscovered Egypt and Assyria; the interest in comparative religions and comparative philology which focused attention on ancient religions and literatures; emergence of the Higher Biblical criticism which brought in its wake a study of the Islamic civilizations that dominated the areas of "sacred geography." In Melville's imagery famous contemporary Orientalists—Belzoni, Champollion, Layard, and Sir William Jones, who died a generation before—are as integral a part of the Near Eastern historical landscape as the pyramids, the hieroglyphs, Nineveh, Zoroaster, and the Persian poets. This contemporaneity of Melville's Orientalism in terms of nineteenth-century scholarship lends an added significance to his use of the material. It reveals the state of popular knowledge about the ancient Near East; it provides a guide to Melville's sources of information; it illuminates the links in his series of "linked analogies."

On the other hand, Melville's voyage to the Near East cannot be regarded as an "authentic symbol for the journey *away* from the Occident."[14] At its public level it was a lit-

14. Baird, p. 13.

erary and cultural trend thoroughly of his place and time. In its personal significance for Melville it was not a vehicle of either romantic or primitivist escape. Wandering Ishmael that he was, Melville had an early recognition that "Orienda" was "another disenchanting isle," as he recorded in his *Journal*. It was just another "grand masquerade of mortality."[15] In the final analysis, his faith in America wavered as little as Whitman's: "We Americans are the peculiar, chosen people—the Israel of our time," he says in *White Jacket*.[16] By contrast, the Orient is doomed: "Oh, Orienda! thou wert our East, where first dawned up song and science, with Mardi's primal mornings! But now, how changed! the dawn of light becomes a darkness. . . . Oh, Orienda, in thee 'tis vain to seek our Yillah!"[17] It must be remembered that Melville's experience of Polynesia as depicted in *Typee* never advanced into the realm of the spirit and left him ailing and longing for escape, even while it filled him with the joy of mere existence and intimations of a state of primeval innocence.[18] The Near East, however, with its load of history, oppressed him both in spirit and body. Its very picturesqueness indicated decay; it was the phosphorescence of decomposition. "That old inertness of the East" signified a state of putrefaction which was infinitely worse than the "vile liberty to reverence naught" and the "juvenile" destructiveness of the West.[19] When he saw it in the flesh, Asia, "grandsire of the nations," looked "like those Asiatic lions one sees in menageries—lazy & torpid."[20]

15. Horsford, *Journal*, p. 114.

16. *White Jacket* (Constable), chap. 36, p. 189.

17. *Mardi*, 2, 271–72.

18. See R. W. B. Lewis, "Melville: The Apotheosis of Adam," *The American Adam* (Chicago, 1955), p. 136.

19. *Clarel*, *1*, 282; 2, 240. On the "juvenile" quality of America or Europe as compared to Asia see also Horsford, *Journal*, p. 153; *Clarel*, *1*, 5, 49.

20. Horsford, *Journal*, p. 105.

Melville's Near Eastern journey must, in effect, be considered as an affirmation of his Western heritage which achieved its triumph in his final work, *Billy Budd*. His experience of the physical and spiritual petrifaction of the Holy Land crystallized his personal problem of Christian faith and doubt into a symbolic complex, which dissociated the meaning of Christianity from its petrified traditional origins and incorporated it into the perennial image of the individual human being striving to keep the spirit above the dust. Within the conceptual interplay of Orient and Occident as the ideal and the real, Melville clearly arrived at the conclusion that New Worlds were not to be discovered by a reversion to the primitive or the old:

> Columbus ended earth's romance:
> No New World to mankind remains![21]

In the end, the meaning of existence must be sought within one's own human condition: "And though in your dreams you may hie to the uttermost Orient, yet all the while you abide where you are."[22]

21. *Clarel*, 2, 250.
22. *Mardi*, 2, 57.

2. The Near East on the American Scene, 1810–1850

Melville's contemporaries were well aware "that over against America . . . was Asia."[1] The Orientalism of the Transcendentalists—Emerson, Thoreau, Alcott—was a significant component of their philosophy. What Emerson vaguely called "Asia" was the home of the oldest philosophic truths. In Zoroastrianism, Buddhism, Persian Sufism, and Hinduism, he and the Concordians found what they were seeking—historical evidence to establish an organic link between Christianity and the mystic creeds of the Orient and to confirm the Transcendentalist concept of the unity of the world, man, and God.

The Orientalist tradition established in New England in the first half of the nineteenth century was characteristically American in its eclecticism and the striving for a spiritual synthesis between East and West. Nevertheless it was an integral part of a general Western preoccupation with "the East" that characterized the larger movement of European Romanticism. In their search for historical evidence to vindicate the basic principles of their thought, the Transcendentalists drew on the same sources which, a generation before, had fed the Orientalism of Goethe, Byron, Sir Walter Scott, and Thomas Moore. As early as 1808 the *Monthly Anthology and Boston Review,* a Boston journal edited by Samuel Cooper Thacher, Librarian of Harvard University

1. *Mardi, 1,* 9.

and successor to the father of Ralph Waldo Emerson as editor, published a list of Oriental literature in the Harvard College Library which included the works of the poet Saadi, in the original Persian, and Herbelot's *Bibliothèque Orientale,* described as "a treasure of useful and ornamental knowledge."[2] Other writings recommended to the American youth "who are fond of oriental literature" were the *Asiatick Miscellany* published in Calcutta (1785) by Sir William Jones, the father of Oriental studies in England; the *Ayeen Akbery,* or the Institutes of Akbar, the Mogul emperor of India, translated by Francis Gladwin, who also translated Saadi's *Gulistan;* the *Forms of Herkern,* a Persian stylist, which appeared in an English translation in Calcutta (1781); the *Poems of Ferdosi,* the great epic poet of Persia, author of the Shah Nameh, in the translation of J. Champion (Calcutta, 1785); the *Institutes of Menu,* a book of Indian laws translated by Sir William Jones, which was among the books bequeathed to Emerson by Thoreau; and, above all, the *Works* of Sir William Jones (1746–94), *"vir omni preditus, et omni laude dignus."*[3]

The American Transcendentalists were not interested in the Orient for the Orient's sake as the romantics were. Their Orientalism was not prompted by a desire to escape anything or to lose themselves in the exoticism and glamour of "the gorgeous East." Emerson, in spite of his enthusiasm for the Orient, was proud of his "manly" Western heritage.[4] He believed in the superiority of the West, which he preferred to the mawkish mystery of the East. The Orientalism of the Transcendentalists was strictly functional. They "used" the Orient to demonstrate the truth of their conviction that there was "a kindred principle at the bottom of

2. *Monthly Anthology and Boston Review,* 5 (1808), 85, 87.

3. Ibid., p. 88. Cf. Emerson, *Journals,* ed. E. W. Emerson and W. E. Forbes (10 vols. Boston, 1909–14), *9,* 419, entry for 1862.

4. See F. I. Carpenter, *Emerson and Asia,* Cambridge, Mass., 1930.

all affinities."[5] They clearly read their own ideas into the East, as may be seen from Emerson's interpretation of Saadi's *Gulistan*, or his translations of Persian poetry from the German of the Austrian Orientalist, Hammer-Purgstall, who inspired Goethe.[6]

It was only toward the end of the nineteenth century that the Orientalist tradition at Harvard which had stimulated the young Emerson acquired an escapist, "romantic" quality. In the second half of the century this tradition was centered around an individualistic coterie of aesthetes, artists, and religious philosophers who studied Sanskrit, Buddhism, and Chinese and Japanese poetry and painting in search of private salvation. The "new" Boston Orientalists at the end of the century, Edward S. Morse, Ernest Fenollosa, Percival Lowell, William Sturgis Bigelow, John La Farge, Henry Adams, and other representatives of "New England's Indian Summer" regarded the East as the gate to spiritual fulfillment—an attitude which Melville, like Emerson, had strongly repudiated a generation before: "Oh, Orienda, in thee 'tis vain to seek our Yillah!"[7]

Another criterion which distinguishes the earlier nineteenth-century Orientalism in American literature and thought from the later is the perceptible shift in the concept of Asia or the East. The European concept of the East as primarily denoting the Near East, western Asia, the classic lands of Judaism, Christianity, Islam, and India was at the turn of the century, for geopolitical reasons, superseded by a spiritual orientation toward the Far East, China and Japan. Emerson's Asia was closely related to the European concept. Melville's included his own immediate experience of Oce-

5. *The Journal of Henry D. Thoreau*, ed. B. Torrey and F. H. Allen (Cambridge, Mass., 1949), entry of February 16, 1840, *1*, 120.

6. See J. D. Yohannan, "Emerson's Translations of Persian Poetry from German Sources," *American Literature*, *14* (1943), 407–20.

7. *Mardi*, 2, 271.

ania, but his intellectual preoccupation with the creeds of the ancient Near East was of European origin, like Emerson's. The mysteries of Zoroastrianism and Persian Sufism, which attracted Emerson and Hawthorne and had a profound influence on *Mardi* and *Moby-Dick,* held the attention of European writers throughout the century.

On the other hand, it must be remembered that Melville's Orientalism, unlike Emerson's, was nurtured in New York among a group of metropolitan literati who "were committed from birth, with no prospect of release, to what historians call 'romanticism.' "[8] The mood of this type of Orientalism was expressed by Hawthorne in *The Journal of a Solitary Man:* "I had a strange longing to see the Pyramids. To Persia and Arabia and all the gorgeous East I owed a pilgrimage for the sake of their magic tales."[9] The Orientalism of New England, though it drew on German and English sources, was transmuted into an essentially American product by Transcendentalism, while that of the New Yorkers, Washington Irving, Poe, and minor writers like Curtis and Bayard Taylor, was not only rooted in the European tradition but in its essence continued as a manifestation of a European literary trend.

The letters discussing American life and manners from Mustapha Rub-a-dub Keli Khan, a Tripolitanian prisoner of war "at large" in New York, to Asem Hacchem and Abdallah Eb'n al Rahab in Irving's *Salmagundi* are typical of the kind of social satire in the form of Oriental pseudo-letters which flourished in Europe in the eighteenth century and of which Montesquieu's *Lettres Persanes* (1721) are the standard example. The popularity of this type of orientalizing in America is also attested in "The Egyptian

8. Perry Miller, *The Raven and the Whale* (New York, 1956), p. 27.

9. "Fragments from the Journal of a Solitary Man," *The Complete Writings of Nathaniel Hawthorne* (Boston and New York, 1900), *17,* 295.

Letters," a series of thirty-one which appeared in the New York *Knickerbocker Magazine* from November 1846 to May 1848. This correspondence purported to be addressed by one Abd 'Allah Omar, an Egyptian traveler temporarily resident in New York, to Seyd Ahhmad El Haji, "Chief Secretary of the Ckadee at Cairo," and invariably bore the Arabic date, e.g., "New York, 13th day of the Moon Regeb, Year of the Hegira, 1260."[10] Washington Irving's interest in Islam, conspicuous in such works as *The Conquest of Granada* (1829), *The Alhambra* (1832), and *Mahomet and His Successors* (1849–50), is natural in view of his personal preoccupation with Spain. But his presentation of the material is purely in the romantic tradition. The emphasis on the barbarity of the Christian conquerors as opposed to the heroism and chivalry of the Moors in *The Conquest of Granada* follows the standard example of Scott, and the legends of *The Alhambra* have the familiar features of the *Arabian Nights,* including the magic carpet and the magic horse.[11] Finally, *Mahomet and His Successors* is the picturesque biography of a hero of Arabian romance rather than an adequate account of the founder of Islam.

The same romantic tradition prevails in the Orientalism of Poe, in whom the tendency naturally inclines toward the Arabesque and the Gothic rather than the historical. The Koranic titles of "Al Aaraaf" (the partition separating paradise from hell) and "Israfel" (an archangel who will sound the trumpet at the Resurrection), the two most conspicuously Oriental among Poe's poems, are duly explained in the type of footnotes that are the trade-marks of romantic writers like Robert Southey and Thomas Moore. Among the tales of Poe, "The Thousand-and-Second Tale of Sche-

10. *Knickerbocker, 28* (1846), 391.
11. See "Legend of Prince Ahmed Al Kamel; or the Pilgrim of Love," "Governor Manco and the Soldier," and "Legend of the Two Discreet Statues" in *The Alhambra*.

herazade" is a variation on the introduction to the *Arabian Nights,* with a characteristically gruesome ending in which Scheherazade loses her life.

The travel books of George William Curtis and Bayard Taylor followed a well-beaten European path to the Near East that was pursued and described by many contemporary American travelers. The superficiality of most of these accounts was assailed in Poe's *Broadway Journal,* where it was contrasted with the "superior brilliancy" of Alexander William Kinglake's famous *Eothen, or Traces of Travel brought Home from the East,* the first book to appear in Wiley and Putnam's Library of Choice Reading in 1845, one year after its original publication in London. "Eothen is a reprint of the most brilliant book of travels that has appeared in England since the time of Childe Harold," said the *Broadway Journal.* "It was nine years after his return from the East before his book was published; our travellers begin to publish the day after they leave home, and give us their sketches as they proceed."[12]

The extent to which the Orientalism of Europe dominated American literary taste by the middle of the nineteenth century is exemplified in William Starbuck Mayo's novel *Kaloolah, or Journeyings to Djebil Kumri* (1849). Like Melville's *Mardi,* which was published two months earlier in the same year, this novel depicts the quest for a white maiden among the North African Berbers. It was "the book of the season, having produced a sensation quite as extended as did the works of Mr. Melville," wrote O'Sullivan's *Democratic Review.*[13] In spite of its Oriental setting, the *Review* extolled it as proof of a "national" American literature. The orientalizing tendency was taken for granted as standard literary equipment—an attitude persist-

12. *The Broadway Journal, 1* (1845), 178.
13. *Democratic Review, 25* (1849), 91.

ently reflected in the most popular American magazines of the time.

Beginning with January 1836, the third year of its publication, the *Knickerbocker Magazine,* "America's foremost literary and critical monthly,"[14] carried articles on Near Eastern lands, life, and manners in almost every number. These pieces ranged from random contributions like the "Characteristics of the Mussulman" by the Reverend Walter Colton—"an officer of the United States Navy" who had composed a "Journal of a Cruise in the Levant" which initiated the magazine's coverage of the Near East—to the authoritative articles on Turkish life and literature by "our oriental correspondent," the well-known American Orientalist J. P. Brown, dragoman of the American Legation at Constantinople, which began to appear in the issue of June 1842 and continued as a constant *Knickerbocker* feature until August 1857, the year in which Brown became Consul-General.[15] The *Knickerbocker's* enthusiasm went so far as to devote considerable space in the "Editor's Table" of June 1845 to the receipt of a talisman from Constantinople in the shape of a signet ring, like the Prophet Mohammed's, with the word "Knickerbocker" engraved in its center in Eastern characters, which Brown "translated" "Neek Er Bakr, (the first Persian, the second Turkish, and the latter Arabic)," meaning " 'The Good Virtuous Man' or rather the 'Good Old Bachelor.' "[16]

The vogue of the Oriental tale in the first half of the nineteenth century, of which *Kaloolah* and *Mardi* were the culmination, is illustrated in the number of February 1836. This issue announces the publication by an anonymous American writer of "Mahmound. A Novel. In Two Volumes . . . a romance upon the model of 'Anastasius,' though

14. Miller, p. 6.
15. *Knickerbocker, 8* (1836), 421; *19* (1842), 497 f.; *50* (1857), 107 f.
16. Ibid., *25* (1845), 549.

greatly inferior in talent to that work," Thomas Hope's
Anastasius, or Memoirs of a Greek (1819) being a best-
selling English account of those "ever interesting regions,
once adorned by the Greeks, and now defaced by the
Turks."[17] The *Knickerbocker's* "Literary Notices" of January 1837 discuss another anonymous New York publication of a related type, entitled "Giafar Al Barmeki, A Tale
of the Court of Harun Al Rashid." The accompanying edi-
torial comment is of great interest because it reveals the
kind of Oriental romance, "within the bounds of nature,"
which Melville originally contemplated in *Mardi,* as a common literary practice of the time:

> Madam Rumor . . . has assigned the authorship of the
> hard-named volumes to a professional gentleman of
> this city, who has never left his native country, and
> whose pursuits and duties have left him little leisure
> to prosecute literary enterprises. This may be, and we
> believe is, indeed true; but most readers will find it
> difficult to credit it. . . . They will find scenes of orien-
> tal splendour, and the manners and customs of the
> East, depicted in such faithful colours, as to lead them
> at once to conclude, that none but an eastern traveler,
> possessed of a quick eye and a ready pen, could have
> spread these pictures before them. . . . The main point
> upon which 'Giafar Al Barmeki' turns—the destruc-
> tion of the Barmecides by Haroun Al Raschid—as is
> well known, is a historical fact. Connected with this,
> however, is an underplot, managed with skill, and ren-
> dered highly exciting by an active imagination—
> which, preserving all the attractions of romance, still
> keeps within the bounds of nature—.[18]

17. Ibid., 7, 211. The novel is attributed by Roorbach *(Bibliotheca
Americana)* to Gardiner Spring, Jr.
18. Ibid., 9, 86–87.

The *Knickerbocker's* rival, the *Democratic Review*, which started publication in October 1837, featured a "Hymn of the Fire-Worshippers" in its second issue of January 1838, with a quotation from Goethe's description of ancient Persian fire worship.[19] The fourth issue, of March 1838, carried the first installment of the "Recollections of Eastern Travel" by J. S. Buckingham (1786–1855), the English traveler who was lecturing in the United States at the time. At Baltimore, reported the New York *Arcturus,* Buckingham even appeared in the national costume of a Turk "to assist, as he said, the imagination of his audience."[20] Buckingham's "Recollections" continued to appear in the *Democratic Review* until June 1838 and included a report of his encounter, in Upper Egypt, with the famous "Sheik Ibrahim," who was actually the Arabian traveler John Lewis Burckhardt. A visit to Lady Hester Stanhope in the Lebanon "by an American" was recounted in the issue of May 1838, with long extracts from the account of a similar visit, in 1832, by the French statesman and poet Alphonse de Lamartine.[21] All these articles represent material that was current knowledge at the time and is reflected in various writings on both sides of the Atlantic.

Original American compositions on Near Eastern subjects begin to appear in the *Democratic Review* a few years later. The issue of March 1844 contained a poem, "The Bedouin," by W. S. Mayo, author of *Kaloolah,* who seems to have had a knowledge of Arabic.[22] Another literary Orientalist, the author of "Giafar Al Barmeki," who had attracted the attention of the *Knickerbocker Magazine* in 1837, appears in the *Democratic Review* of January 1845 as

19. *Democratic Review, 1,* 182–83.
20. *Arcturus, 1,* December 1841. This volume was borrowed by Melville from Evert Duyckinck in 1850 (Leyda, *Log,* p. 377).
21. *Democratic Review, 1* (1838), 421–22; 2 (1838), 187–95, 247–59.
22. Ibid., *14,* 289–90. Arabic terms are explained in footnotes.

a contributor of a series of stories entitled "The Sheik of Alexandria and His Slaves," translated from the German of Hauff. "Giaffer Al Barmeki" was still going strong in New York in 1849 when the *American Review* published a poem on the subject.[23]

Whatever the literary and political merit of the *Knickerbocker Magazine,* its Oriental coverage was the most distinctive of all American periodicals. One example is the report in the "Editor's Table" of March 1847 on the "Extraordinary Antiquarian Researches and Discoveries in the East" of Sir Austen Henry Layard, the excavator of Nineveh whose work engaged the attention of Melville. The *Knickerbocker* reprinted Layard's letters from the site of ancient Nineveh to "Mr. Kellogg, an American gentleman, a citizen of Ohio, now travelling on the Continent, who transmits them to his brother, resident at Cincinnati."[24] In October of the following year Duyckinck's *Literary World* included a short notice of "Assyrian Antiquities" in which it reprinted a letter of Layard to the London *Literary Gazette.* This notice was followed up, in the numbers of February 10 and February 17, 1849, with a lengthy reprint from the London *Examiner* in which Layard's discoveries were discussed in connection with the publication of *Nineveh and Its Remains* at the beginning of that year.[25] On March 17, 1849, the *Literary World* published a letter, "The Discoveries at Nineveh," by the famous American Dr. Edward Robinson of Union Theological Seminary, author of *Biblical Researches in Palestine, Mount Sinai and Arabia Petraea* (New York, 1838), a book that "was looked upon, by the few who at that time made a careful study of Palestine,

23. *American Review, 9* (1849), 384.

24. *Knickerbocker, 29* (1847), 267.

25. *Literary World, 2,* 233–34; *4,* 127–30, 153–54. "Layard's Nineveh" is listed by Duyckinck in a manuscript "Authors', Readers' and Publishers' Gazette" (New York Public Library, Duyckinck Papers).

as the turning point in the whole matter of Palestine research."[26] Dr. Robinson's letter was to appear as a preface to the forthcoming American edition of *Nineveh and Its Remains*. The edition was brought out by Wiley and Putnam a few weeks later and discussed in an extensive article by the *Democratic Review* in its issue of April 1849.[27] Another review of the work, covering thirty-two pages, appeared in the Boston *North American Review* in July 1849. The series of articles on Layard in American magazines was concluded in the *Literary World* on April 20, 1850, with a reprint from the London *Times*.[28]

Most of the articles on the Near East in American periodicals were written in connection with book reviews, of which those in the *North American Review*, for example, were of considerable length. In its early numbers this magazine carried extracts from Sir John Malcolm's account of Persia, an essay on "Von Hammer's Constantinople," and articles on "The Zodiac of Denderah" and "Hieroglyphics."[29] In the 1840's there were articles on the Nestorian Christians of Persia, a comprehensive review of Robinson's *Travels in Palestine and Arabia,* and lengthy surveys of contemporary Egypt and Turkey.[30]

Of special significance is the publication, in the New York *American Review*, of two articles on the Persian poets Saadi and Firdausi, in September 1848 and January 1849.[31] The interest in Persian poetry which is apparent in *Mardi* was obviously in the air when Melville was writing his ro-

26. H. V. Hilprecht, *Explorations in Bible Lands during the 19th Century* (Philadelphia, 1903), p. 585.

27. *Democratic Review, 24,* 355–62.

28. *Literary World, 6,* 395–96.

29. *North American Review, 3* (1816), 169–74; *7* (1823), 203–21; *8* (1823), 233–42; *32* (1831), 95–126.

30. Ibid., *53* (1841), 175–211; *57* (1843), 156–84; *65* (1847), 56–84.

31. *American Review, 8,* 275–82; *9,* 54–67.

mance. Evidently the Persian poets were a favorite subject not only with Emerson but with the average literary New Yorkers.

A revival of interest in the *Arabian Nights* is also noticeable in the New York magazines of these years as a result of the publication of new American editions of the tales. In December 1847 the *American Review* had an article entitled "The Thousand and One Nights," announcing the publication, by C. S. Francis and Co., of a New York edition in the translation of the Reverend Edward Forster.[32] A series on the *Arabian Nights* is also found in the *Literary World,* written on the occasion of Francis' edition and a reprint of Edward Lane's translation by Harper and Brothers. These articles, by one "Sahal-Ben-Haroun," in the issues of February 12, February 26, March 18, March 25, May 13, and October 14, 1848, represent the most exhaustive and competent treatment of the subject in any American magazine in the first half of the nineteenth century.[33]

It must be remembered that any subject of interest to Evert Duyckinck, reader at Wiley and Putnam's, the American publishers of *Typee* (1846), and later editor of the *Literary World,* was bound to swim into Melville's ken when, at the age of twenty-five, he left the sea for a career of authorship. The most cursory perusal of the reading matter in American periodicals from 1810 to 1850 is sufficient to show that the Near East was a literary force in New York when it became Melville's Yale and Harvard.

32. Ibid., *6,* 601–18.
33. *Literary World, 3,* 26, 63, 123, 144, 284. On the identity of "Sahal-Ben-Haroun" see below, p. 36.

3. Melville's Reading

The books which have survived from Melville's own library or are known to have been read by him from a listing of his borrowings and purchases do not cover the most significant period in Melville's creative life, the years from 1846 to 1852 in New York and Pittsfield. As is well known, "the vicissitudes of Melville's life affected the accumulation and survival of his library." Most of the books that have come down to us date from the final period in New York, the years from 1863 to 1891. There are seven travel books on Egypt and Palestine in Merton Sealts' *Check-List of Books Owned and Borrowed by Melville*. All of them were acquired *after* his trip to the Levant in 1856–57 and were used as material for *Clarel*. We know of only two Oriental romances in Melville's library at the time when he was writing *Moby-Dick:* Beckford's *Vathek* and Hope's *Anastasius,* both of which he obtained on his trip to Europe in 1849. Melville's annotated copy of *Anastasius* has survived, and so has Saadi's *Gulistan,* in the translation of Francis Gladwin, bought on September 29, 1868. Three editions of Fitzgerald's *Rubáiyát of Omar Khayyam* in Melville's possession date from the years 1878 and 1886.

For the rest, the evidence of Melville's reading on the Islamic Orient as attested by Sealts must rely on material in the periodical publications listed, such as *The Literary World* and *The Edinburgh Review,* books of general interest like the Oriental poems of Byron, Moore, Matthew Arnold, Sir Edwin Arnold, James Thomson, and the material in Bayle's *Historical Dictionary*, Gibbon, and Carlyle. But the purely objective evidence, as Sealts has emphasized, "does not tell the full story." Numerous indications emerge from references and allusions in Melville's works and from reading material available to him at the libraries which he is known to have used. However unique in his probes at the axis of reality, Melville was a nineteenth-century writer of "Romance" by his own proclamation. There were certain books and writers which formed the stock-in-trade of the literary tradition that launched him on his career as an author. Enlarged and transmuted to serve his symbolic purpose, they left their stamp on his most mature writings. Almost inevitably, Melville's first acquaintance with Oriental literature leads us to the *Arabian Nights*.

THE *ARABIAN NIGHTS*

We do not know whether Melville, like Byron, the hero of his youth, read the *Arabian Nights* before he was ten years old. That he had read the tales by the time he was twenty is evident from the influence they exerted on him in his first published pieces of writing, "Fragments from a Writing Desk" (1839).

In Albany, where the family moved from New York in 1830 when Herman was almost eleven years old, the *Arabian Nights* left its traces in the Gansevoort-Melville households, for it now appears that a copy of the book was withdrawn by Melville's uncle, Peter Gansevoort, from the Albany Library on June 14, 1836.[1] Besides, a six-volume

---

1. This has been established by an examination of the manuscript "Charging-Book, 1829–1837" of the Albany Library, in the New York State Library, Albany, in which the borrowings are listed by shelf number. Among the books withdrawn by Peter Gansevoort in the period 1834–36 is number "358" (Charging-Book, p. 454), i.e. "Arabian Nights' Entertainments, 4 v.", according to the Albany Library Catalogue (July 1828), p. 9. The four-volume edition may have been in the translation of Edward Forster, published in Philadelphia in 1812. The library possessed another edition, in six volumes, in the translation of Jonathan Scott (shelf number 826). The standard six-volume edition of Scott's translation was published in Philadelphia, 1826.

edition, probably in the translation of Jonathan Scott, was available to Melville in the reading room of the Albany Young Men's Association, of which he became a member in 1835.[2]

The evidence which is contained in the "Fragments" themselves has been examined in William Gilman's *Melville's Early Life and "Redburn."* The "Fragments" are permeated by an Oriental exoticism derived from Byron, Scott, and Thomas Moore. But there are indications, particularly in "Fragment 2," that the *Arabian Nights* also had a direct impact on the composition of these pieces.

"Fragment 1" is a "strange effusion," as William Gilman has called it, written in the form of a letter by a young "distingué" to his mentor, a sophisticated and scholarly man of the world. The hero is modeled on Lord Chesterfield's precepts for a young man about town, and his polished wit dazzles all "like the glittering edge of a Damascus sabre." The piece is mainly devoted to a voluptuous description of three beautiful girls. Of these the beauty of the second girl is exotic and Eastern.

> Her complexion has the delicate tinge of the brunette, with a little of the roseate hue of the Circassian . . .
>
> And then her eyes! They open their dark, rich orbs upon you like the full noon of heaven, and blaze into your very soul the fires of the day! . . . so, a single glance from that Oriental eye as quickly fires your soul, and leaves your bosom in a perfect conflagration! . . . But it is well . . . that this glorious being can . . . give to the expression of her eye a melting tenderness. . . .

2. *Catalogue of Books in the Library of the Young Men's Association of the City of Albany* (cited as *YMA*) (Albany, 1837), No. 88, p. 3: "Arabian Nights' Entertainments, 6 vols." Cf. entry "Arabian Nights' Entertainments (Scott's 6 v.)" in Albany Library Catalogue, July 1828.

If the devout and exemplary Mussulman, who dying
fast in the faith of his Prophet, anticipates reclining on
beds of roses, gloriously drunk through all the ages of
eternity, is to be waited on by Houris such as these:
waft me, ye gentle gales, beyond this lower world.[3]

The Oriental beauty of Melville's second lady stems from
Byron and Moore. The Fragment refers the reader to "the
latter portion of the first canto of *Childe Harold*" in which
feminine beauty is described in terms of houris, Spain's
dark-glancing daughters, and the wise Prophet's paradise.
Byronic images are offered in Melville's paean to the dark
lady. To these ingredients are added flavors of Thomas
Moore's *Lalla Rookh* (first published in 1817) which is
steeped in the roseate hues of Circassian beauties, the darkness and melting tenderness of Oriental eyes, and the voluptuous delights of the houris, roses, and wine in the Prophet's
paradise.

Even the Nordic beauty of the third lady in Melville's
Fragment, whose eyes "effuse the mildness of their azure
beam," has been affected by Moore's Persian heroine whose
"mild eyes" quite overcome her lover "beaming that blest
assurance."[4]

As Gilman has shown, "Fragment 1" among a wealth of
literary allusions contains references to *The Siege of Corinth* and *The Bride of Abydos,* both of which were based
on Byron's reading in Turkish history and the *Arabian*

3. "Fragment 1" in *Billy Budd and Other Prose Pieces* (Constable),
pp. 387–88.

4. Cf. Byron, *Works* (London, 1823–25), *1,* 50–51; "Lalla Rookh" in
Moore's *Poetical Works* (Philadelphia, 1829), pp. 35, 70, 71. An unidentified quotation in "Fragment 1" referring to the glittering edge
of a Damascus saber which "dazzled all it shone upon" may be a paraphrase of a line in Byron's dedication to *Childe Harold* "To Ianthe"
whose eye "dazzles where it dwells," combined with a line from *The
Siege of Corinth,* "and envied all he gazed upon" (*Works, 1,* 15; *3,* 189).

Nights. By 1839, when Melville wrote his pieces for *The Democratic Press and Lansingburgh Advertiser,* he was well versed in Byron's Oriental romances—a fashionable taste which he shared with his brother Gansevoort and his sister Helen. Byron's notes and prefaces to his poems must have been the earliest guide to Melville's exploration of the Near East.[5]

In "Fragment 2" the *Arabian Nights* is explicitly mentioned. The piece describes an amorous adventure in an Oriental setting which is closely patterned on a typical scene in the *Arabian Nights.* A handsome young man receives a mysterious summons from an unknown "Inamorata." With great secrecy, a female go-between conducts him to the lady's palatial abode. This go-between, "a figure effectually concealed in the ample folds of a cloak," is a character straight out of such tales as "The Story of the Barber's Second Brother," "The Story of the Barber's Fifth Brother," and "The History of Aboulhassen Ali Ebn Becar and Shemselnihar, the Favourite of Calif Haroun Al-Raschid." In the stories of the Barber's brothers the go-between walks before the hero, and he follows at a distance. In the story of Aboulhassen and Shemselnihar one of the parties tries to overtake the other. Melville's account in "Fragment 2" is a combination of elements from both tales: "the stranger, regulating her movements by mine, proceeded at a pace which preserved between us a uniform distance, ever and anon looking back like a wary general to see if I were again inclined to try the mettle of her limbs." The "sundry misgivings" of Melville's hero about the outcome of his gallant adventure echo a similar feeling of apprehension in Scheherazade's "Story told by the Sultan of Casgar's Purveyor." But Melville's "mysterious affair" is soon

5. See Edward Fiess, "Byron and Byronism in the Mind and Art of Herman Melville," doctoral dissertation, Yale University, 1951.

brought to an "éclaircissement." In the classic manner of
Arabian lovers entering a harem, Melville's hero is smuggled into the lady's apartment by faithful servants:

> my leader suddenly halted beneath a lofty window, and
> making a low call, I perceived slowly descending there-
> from, a thick silken cord, attached to an ample basket,
> which was deposited at our feet. Amazed at this appari-
> tion, I was about soliciting an explanation: when laying
> her fingers impressively upon her lips, and placing her-
> self in the basket, my guide motioned me to seat myself
> beside her. I obeyed; but not without considerable
> trepidation: and in obedience to the same low call
> which had procured its descent our curious vehicle,
> with sundry creakings, rose in air.[6]

The apartment into which the hero is introduced is one of
"Eastern splendour," a type which Melville later described
in *Redburn,* as "Aladdin's Palace," the London gambling-
house. Our lover beholds "a spectacle as beautiful and enchanting as any described in the *Arabian Nights.*" Like
Zuleika's chamber in *The Bride of Abydos,* the room is
"redolent of the most delicious perfumes," in its "angles,"
with "luxurious couches, covered with the finest damask."
Like Byron's Zuleika, Melville's lady reclines on an "ottoman," duly equipped with a lute. The Oriental accessories
of her dress are of the type found in Byron's *Don Juan,*
though Melville, obviously spoofing, could not refrain from
giving them an emblematic touch: "Her zone was of pink
satin, on which were broidered figures of Cupid in the act
of drawing his bow; while the ample folds of her Turkish
sleeve were gathered at the wrist by a bracelet of immense

---

6. "Fragment 2" in William H. Gilman, *Melville's Early Life and
"Redburn"* (New York, 1951), Appendix B, pp. 265–71.

rubies, each of which represented a heart pierced thro' by a golden shaft."[7]

The matchless exotic beauty of the lady, complete with "lustrous orbs" and "long dark lashes," smothers the hero with its fires. But like many a tale in the *Arabian Nights,* Melville's idyl has an unhappy ending. In Arabian romance the lovers are usually separated by the lady's father, husband, or the khalif in person, if the lady happens to be the khalif's concubine, and the lover has to flee for his life.[8] Melville devised a more dramatic and poignant ending. At the climax of his passion, the hero discovers that the beautiful stranger is deaf and dumb, and he flees in horror. Melville's extraordinary dénouement has been appropriately called the first of his variations on the theme of a frustrated quest. The final anticlimax is the earliest demonstration of his irresistible impulse to prick the rosy bubble of romance and to reveal its terrible core of tragic reality. But the theme of the deaf and dumb mistress is not original. It, too, reflects the influence of the *Arabian Nights,* for in "the Story of Beder, Prince of Persia and Giahure, Princess of Samandal," a king falls in love with a woman whom he imagines to be dumb.

There is also an American model for Melville's story which has not been previously noted. The subject of the deaf and dumb mistress is the theme of *Amir Khan,* a popular Oriental verse romance by a young American poet, Lucretia Maria Davidson who died in 1825 at the age of sixteen. *Amir Khan and Other Poems* was published posthumously in 1829 and is included in the Catalogue of Books

7. Cf. *Bride of Abydos,* canto II, stanza 5; *Don Juan,* canto III, stanzas 64–76.

8. Cf. "The Story of the Lady of Cairo and Her Four Gallants" and "History of Abouhassen Ali Ebn Becar, and Shemselnihar, Favourite of the Caliph Haroun al Rusheed," *Arabian Nights* (Philadelphia, 1826), 2, 265 f.; *6,* 269 f.

in the Library of the Young Men's Association of the City of Albany on which our ideas of Melville's early reading are based. In the context of Melville's early interest in Oriental romance, *Amir Khan* is one of the most interesting books in the Albany catalogue.[9]

The heroine, Amreta, is a Circassian maid whose lover, Amir Khan, is the noble Governor of Cashmere. The tale of the lovers is developed with the help of the popular Oriental machinery which Melville later used in *Mardi*—peris (good spirits), bulbuls (nightingales), gulnares (roses)—all dutifully explained in notes on the model of Moore's *Lalla Rookh*. *Amir Khan* is remarkable for the youth of its author and the praise it earned from Robert Southey, author of another famous Oriental romance, *Thalaba*.[10] But its main claim to attention lies in its theme, which may have had some bearing on Melville's composition. Like the Inamorata of Melville's Fragment, Amreta, the heroine, is deaf and dumb and is characterized by "long dark lashes" and an appropriately amorous name. The passionate ardor of Amir Khan meets no response in the beauteous damsel. But Amir Khan finally resorts to a ruse. With the help of a magic herb, he pretends to be dead and succeeds in evoking speech in his mistress. Unlike Melville's Fragment, the story ends happily.

But Melville's tale is clearly a parody of sentimental "romantic" feeling. The sentimentality of Oriental romance on native American grounds is nowhere more evident than in Miss Davidson's Arabian poem, where the deaf

9. *YMA* (1837), p. 3, No. 1258: *Amir Khan and Other Poems: The Remains of Lucretia Maria Davidson, who died at Plattsburgh, N.Y. August 27, 1825, aged 16 years and 11 Months. With a Biographical Sketch by Samuel F. B. Morse,* New York, 1829.

10. See Washington Irving, *Biography and Poetical Remains of the Late Margaret Miller Davidson* (Philadelphia, 1841), p. 2. Margaret Miller Davidson was Lucretia Davidson's younger sister and a poet in her own right.

and dumb lady is moved to tears at the sight of her lover's apparently lifeless body, Amir Khan awakes from a self-induced trance in the nick of time to prevent her from suicide, and the lovers are blissfully united after a series of melodramatic scenes. Miss Davidson was inspired by the *Arabian Nights* and even more by Thomas Moore, the Western prophet of Oriental romance. One cannot help feeling that *Amir Khan* may have given Melville a special impetus for his "hoax." That he knew the book is likely in view of its local interest. The Albany Young Men's Association had literary aspirations, and Miss Davidson had attended school in both Troy and Albany and was known as a literary prodigy. We know from Washington Irving that her brief poetical career was "celebrated in literary history."[11]

However atypical in feeling and tone, Melville's first attempts at writing are steeped in the rosy tints of Arabian romance which were the trade-marks of "literature" in his time. It was only natural that a young man aspiring to authorship should use them profusely. The Oriental beauty in "Fragment 1" has a "roseate" hue, as she ought, and the hero, in "Fragment 2," is summoned by a "rose-coloured" billet-doux. "Roseate" and "rose-coloured" were *de rigueur* as the two favorite adjectives of the romantics. *Lalla Rookh*'s heroine is characterized by a "rose-coloured" veil; the whole poem is studded with roseate lips and roseate hues. Melville, as we know, was soon forced to abandon the rosy haze of fantasy for the unique experience which made him famous as the man who had lived among the cannibals. The tone which radiates from his first book, *Typee,* is "golden-hued," like the sensuously lived South Sea experience which he recorded. But his fifth book, *Mardi* (1849), marks a return to the tints of the *Arabian Nights:* Yillah's emblem is a "rose-coloured" pearl at her bosom.

11. Ibid., p. 12.

Mardi was planned as a story of Polynesian adventure, a sequel to *Omoo,* but was turned into a "Romance" for reasons which have not yet been fully explored. To plume his powers for a mystic flight, but also no doubt to catch the attention of readers in doing so, Melville deliberately steeped *Mardi* in "the roseate air of romance," which was held up to the American reader as an ideal by the *Knicker-bocker Magazine.*[12] In continuing his "romance" Melville went to work heart and soul at what was to him the essence of writing, to convey "hidden" meaning in an allegorical guise. It looks as if he found not only the machinery of romance but an esoteric vocabulary of "meaning" in a renewed exploration of the *Arabian Nights.*

The years in which Melville wrote *Mardi* were marked by a special interest in the *Arabian Nights* among the New York literati. In 1847, the New York firm of Charles S. Francis and Co. published a three-volume edition of the *Arabian Nights' Entertainments,* followed by separate illustrated volumes of *The Story of Aladdin* and *The Seven Voyages of Sindbad the Sailor: and The Story of Ali Baba and the Forty Robbers.*[13] Another American edition of the *Arabian Nights* appeared in the week between March 11 and March 18, 1848.[14] It was published by Harper and Brothers, Melville's publishers, and was reprinted from the second English edition of Edward Lane's classic translation,

12. Miller, *The Raven and the Whale,* pp. 28–29.

13. See announcement of books "just published" by Francis and Co. in *Literary World,* 2 (1848), 526; 3 (1848), 26. A copy of Francis' edition of *The Seven Voyages of Sindbad the Sailor: and The Story of Ali Baba and The Forty Robbers* (New York, 1848), which belonged to Catherine Gansevoort Lansing, Melville's aunt, is in the Oriental Room of the New York Public Library (Gansevoort-Lansing Collection).

14. See "List of Books Published in the United States, from March 11 to March 18," in *Literary World, 3,* 132. An illustrated excerpt from Harper's edition appeared ibid., pp. 724–25.

brought out by John Murray, the English publisher of *Typee,* in 1847.

We know that by January 1848 Melville had embarked upon a "Romance of Polynesian Adventure." He had abandoned his original plan of writing a continuation of *Omoo,* the "bona-fide narrative" of his adventures in the South Seas which constitutes the beginning of *Mardi.* His new venture was to be "a *real* romance" and was to be packed with what later reviewers called "oriental delights" which, notwithstanding Melville's protestations to the contrary, were borrowed from the well-known Circulating Library of Oriental tales:[15] Yillah, the maiden, is a peri with a "rose-coloured" pearl at her bosom; Taji, the hopelessly pursuing lover, looks like an Arabian Emir; Hautia and her dark-eyed damsels entice the hero to the sensuous delights of a Mohammedan paradise.

The change in Melville's "determinations," as Merrell R. Davis has shown, is reflected in the books which Melville borrowed from his friend, Evert Duyckinck, in the early months of 1848.[16]

Melville's name is not mentioned by Duyckinck among those of his friends to whom, at one time or another, he lent the *Arabian Nights.* But Duyckinck's interest in the book is well attested. An English version of Galland's original French translation was published by Duyckinck's father, Evert Duyckinck, in 1815.[17] Duyckinck's loans of at least

15. Letters to John Murray of January 1 and March 25, 1848, in *Letters,* pp. 68, 70–71.

16. Merrell R. Davis, *Melville's "Mardi"* (New Haven, 1952), pp. 60–78.

17. "Arabian Nights entertainments. Consisting of a collection of stories, told by the Sultaness of the Indies . . . containing a better account of the customs, manners, and religion of the eastern nations . . . than hitherto published. Translated into French from the Arabian mss. by Mr. Gallard and now into English, from the Paris edition. New York, E. Duyckinck, 1815."

two editions of the *Arabian Nights* appear in his list of "Books Lent." One copy, in four volumes, was lent to C. Wolfe and Cornelius Mathews, fellow editors and literati, and is now in the possession of the New York Public Library. Lane's translation, in three volumes, was lent to Washington Irving in the spring or summer of 1849.[18]

When we consider Melville's reading during the significant months of 1848, it is striking to find that several articles on "The Origin of the Arabian Nights' Entertainments" appeared in Duyckinck's *Literary World* at that very time. These articles were published in lengthy installments, beginning February 12, 1848 and ending in the number of May 13 of the same year.[19] The famous collection of romances was discussed by "Sahal-Ben-Haroun," the pseudonym of E. G. Langdon, who was a regular contributor to the *Literary World* on Oriental subjects.[20] The articles were a commentary on the two contemporary American editions of the *Arabian Nights:* the edition of C. S. Francis, which is mentioned as "being now before the public," and the reprint of Lane by Harper and Brothers, announced in the first article as "nearly ready for issue."[21]

There is no external evidence to show that Melville read the *Arabian Nights* while writing *Mardi,* though its Arabian overtones are clearly apparent to every reader. Aside

18. See List of "Books Lent" in New York Public Library, Duyckinck Papers. Entry of loan to Washington Irving listed after April 13, 1849; to "C.M." after September 20, 1855.

19. *Literary World, 3,* 26–28, 63–65, 123–25, 144–46, 284–86.

20. The identity of "Sahal-Ben-Haroun" appears from a manuscript letter in the Duyckinck Papers of the New York Public Library, "Letters 1845–1854." The Letter, dated January 16, 1851, was addressed to E. A. Duyckinck by E. G. Langdon, alias "Sahal-Ben-Haroun." A person by the name of "Langdon, Edmund G., author" is listed in Rode's New York City Directory, 1850–51.

21. *Literary World, 3,* 26.

from a commonplace allusion to the "Story of Ali Baba and the Forty Robbers," there is no reference to the tales in *Mardi* itself. In *Redburn,* which was published in the same year, Melville does mention the effect of reading the *Arabian Nights.*[22] Also, the mysterious London den to which Redburn is taken is "Aladdin's Palace."

Nevertheless, there are indications that Melville was reading the *Arabian Nights* at this time. He may even have read the tales in one particular edition—namely, in Lane's translation, its first London edition, published by Charles Knight in 1841. The suggestion arises from Melville's use of Arabian names for his main characters in *Mardi*—(Taji, Yillah, Yoomy, Babbalanja)—from his way of transliterating what are obviously meant to be Arabic sounds, and from a possible explanation of these names.

It can hardly be doubted that Melville saw the articles on the *Arabian Nights* which began to appear in the *Literary World* in February 1848. The first article, of February 12, announced Harper's edition of Lane and also mentioned two other versions of the *Arabian Nights,* one translated by the Reverend Edward Forster and another, from the version of the Austrian Orientalist, Hammer-Purgstall, in the translation of the Reverend George Lamb.[23] Nevertheless, all translations of the *Arabian Nights* with the exception of Lane, as well as Lane's version in the American edition of Harper and the English edition of Murray, must be discarded as possible source material for *Mardi.* The reasons for this will appear below, but a contributory factor for the exclusion of these editions is their small type as compared with the large and clear type of Knight's first London edi-

22. *Redburn,* chap. 8.
23. Charles Knight was also the publisher of "Knight's London," an unidentified edition of which, in three octavo volumes, Melville bought in London on December 15, 1849 (Leyda, *Log,* p. 348).

tion. The legibility of the type is important in considering Melville's sources for *Mardi*, for we know that he suffered from weak eyesight at the time and was therefore likely to select the edition with clearer type for his reading.[24]

The clue which points to the possible use of Lane's first edition is Melville's way of transliterating Arabian sounds in names like Aleema, Yoomy, Yillah. This transliteration is in complete agreement with Lane as published by Knight, while all other translations and editions of Lane at that period employed an entirely different system, which is also reflected in Melville's other works, e.g. *Clarel,* and the writings of his contemporaries.[25]

The pertinence of this matter will be apparent from the following: In the preface to Knight's first edition Lane explained the problem of transliterating Arabic sounds in a way "congenial" with English. Lane's system, which he illustrated by a table of vowels, was a deliberate deviation from the accepted nineteenth-century way of transliteration in which English writers used the Italian and French equivalents for reproducing Oriental sounds. According to Lane's table, "ee" should be written for the sound to be pronounced as in "bee" (cf. Aleema); "oo" as in "boot" (cf. Yoomy); "i" as in "bid" (cf. Yillah); and the letter "y" is to be pronounced as in "you" (cf. Yoomy, Yillah).[26] This

24. On Melville's weak eyesight see letter of Elizabeth Melville to her stepmother, December 23, 1847 (Leyda, *Log,* p. 266).

25. Cf. Eliot Warburton's disagreement with Lane in the preface to *The Crescent and the Cross,* published in 1845 by the New York firm of Wiley and Putnam, publishers of *Typee:* "I should also, perhaps, apologize for using *our* old Oriental appellations, instead of those which the Arabic mode of pronunciation has now rendered customary. I scarcely fear, however, that the reader of the Arabian Nights will object to hear of Viziers, Sultans, Cairo and Damascus; instead of Wezeers, Sooltauns, Masr, and El Shām" (p. xiv).

26. *Arabian Nights' Entertainments* (3 vols. London, 1841), *1,* "The Translator's Preface," p. xx.

preface was omitted in the second London edition of Lane's *Arabian Nights,* published by Murray in 1847, and in Harper's American reprint of Murray's edition (1848). In an "Advertisement" the publishers declare that the spelling of Arabic words and names was "restored to their more usual forms" during Lane's absence in Egypt, without the translator's concurrence or knowledge. "It appeared to them that the words alluded to would be not only more intelligible in their old orthography but more agreeable to the eye and ear, and more consonant with the spirit of our language."[27] Accordingly, "ou" was restored for Lane's "oo"; "i" for "ee," etc., which would have turned Melville's "Aleema" into "Alima," and "Yoomy" into "Youmy." From the exactness with which the sounds in the Arabian names of Melville's characters are rendered into English in accordance with Lane's prescriptions, it seems likely that he had come across Lane's table in Knight's edition of the *Arabian Nights.* From the preface to *Typee* we know that Melville was aware of the problem of transliteration: "In the Polynesian words used in this volume," he writes, "—except in those cases where the spelling has been previously determined by others—that form of orthography has been employed, which might be supposed most easily to convey their sound to a stranger." Melville's ear frequently misled him in the rendering of Polynesian words and names which he thought he knew from personal experience. In coining his Arabian names, however, he seems to have relied on his reading, and it would have been natural for him to follow the best available model—Lane's amply annotated translation of the *Arabian Nights,* which, to his contemporaries, was not only the classic source of Oriental romance but a handbook on the customs and manners of the East.

It is also possible, of course, that Melville saw the table

---

27. *Arabian Nights' Entertainments* (3 vols. New York, 1848), *1*, iii.

of transliterations in the third edition of Lane's standard work on the *Manners and Customs of the Modern Egyptians,* to which frequent reference is made in the Explanatory Notes to the *Arabian Nights.* Still another consideration, however, seems to bear out the contention that Melville read Lane' translation. Lane includes a tale which does not appear in the older versions of Lamb and Forster but is of great interest in connection with *Mardi:* "The Story of Taj-el-Mulook and the Lady Dunya," whose Arabic names mean "The Crown of the Kings" and "the Lady World." The relationship of this romance to *Mardi,* which will be examined later, provides one of the most interesting landmarks in the exploration of Melville's acquaintance with the *Arabian Nights,* for it seems to throw light not only on the romantic machinery in the novel but on its symbolic structure and theme.

With regard to Melville's later writings, the *Thousand and One Nights* have no particular significance—for instance, in the story "Poor Man's Pudding and Rich Man's Crumbs," published in 1854 and based on his London experience of watching beggars fight for the remnants of the Lord Mayor's Banquet, Melville bethought himself of the *Arabian Nights* to suggest the opulence of the rich.[28]

Of greater interest is a reference in the *Confidence-Man* (1856) that alludes to "a pleasing Arabian romance" on the subject of hospitality. The allusion is made in a context that suggests Melville was thinking of "The Barber's Story of his Sixth Brother" in the *Arabian Nights.* Here a hungry man is entertained with imaginary food and drink at an imaginary table by a friendly impostor in the manner of the cheating tailor in Hans Andersen's *The Emperor's New Clothes.* Instead of food and wine, the starving hero is of-

---

28. *The Complete Stories of Herman Melville,* ed. Jay Leyda (New York, 1949), p. 177.

fered what Melville, in his context, calls "untried abstractions," conveyed by gesture and mimicry. The theme of the relevant passage in the *Confidence-Man* is the deceptive appearance of benignity and of warnings against evil designs "which do not forewarn, but in mockery come after the fact." This, precisely, is the situation in the story of mock hospitality in the *Arabian Nights*. The hero sees through the mockery from the beginning but pretends to be duped by his host until he has an opportunity of turning the tables on his "benefactor." The moral of the Arabian story corresponds to Melville's point: "Whatever latent design your impostor friend might have had upon you," says a stranger to the cosmopolitan on the subject of abused confidence, "it as yet remains unaccomplished. You read his label!"[29]

Arab hospitality was, of course, proverbial and was frequently alluded to in the literature of the time. Arabian stories of hospitality were recounted by Emerson in his *Essays* and *Journals*. The story in the essay "Heroism" deals with the hospitality of the city of Soghd, in Bukhara, and was taken by Emerson from the *Oriental Geography* of a tenth-century Arab writer, Ibn Haukal. The tale Emerson copied in his *Journals* concerns the legendary hospitality of Hatem Tai, the pre-Islamic hero and poet, which Emerson probably took from von Hammer's translation of the *Arabian Nights*. But aside from the general theme of hospitality there is no particular relevance in these stories to the subject of the *Confidence-Man*. On the other hand, the appropriate theme is provided by "The Story of the Barber's Sixth Brother" in which, significantly, the subject of hospitality is linked to a breach of confidence and a masquerade.

29. *Confidence-Man*, chap. 36. See also Elizabeth S. Foster, Explanatory Notes to *Confidence-Man* (New York, Hendricks House, 1954), p. 356.

TRAVEL LITERATURE AND ROMANCE,
1835–1850

The library of the Albany Young Men's Association
which Melville joined on January 29, 1835, provided him at
the age of fifteen with the opportunity to indulge, like his
hero Byron, in his favorite reading of travel literature and
romance. The library, whose "peculiar aim" was "to cherish
. . . a taste for literary pursuits" had a collection of books on
the Near East which compared favorably with the larger
Albany Library of which Melville's uncle, Peter Gansevoort, was a member. By the side of the *Arabian Nights,* in
the six-volume translation of Jonathan Scott, there were
Beckford's *Vathek* and Hope's *Anastasius,* which in their
Oriental flavor rivaled the popularity of the authentic
Arabian tales. Melville's acquisition of the two books fourteen years later in Europe may thus have been the culmination of an acquaintance which began in the Albany reading-
room. The most recent travel book in the library at the time
when Melville became a member was Adolphus Slade's
*Records of Travels in Turkey, Greece, &c. and of A Cruise
in the Black Sea, with The Captain Pasha, in the Years 1829,
1830, and 1831,* published in Philadelphia in 1833. Slade,
an English admiral in the Turkish service, covered the same
territory as Thomas Hope's fictitious Greek, Anastasius.
The attraction of "these ever interesting regions" to the
nineteenth-century West was not unduly romanticized by
Slade: "The Turkish empire is as interesting now, that it is
crumbling to pieces, as it was in the 16th century, when a
Tartar could ride with the Sultan's firman, respected all the
way, from the banks of the Volga to the confines of Morocco
—when its armies threatened Vienna, and its fleet ravaged

the coasts of Italy. It then excited the fears of civilized
Europe: it now excites its cupidity."[1]

Of special significance in relation to Melville's later reading are a *History of Algiers,* listed in the YMA catalogue;
an unnamed two-volume work on the Holy Land; and an
unnamed book on Persia.[2] The library also possessed *The
Adventures of Gaudentio di Lucca,* an account of travel in
Africa by Simon Berington (1680–1755), written in the
guise of a report to the Bolognese Inquisition, and "The
African Travels" of Mungo Park (1771–1806), the Scotsman
who explored Africa in 1795 in the service of the English
African Association. These books, as well as John Morgan's
History of Algiers, are mentioned in *White Jacket, Mardi,*
and *Redburn* and may have floated into Melville's ken when
he swam through his first library.

In addition to travel literature and romance, the Albany
Young Men's Association also owned books on the Near
East which were respectable from the scholarly point of
view. George Sale's translation of the Koran, with its "Preliminary Discourse" on the history and religion of Islam,
was a standard source book on Islamic subjects. A two-
volume *History of the Saracens,* listed in the catalogue beside Charles Mills' *History of the Crusades,* was probably by
Simon Ockley. The book was Gibbon's authority in his
chapters on Mohammed and the rise of Islam and was frequently consulted by Emerson.[3] Other sources for an early

1. "Slade's Travels in Turkey, 2 vols.," shelf number 1242, *YMA*
(1837), p. 28. By 1848 the YMA Library had two copies of this work
(1848, p. 33).

2. *YMA* (1837), shelf numbers 1081, 125, 1622. The Catalogue of
1848 lists one volume of a *History of Algiers* by J. W. Stevens, Brook-
lyn, 1800.

3. The first edition of Ockley's *History of the Saracens* was published in two volumes in 1708–18. *YMA* (1848) lists a one-volume edition, New York, 1847. Emerson mentioned Ockley among his reading
in 1840 (*Journals, 5,* 502).

acquaintance with the Near East in Albany were Gibbon's *Decline and Fall of the Roman Empire*, the works of Isaac D'Israeli and, of course, Washington Irving, including separate editions of *The Conquest of Granada* and *The Alhambra*. Lord Teignmouth's famous *Life of Sir William Jones* was also available to the young Melville. It was published in 1807 and included a collection of Jones' letters and writings.

Though the *American Quarterly Review* complained of the "juvenile enthusiasm" of Sir William Jones for things Oriental, the name of "Asiatic Jones," as Emerson called him, was a byword with those who were interested in the Orient in the first half of the nineteenth century.[4] In the last decade of the eighteenth century, Jones, a judge in India and founder of the Bengal Asiatic Society, had opened up the field of Oriental studies in England. His encyclopaedic knowledge of Oriental languages, thought, and jurisprudence had become proverbial. His pioneering work of translating Oriental poetry from Arabic, Persian, and Sanskrit deeply affected the romantic poets of the West. Its function in creating the concept of a world literature is best studied in Emerson, whose adaptations of Persian poetry, though based on the German versions of Hammer-Purgstall, owed their inspiration to Jones. A year after his graduation, in 1822, Emerson copied lines of Jones' translation of "Narayena" into his *Journal*. Regular records of readings of Jones begin to appear in the *Journals* in 1837.

To Melville, Jones was a wise man, an explorer and decipherer of mysteries like Belzoni and Champollion. At first, in *Typee*, he thought of him simply as a famous grammarian, a reputation which Jones had acquired while he was still in England, in 1771, by publishing a famous *Persian Grammar*.[5] The image of Jones, like that of Belzoni, soon

4. *American Quarterly Review, 8* (1830), 8–9.
5. See A. J. Arberry, *Asiatic Jones*, London, 1946.

acquired symbolical stature as Melville's writings began to concern themselves more and more with man's tragic ignorance of the profounder meanings of life: "Physiognomy, like every other human science, is but a passing fable," we read in *Moby-Dick*. "If then, Sir William Jones, who read in thirty languages, could not read the simplest peasant's face in its profounder and more subtle meanings, how may unlettered Ishmael hope to read the awful Chaldee of the sperm whale's brow?"[6]

After leaving Albany in 1837 Melville did not join another library till over a decade later, when he bought a membership in the New York Society Library from the absent George Duyckinck on January 17, 1838. Before that, for the composition of *Typee* and *Omoo*, on his return from his voyages before the mast he had drawn on a wide range of travel books on the South Seas, some of which he characteristically disavowed. But *Typee* also discloses an interest in the Near East—in Belzoni's explorations in Egypt and Sir William Jones' legendary knowledge of Oriental languages. In *Omoo*, Melville shows a familiarity with terms like "Hegira" and the indications of Ottoman military rank —Doctor Long Ghost is "a Bashaw with Two Tails." Indeed, when *Typee* and *Omoo* were compared by Horace Greeley to Stephens' *Travels*, it must be remembered that "the American traveler" had also visited the Near East.[7]

Melville's early predilection for Oriental romance had been evidently widened by his travels to encompass data on the manners and customs of the Near East. They lent his early writings an air of fashionable erudition but gave his

6. *Moby-Dick*, chap. 79.
7. See Leyda, *Log*, p. 248; John Lloyd Stephens, *Incidents of Travel in Egypt, Arabia Petraea, and the Holy Land. By an American*, 2 vols. New York, 1837. Other volumes by Stephens (1802–52) cover Greece, Turkey, and Eastern Europe; Central America; and Yucatan.

later work an increasingly complex symbolic significance. The books charged to Melville in the ledgers of the New York Society Library are only four in number and have no bearing on the Near East. Melville's membership expired on September 11, 1848, but was renewed from April 17 to October 7, 1850, when he was writing *Moby-Dick*.[8] In both *Mardi* and *Moby-Dick* there is a catalogue of seventeenth-century travel books on the Orient, some of which he must have consulted in the Library building, for they are books not easily available in a private library. In the Library Catalogue of 1850 such books are marked by an asterisk, which indicates that they "shall not, but with the consent of the library committee, be lent out, but must be read only in the library rooms."[9] Among these books, for example, are "the *Oriental Pilgrimage* of pious old Purchas" and "the fine old folio *Voyages*" of Hakluyt, and Thevenot.[10]

Other old accounts, well-known from *Moby-Dick*, which Melville read in Harris' *Collection of Voyages* were Leo Africanus' description of the kingdoms of North Africa, Tavernier's "Travels into Persia and India," and Sir Thomas Herbert's "Travels into Africa and Asia." George Sandys' *A Relation of a Journey Begun An:Dom: 1610*, part of which was reprinted in Harris, was later mentioned by Melville in the *Journal* of his visit to the Levant.[11]

The English had traded in the Levant throughout the sixteenth century, fighting their way through a Mediterranean which, as Melville later noted in his reading of Stanley's *Sinai and Palestine*, was "the boundary and the terror of the

8. Leyda, *Log*, pp. 269, 280, 372, 398.
9. *Alphabetical and Analytical Catalogue of the New York Society Library* (New York, 1850), p. xxx.
10. *Mardi, 1*, 266.
11. On the identification of Sandys from Melville's reference to "Saunders" see Horsford, *Journal*, p. 139, n. 7.

eastern nations."[12] In his famous collection of voyages
Richard Hakluyt, an advocate of colonization and discovery
who never went to sea himself, devoted special attention to
publicizing the Levant trade. He faithfully recorded the
personal observations and experiences of every English
traveler to the East, including accounts of foreign travelers
like the Venetian Giovanni Battista Ramusio (1485–1557),
whom Melville also mentions.[13] Samuel Purchas (ca. 1577–
1626), who followed in Hakluyt's footsteps, has been described as a kind of world gazetteer. Like Milton and Coleridge, Melville was obviously a fascinated reader of Purchas.
The reference to "the Oriental Pilgrimage of pious old Purchas" in *Mardi* is clearly to *Purchas His Pilgrimage, or Relations of the World and the Religions Observed in All
Ages,"* the first work, published in 1613. Marco Polo's
travels found a place in *Hakluytus Posthumus, or Purchas
His Pilgrimes, Containing a History of the World in Sea
Voyages and Land Travel by Englishmen and Others.* This
work appeared in 1625 and was a collection of Hakluyt's
unpublished material that had somehow passed into the
possession of Purchas after Hakluyt's death.

Hakluyt had also given his assistance to a great international collection of voyages, the *Peregrinations* of the Dutchman Theodor de Bry, published in several volumes in
Frankfurt am Main, 1590–1602. Aiming at the reading
public of all Europe, de Bry brought out English, French,
German, and Latin versions of his text, accompanied by
many illustrations. One of these, in the so-called "Small
Voyages" dealing with the East Indies, shows the Asiatic

12. This sentence is checked in Melville's annotated copy of Arthur
Penrhyn Stanley's *Sinai and Palestine in Connection with Their
History* (New York, 1863), p. 113. The book is in the New York Public
Library, Osborne Collection.

13. *Mardi, 1,* 266.

temples about which Melville claims to have read in the *Voyages* he catalogues in *Mardi*.[14]

"Old Harris' collection," repeatedly quoted by Melville, was a compilation commissioned by the London booksellers from John Harris (*ca.* 1667–1719), a divine and topographer who also compiled the first English Dictionary of Arts and Sciences. Harris' *Navigantium atque itinerantium bibliotheca; or, A Compleat Collection of Voyages and Travels* was published in two volumes in 1705 and went through three editions. It claimed to consist "of above four hundred of the most authentick writers" in the English, Latin, French, Italian, Spanish, Portuguese, German, and Dutch tongues. It included extracts from the Persian and Indian voyages of Jean-Baptiste Tavernier (1605–89) and the Levantine travels of Jean de Thevenot (1633–67), two jewel-trading Frenchmen who found themselves a comfortable nook at the Ottoman court and wrote detailed reports on the intimate household of the Turkish sultan "nevr before expos'd to publick view."[15]

Sir Thomas Herbert (1606–82), quoted in "Extracts" in *Moby-Dick,* concerned himself "especially with the territories of the Persian monarchie."[16] He has been consid-

14. Plate XXI, "Idolum Indorum Pagodes, & Templa Mahumetanorum" in Vol. 1 of Johann Theodor de Bry, *Collectiones Peregrinationum in Indiam Orientalem et Indiam Occidentalem,* 3 vols. Frankfurt am Main, 1590–1602.

15. See *The Travels of Monsieur de Thevenot into the Levant. In Three Parts,* 3 vols. London, 1687.

16. William Foster, "Introduction" to his edition of *Thomas Herbert, Travels in Persia: 1627–1629,* New York, 1929. The first edition of Sir Thomas Herbert's *Travels* was published four years after his return to England under the title *A Description of the Persian Monarchy Now Being, the Orientall Indyes, Isles, and Other Parts of the Greater Asia and Africk. By Th. Herbert, Esq.,* London, 1634. Part of the account was reprinted in Harris' *Collection of Voyages and Travels, 1,* chaps. 20–27, particularly chap. 23: "Sir Thomas Herbert's Travels into Persia."

ered "one of the most lively writers who ever put Persia on
an English bookshelf."[17] As Harris points out, Sir Thomas
began his travels in the year Purchas ends his Pilgrimage,
1626. Following the practice of gentlemen of his day, he
embarked for Persia in the suite of the English ambassador
to the Persian court, and he kept a journal throughout his
travels. On returning to England he followed another common practice by using his journal to compile an account of
the trip. This genre of travel books, describing British embassies to the Persian court and vice versa, included the
trappings which Melville later used to embellish the plot
of his unfinished tale " 'Under the Rose' (Being an extract
from an old Ms. entitled 'Travels in Persia' (Iran) by a servant of My Lord the Ambassador)."[18]

Of eighteenth-century travelers, James Bruce (1730–94),
the famous explorer of Abyssinia, is mentioned in *Mardi* in
a context that indicates Melville must have read the American edition of Bruce's travels: *Interesting Narrative of the
Travels of James Bruce, Esq. into Abyssinia, to Discover
the Source of the Nile*. This edition, published in Boston
in 1798, was an abridgment of the original work in five
volumes that had appeared in Edinburgh in 1790. Bruce—
to quote his biographer—was the poet, and his work the
epic, of African travel.[19] Like Purchas he was one of Coleridge's guides on the road to Xanadu. By the time Melville
was writing *Mardi*, Bruce's travels to Abyssinia had become
a literary *cause célèbre*. We know from Poe's *Broadway
Journal* of 1845 that the detractors of Bruce considered the
account of his journeyings "apocryphal," while Bruce's de-

17. Ed. Arthur J. Arberry, *The Legacy of Persia* (Oxford, 1953), p.
367.

18. See *Billy Budd and Other Prose Pieces*, pp. 339–45.

19. Richard Garnett in *DNB*, as quoted in John Livingston Lowes,
The Road to Xanadu (New York, 1959), p. 338.

fenders—the *Broadway Journal* among them—pointed out
that the *Travels* had been published in his own name and
was accompanied by numerous original drawings from
direct observation.[20] Melville, himself a traveler, keenly
felt for Bruce, as we see in the chapter "The Tale of a
Traveller" in *Mardi:* "But stay-at-homes say travellers lie.
Yet a voyage to Ethiopia would cure them of that; for few
sceptics were travellers; fewer travellers liars, though the
proverb respecting them lies. It is false, as some say, that
Bruce was cousin-german to Baron Munchhausen; but true,
as Bruce said, that the Abyssinians cut live steaks from their
cattle."[21]

In the preface of the American edition Bruce is defended
against "suspicious hints . . . invidiously thrown out by his
enemies" to cast doubt upon the truthfulness of his account.
A refutation of these insinuations by one of Bruce's friends,
printed verbatim, takes special issue with the objections to
Bruce's report "that the Abyssinians cut a slice from the
living ox, esteeming it one of their greatest delicacies."
Bruce's narrative tells how "he saw, with the utmost aston-
ishment, two pieces, thicker and longer than our ordinary
beef steaks, cut out of the higher part of the buttock of the
beast."[22] Bishop Samuel Gobat, whose *Journal of a Three
Years' Residence in Abyssinia* (first published in London in
1834) Melville is known to have read,[23] could "scarcely
persuade" himself that Bruce's account was true. "Whenever I have inquired whether it now is, or ever was, their
custom to cut pieces of flesh from the bodies of living ani-
mals for the purposes of food," writes the venerable Bishop
naively, "they [the Abyssinians] have uniformly expressed

20. *Broadway Journal* (May 10, 1845), 298.
21. *Mardi, 1,* 346.
22. James Bruce, *Travels in Abyssinia* (Boston, 1798), pp. xii, 205.
23. Horsford, *Journal,* p. 156.

the utmost horror and disgust at the suggestion."[24] It was Dr. Edward Daniel Clarke (1769–1822), Fellow of Jesus College, Cambridge, another famous traveler of the time, who played an important part in clearing Bruce's name. "I have had an opportunity to converse with an inhabitant of Abyssinia," wrote Clarke from Cairo in 1801, "the rest of which conversation proves beyond doubt, that Bruce's writings are not only correct as to the observance of truth, but that few travellers have written with more veracity than he has done."[25]

Melville's attention must have also been drawn to Bruce by an article in the *Edinburgh Review* of 1824 which discussed a *Journal of a Visit to Some Parts of Ethiopia* by two Englishmen. The article followed a piece on the "Abolition of Impressment" that Melville used when he borrowed this particular volume of the *Edinburgh Review* from Duyckinck during the composition of *White Jacket*.[26]

In *Redburn*, published in the same year as *White Jacket* and *Mardi*, there is a facetious reference to an "Arabian traveller." This personage, whose distinguishing feature was his big eyes and who was pointed out to Redburn by an aunt "one Sunday in church," haunted the hero's imagination, for "when he was almost dead with famishing in the desert, he all at once caught sight of a date tree, with the ripe fruit hanging on it." Redburn had read about his adventures in "Stony Arabia," in a book whose very appearance evoked an image of the Arabian desert: "an arid-looking book in a pale yellow cover."[27]

24. S. Gobat, *Journal of a Three Years' Residence in Abyssinia* (New York, 1850), p. 463.

25. Letter to the Rev. Robert Tyrwhit in William Otter, *The Life and Remains of the Rev. Edward Daniel Clarke* (London, 1824), p. 490.

26. Leyda, *Log*, p. 309.

27. *Redburn*, chap. 1.

Whatever the possible identity of this particular Arabian traveler, the two most famous travelers to Arabia in Melville's time were the Dane Carsten Niebuhr and the Swiss John Lewis Burckhardt, the discoverer of Petra, of whom Melville speaks at some length in *Clarel*. Carsten Niebuhr was the father of the famous nineteenth-century historian Barthold Georg Niebuhr (1776–1831), whom Melville, also in *Clarel*, "wished to the dogs" for having "Niebuhr-ised" Rome, i.e. destroyed the beauty of faith and myth by his scientific analysis of Roman history.[28]

Niebuhr's *Travels through Arabia and Other Countries of the East* (1792), an account of a Danish expedition to Arabia in 1760–67 from which he returned as the only survivor famishing in the desert much like Redburn's Arabian traveler, was a classic of the age. Niebuhr's "Life" by his famous son had appeared in a volume called *Lives of Eminent Persons*, published in 1833 by "The Society for the Diffusion of Useful Knowledge," also publishers of the popular *Penny Magazine*. Hawthorne had borrowed from Niebuhr's account of the Parsis in Bombay in the article "Fire-Worshippers," which he wrote in 1837 for his "American Magazine of Useful and Entertaining Knowledge." The article, it has been shown, was a forestudy for the sketch on "Fire-Worship" in *Mosses from an Old Manse*, which Melville reviewed in the *Literary World* in August 1850.[29] It is more than likely that Niebuhr, who had aroused such interest in Hawthorne, contributed to Mel-

28. *Clarel, I,* 136. Horsford, *Journal,* p. 167.

29. See Millicent Bell, "Hawthorne's 'Fire-Worship,' Interpretation and Source," *American Literature, 24* (1952), 37–38. Arlin Turner, *Hawthorne as Editor* (University of La., 1941), pp. 254–55. Miss Bell has shown that Hawthorne borrowed from Niebuhr's chapter "Of the Persees," in *Travels through Arabia* (2 vols. Edinburgh, 1792), 2, 430–31.

ville's preoccupation with Persian fire-worshipers in *Moby-Dick*.

While Melville was writing *Typee* and *Omoo*, the startling discoveries of Sir Henry Austen Layard (1817–94) restored the lost civilization of the Assyrian empire to an astonished world, provoking a flood of articles on both sides of the Atlantic. Layard's account of his excavation of Nineveh in 1846 and 1847 appeared in several illustrated volumes in 1848–49. No wonder that Melville had Layard on his mind in the summer of 1849 when he was writing *White Jacket*.[30]

An inevitable "eagerness to experience for himself the wonders of the magical East" began to show itself in October 1849, when he embarked for Europe to find a publisher for *White Jacket*. On board the *Southampton*, which took him across the Atlantic, he was seriously considering "a glorious Eastern jaunt." He and two traveling companions "sketched a plan for going down the Danube from Vienna to Constantinople; thence to Athens on the steamer; to Beyrouth & Jerusalem—Alexandria & the Pyramids." Though Melville had no doubt this could be done "at a comparatively trifling expense," in the end he was compelled to abandon the plan, "by something of a pecuniary nature." Lack of funds and a longing for his young wife and son brought him home in February 1850.[31]

But he had experienced a whiff of the East in his meetings with Albert Smith and Alexander William Kinglake, and in his luggage when he returned were Beckford's *Vathek* and Hope's *Anastasius*, which he had received as gifts from Bentley, his London publisher.

Melville met Albert Smith—"the comic writer" whose "Natural Histories" of the Ballet Girl and the Gent he

30. *White Jacket,* chap. 86.
31. Ed. Eleanor Melville Metcalf, *Journal of a Visit to London and the Continent* (Cambridge, Mass., 1948), pp. vii f., 10.

was, decades later, to present to his wife—at a London supper party. Smith, recorded Melville, was just from the East, sported a blazing beard, told funny stories about his adventures, and purposed writing something "funny" about it.[32] *A Month at Constantinople* duly appeared in 1850. But by that time Smith had decided that "the funny school" had been "a little overdone of late,"[33] so that his book was simply another account of Eastern travel added to swell the catalogue of those already published. Of these the most famous was *Eothen, or Traces of Travel brought Home from the East,* published in 1844. When Melville met "Mr. Kinglake (author of Eothen?)" at a literary breakfast he had "a very pleasant morning" but obviously disliked the man.[34] He could not have warmed to the elegant smoothness and worldly wit of *Eothen,* a book that reflects the wellborn Englishman's traditional condescension in his contact with "natives." Years later, reading Arnold's *Essays in Criticism,* he emphatically marked Arnold's censure of Kinglake's style:

> It has not the warm glow, blithe movement, and soft pliancy of life, as the Attic style has; it has not the over-heavy richness and encumbered gait of the Asiatic style; it has glitter without warmth, rapidity without ease, effectiveness without charm. Its characteristic is, that it has no soul; all it exists for, is to get its ends, to make its points, to damage its adversaries, to be admired, to triumph.

["The style is (in the case of Mr. Kinglake) eminently the man," noted Melville.][35]

32. Leyda, *Log,* p. 800. Metcalf, *Journal,* pp. 37, 41.

33. A. Smith, *A Month at Constantinople* (Boston, 1852), p. iii.

34. Metcalf, *Journal,* pp. 81, 161–62.

35. Melville's copy of Matthew Arnold, *Essays in Criticism* (Boston, 1865), p. 68. Houghton Library, Harvard University.

However, *Eothen* was generally hailed as the most original travel book. *The Quarterly Review* bestowed on it the
highest contemporary praise by admiring it for rivaling
Vathek in its gorgeous descriptions and power of sarcasm
and for having caught the character and humor of the
Eastern mind as completely as *Anastasius*.[36] Both books
had appeared in Bentley's edition of "Standard Novels"
and were classics of Western literature.

When Melville got them "out of" Bentley in December
1849, he had probably told the publisher the story of his
Paris *Anastasius*. About a week before his interview with
Bentley he had bought a copy of *Anastasius* in Paris, which
had been seized by the English customs as "food for fire."[37]

The "fine" copy at whose seizure Melville was "much en-
raged" may have been the reprint in Baudry's Foreign
Library (2 vols. Paris, 1831), for by the law of copyright
between England and France there was "an absolute prohibition" against the importation of "books wherin the copyright shall be subsisting, first composed or written or printed in the United Kingdom, and printed or reprinted in any
other country." Any person importing such a book was
liable to have it forfeited, seized, and destroyed by any officer of the customs or excise.[38] The peculiar interest and

36. London *Quarterly Review*, 75 (1845), 760.

37. Metcalf, *Journal*, pp. 68, 85.

38. See Copyright Act, 1842, in E. J. Macgillivray, *A Treatise upon
the Law of Copyright* (London, 1902), p. 323. The suggestion that
Melville's copy of *Anastasius*, which was confiscated, was a Tauchnitz
edition (Sealts, 6, 1952, 244, No. 281) is invalid, as Hope's *Anastasius*
is not included in the list of publications of the Tauchnitz Collection
of British and American authors given by Bernhard Tauchnitz in
1860 *(Five Centuries of the English Language and Literature*, Leipzig,
Tauchnitz, 1860, "Preface by the Editor," p. ix). On the other hand,
"Baudry's European Library" also published *Vathek* with Beckford's
Italy (Paris, 1834), and, in 1849, pirated and reprinted a copy of
Redburn (Baudry's *British Library of Travels*, Vol. 2). See Leyda, *Log*,
p. 356.

tension that were attached to *Vathek* and *Anastasius* in the nineteenth century rivaled the fame of Byron. But *Vathek* had "the lustre of priority." It was the chief ingredient in the outburst of literary Orientalism that overflowed in Moore's *Lalla Rookh* and Byron's Oriental poems.

Vathek was published by the Reverend Samuel Henley, Beckford's tutor, in 1786 as a rendering from the Arabic. Beckford had originally composed it in French, and Henley had been entrusted with the preparation of an English version. Needless to say, though there was a Khalif Watik (842–847), son of al-Mutasim and grandson of the famous Harun al-Rashid, Beckford's romance had nothing to do with an Arabic original. It was an Oriental fantasy, one of the "gang of wild and *fauve* romances," (by Monk Lewis, Mrs. Radcliffe, Horace Walpole) as Sacheverell Sitwell has aptly called them, the collective appearance of which marked the break-up of eighteenth-century classicism.[39]

Beckford's extravaganza was meant to reproduce "the luxuriant imagery and wild incidents of an Arabian tale." It is the story of a Khalif who sells his soul to the devil "from the insolent curiosity of penetrating the secrets of Heaven." The Khalif's satanic pride leads him into extravagant cruelties perpetrated to achieve his purpose—to possess the treasures of the pre-Adamite Sultans. He finally obtains his goal by being admitted to the subterranean halls of Eblis, the Arabian Prince of Darkness. But there he discovers the vanity of his search after "forbidden power." Eternal torture is his punishment for "that blind curiosity, which would transgress those bounds the wisdom of the Creator has prescribed to human knowledge . . . and that restless ambition, which, aiming at discoveries reserved for beings of a supernatural order perceives not, through its infatuated

39. Sacheverell Sitwell, *Beckford and Beckfordism* (London, 1930), p. 34.

pride, that the condition of man upon earth is to be humble and ignorant."[40]

Vathek is, of course, stuffed with "Oriental delights" culled from the *Arabian Nights;* the *Mogul Tales* by Thomas Simon Gueullette, a facile and prolific French writer of pseudo-translations from Oriental languages; the *Adventures of Abdallah, Son of Hanif,* a complicated tale of an Arabian hero's search for the fountain of youth, by Jean Paul Bignon; and a whole library of Oriental or pseudo-Oriental works.[41] It is impossible to say how much Arabic or Persian Beckford knew when he wrote his romance at the age of twenty-two, though ten years later, when "the caliph of Fonthill" bought Gibbon's library at Lausanne, we find him railing at Gibbon's "ignorance of the Oriental languages."[42] *Vathek,* at any rate, has the trappings of Oriental scholarship in an elaborate machinery of notes drawn from Sir William Jones, Herbelot's *Bibliothèque Orientale,* Sale's Koran, Richardson's *Dissertation on the Languages of Eastern Nations,* and other widely used but respectable sources that were an invaluable reservoir to Byron and Moore and certainly came to Melville's attention.

Thomas Hope's *Anastasius, or Memoirs of a Greek Written at the Close of the Eighteenth Century* was published anonymously in 1819 as the story of an utterly unscrupulous though courageous and able man whose adven-

40. William Beckford, *Vathek: An Arabian Tale, with Notes, Critical and Expository,* London, Bentley, Standard Novels, 41 (with *The Castle of Otranto* and *The Bravo of Venice*). The date of the first American edition of *Vathek* is 1816. The only known copy of this edition is in the possession of James Babb, Librarian of Yale University, who kindly lent it to me.

41. See Martha P. Conant, *The Oriental Tale in England in the Eighteenth Century* (New York, 1908), pp. 37–41.

42. Lewis Melville, *The Life and Letters of William Beckford of Fonthill* (London, 1910), p. 272. See also H. A. N. Brockman, *The Caliph of Fonthill,* London, 1956.

tures take him to Albania, Turkey, Egypt, and the Arabia of the Wahabis. A writer in *Blackwood's Magazine* confidently attributed the work to Byron as the only person capable of producing a romance of Eastern travel that not only showed an intimate knowledge of Turkey, Egypt, and Greece but was "full of a clever innate scoundrelism . . . calculated to profane many serious and sacred things."[43] Byron himself had confided to Lady Blessington that he had wept bitterly over many pages of *Anastasius,* and for two reasons—first that he had not written it; and, secondly, that Hope had.[44] When Thomas Hope finally came forward as the author, the revelation caused a furor in the literary magazines. Hope was known as an antiquarian who had spent eight years in Eastern travel and published a book on household furniture which had introduced ancient Egyptian forms into furniture design.[45] Hope said that he wrote *Anastasius* as an account of real experience within a fictitious autobiographical superstructure "in order to enable the author to record his observations on the East in a form less trite than that of a journal."[46] But his contemporaries simply refused to credit this "nick-knacky gentleman" with either a picaresque narrative or an imaginative understanding of the East.

There can be no question that Melville had come across *Vathek* and *Anastasius* long before he acquired the books for his own library. Both works, as we have seen, were available in the library of the Albany Young Men's Association of which he had been a member in his youth. We may safely assume that they were part of the early phase of

43. *Blackwood's Magazine, 10* (Edinburgh, 1821), 201.

44. Samuel Smiles, *Memoir and Correspondence of the late John Murray* (2 vols. London, 1891), 2, 74–76.

45. Thomas Hope, *Household Furniture and Interior Decoration,* London, 1807.

46. *Blackwood's Magazine, 10,* 312.

Byronic Orientalism in Melville which expressed itself in the early "Fragments." In the notes to the *Siege of Corinth* Byron says that he never recurred to *Vathek* "without a renewal of gratification"; in *Childe Harold* he invokes "Vathek! England's wealthiest son." Byron's fascination with Beckford was such that "had these two men been able to exchange, the one his talent and his peerage, and the other his wealth," writes Sacheverell Sitwell, "it is probable that we should have had very much the same Fonthill by Byron, and very much the same poetry by Lord Beckford."[47]

To Melville the main fascination of *Vathek* must have lain in the air of demoniac evil and arrogant godlessness it exhales. In *Anastasius* he found a combination of realism with romance and philosophy—the ingredients of his own intellectual chowder. *Vathek* and *Anastasius* are "wicked books." They are tales of despotism and corruption that violate "the most sacred associations of life." In *Moby-Dick*, philosophically and symbolically developed, he made use of both the essence and the machinery of these novels. The exotic hell-fire in which they were broiled was their most significant contribution to Melville's own "wicked book."

MATERIAL FOR *CLAREL*

The evidence of Melville's reading on the Near East acquires its most concrete shape after his journey there. This is partly due to an external fact. Most of the books that have come down to us from his library date, as we have seen, from the most settled period in his life, the final years in New York, 1863 to 1891. But there are also internal indications to show that his reading on the Near East was not greatly expanded in the five years between the publication of *Moby-Dick*, in October 1851, and the journey to

47. Sitwell, *Beckford and Beckfordism*, p. 9.

Europe and the Levant on which he set out in October 1856. *Pierre, Israel Potter, The Piazza Tales, The Confidence-Man* do not reveal any new acquaintance with Near Eastern material, reweaving, for the most part, the familiar imagery of the earlier books into Melville's thematically recurrent symbolical patterns.

After his return from Palestine, there is a natural expansion in his approach to the Near East, though its metaphorical and symbolical content remained profoundly unchanged. At the deepest level, in the imaginative and artistic grasp of the Near Eastern scene, the journey marked a conclusion not a beginning for Melville, but it brought detailed and accurate knowledge of the terrain—physical, intellectual, and spiritual—and led to a closer association of basic images with their original Oriental sources.

Melville returned from his trip on May 19, "about the time the *Confidence Man* was published in 1857—and with much improved health," as his wife noted in her diary. We know from his journal that he intended to make literary use of his traveling experience. Not only was this his usual manner—but he also had the example of numerous contemporary writers, both English and American, who had taken the same route to the Near East. In addition, there were his perpetual financial straits, which in 1849 had induced him to write *Redburn,* and the expectations of his family. "It would be a luxury to hear from him a Narrative of his recent tour on the borders of the Mediterranean & Constantinople," wrote his uncle, Peter Gansevoort, in December 1857. "I am surprised that he has not made his travels the subject of a Lecture, to be hereafter woven into a Book . . . which would be not only instructive to others, but very profitable to him."[1]

In the end, Melville's only sustained effort to use his

1. Leyda, *Log,* pp. 578, 587.

experience of the Near East was an extraordinary poem, *Clarel*, which, in two volumes, describes the physical and spiritual pilgrimage of a "pilgrim infidel" in the company of an international band of Christian, Jewish, and Moslem "pilgrims." *Clarel* appeared anonymously in 1876, almost two decades after Melville's Palestine journey. It was published with the financial assistance of Peter Gansevoort, after a period in which it had remained in manuscript, "though not undivulged." The writing of *Clarel* extended from the early 1860's to the 1870's and proceeded with the help of Melville's own observations, recorded in his journal, and a number of books which he acquired in 1859, 1870, and 1872.

The earliest recorded purchase connected with *Clarel* is William McClure Thomson's *The Land and the Book; or, Biblical Illustrations Drawn from the Manners and Customs, the Scenes and Scenery of the Holy Land,* which was bought in 1859, the year of its American publication, by Allan Melville, Herman's brother.

William McClure Thomson (1806–94) was an American missionary in Syria and Palestine whose claim to fame, aside from his dedicated life and his book, rests on his connection with Lady Hester Stanhope, the legendary Queen of the Lebanon. It was Thomson whom the British consul at Beirut requested to perform the religious service at the funeral of that "most eccentric Lady" at her palatial retreat in the Lebanon mountains in 1839.

In *The Land and the Book,* a two-volume "pilgrimage" like Melville's, Thomson describes the fantastic funeral "under circumstances so novel and bewildering" as to be worthy of *Vathek.* The funeral procession, with torches and lanterns, got lost in the mazes of Lady Hester's labyrinthine gardens. When it finally emerged in the arbor where the lady was to be buried, it came face to face with "a ghastly heap," the bones of a French general, "with the head on top, having a lighted taper stuck in either eye-socket—a hideous, grinning spectacle."

"Such was the end of the once gay and brilliant niece of Pitt . . ." writes Thomson. "There was no end to her eccentricities. . . . She read the stars, and dealt in nativities and a sort of second-sight, by which she pretended to foretell coming events. . . . She had a mare whose back-bone sank suddenly down at the shoulders, and rose abruptly near the hips. This deformity her vivid imagination converted into a miraculous saddle, on which she was to ride into Jerusalem as queen by the side of some sort of Messiah, who was to introduce a fancied millennium."[2]

Melville vividly remembered the passage when, in *Clarel*, he wrote of "Pitt's sibyl-niece" who "read the stars," prophesied of wars, and kept a saddled steed waiting for some Messiah's call that never came.[3]

The Land and the Book was published during one of Thomson's visits to America and achieved instant success, selling more copies than any previous American book except *Uncle Tom's Cabin*.[4] The book is a description of Syria and Palestine in the usual form of personal journals but with constant and elaborate references to the Bible and numerous illustrations not only of manners and customs and famous sites, but of fauna and flora as well. The illustrations, as the author himself felt, added greatly to the value of the work and doubtlessly enhanced its importance to Melville, whose imagination, as we know from his use of other books, was particularly sensitive to the pictorial. Many of Thomson's illustrations were original, but most were drawn from "the best existing sources," among them Lane's *Modern Egyptians* and Bartlett's *Walks about Jeru-*

2. W. M. Thomson, *The Land and the Book* (New York, 1859), pp. 110–15.

3. *Clarel*, 2, 76.

4. *DNB, 18,* 490.

salem, on whose drawing of Tombs in the Valley of Jehoshaphat, reproduced by Thomson, Melville, as we shall see,
particularly relied.[5] *The Land and the Book* also contained
an illustration of the desert convent Mar Saba, which Melville had visited on his trip from Jerusalem to the Dead Sea
and which inspired the second volume of *Clarel.* A picture
of the Cave of the Nativity in Thomson represents the "silent shapes" kneeling "like statues" in adoration, which
Melville described in one of his cantos in the final part,
"Bethlehem."

Occasionally there is also an echo of Thomson in Melville's vocabulary in *Clarel.* "Wearied with a long ride from
Jaffa, I approached from the west when the shadows of
evening were falling heavily over the blank walls and un-
picturesque ramparts of Zion," writes Thomson. When in
the first canto, "The Hostel," Clarel muses on his first view
of Jerusalem spread out beneath him in the light of the
setting sun, "Thy blank, blank towers, Jerusalem" lie
heavy on his soul.[6] It is Thomson, too, who, like Melville,
describes Masada, the cliff fortress of the Maccabees in their
heroic fight against the Greeks, as a "crag." Thomson did
not see Masada himself, but he included an illustration of
the rock and told the story of the mass suicide (which we
find in *Clarel*) from the *Jewish Wars* of Josephus.[7]

But Thomson's most interesting effect on *Clarel* does not
appear in details of description or illustration. Thomson,
as we have seen, called his work a "pilgrimage" through the
Land of the Bible, designed "to illustrate the Word of
God." Throughout the book the "truth" of the Bible is
constantly reiterated in the face of descriptions which, by
force of their own truthfulness, turn the essence of biblical

5. See William Bartlett, *Walks about the City and Environs of
Jerusalem* (London, Virtue, n.d.), pp. viii, lv.
6. Thomson, Bk. II, p. 467. *Clarel, 1,* 4.
7. Thomson, Bk. II, pp. 418–19. *Clarel, 1,* 293.

truth into stale and bitter waters. Thomson admits that he "was seized with an almost irrepressible propensity to laugh" in the Church of the Holy Sepulchre at the sight of the cruelty and irreverence that prevailed there—an experience which came to Melville's mind when he wrote of the need "to check the hilarious heart" before the memorable Church. But after describing one of the reputed holy places, the tomb of Lazarus, as "a wretched cavern, every way unsatisfactory, and almost disgusting," Thomson heroically marshaled his forces: "I have never been so painfully impressed as to day with the importance of the advice not to allow mere topographical controversies to rob one of the delightful and precious influences which these sacred scenes ought to afford."[8]

Melville may have been originally inspired by Thomson in his decision to call *Clarel* a "pilgrimage" in the Holy Land and in his scheme of relating his own "travelogue" closely to scripture. The fundamental difference in his approach was, no doubt, only strengthened by Thomson. For Melville was concerned not with the correspondence and reconciliation of "nature and evangel" but with their devastating physical and spiritual clash.[9]

The books Melville bought in 1870 and 1872 when he was deeply engaged in composing his poem were three works by William Bartlett, Dean Stanley's *Sinai and Palestine*, Macgregor's *The Rob Roy on the Jordan*, and E. H. Palmer's *The Desert of the Exodus*. Of these, the works by Bartlett and Stanley are most important not only because they have survived with Melville's markings and annotations but also because they were standard works on which the other writers whom Melville read drew.

William Henry Bartlett (1809–54) was a "topographical draughtsman." He was a widely traveled Englishman and

8. See Thomson, "Author's Preface," pp. v, viii.
9. Thomson, Bk. II, pp. 556, 599; cf. *Clarel*, *1*, 21.

a friend of Melville's friend, the New York writer and editor N. P. Willis. Between 1834 and 1854 he made three journeys to the Near East, exploring Turkey, Greece, Asia Minor, Syria, Palestine, Egypt, and the Arabian desert. His accounts of these journeys accompanied by excellent drawings were published in a series of volumes of which *Walks about . . . Jerusalem* appeared in 1844, *Forty Days in the Desert, on the Track of the Israelites; or, A Journey from Cairo, by Wady Feiran, to Mount Sinai and Petra* in 1848; and *The Nile-Boat, or Glimpses of the Land of Egypt* in 1849.[10]

Melville bought *Forty Days in the Desert* and *The Nile-Boat*, in their fifth edition, on January 31, 1870, and gave *Walks about Jerusalem* to his wife on Christmas of the same year.[11] Being a Christmas present and the property of Elizabeth Melville, it was not marked, but its influence, like that of the other two books, is clearly discernible in *Clarel*, not only in the description of scenes and sites of the Palestine landscape but in such matters as the structural details of the poem itself.

On publishing this his first work, Bartlett stated that he wished to render it "useful" by identifying the scenes described in the Bible and presenting a "series of Views chosen with express reference to historical illustration."[12]

10. W. Beattie, *Brief Memoir of the late William Henry Bartlett*, London, 1855. Bartlett visited the U.S. in 1835–36, 1837–38, 1839, and 1852. On his visits he stayed with N. P. Willis. An interesting comment on his drawings was made by G. W. Curtis: "But in all the Eastern illustrations of that accomplished artist, the desert and river are too much adapted to the meridian of the drawing-room. . . . The grand pathos of the Syrian landscape is not there" (*The Howadji in Syria*, New York, 1852, p. 173).

11. Leyda, *Log*, pp. 709, 716. This copy, which Melville gave to his wife, is in the New York Public Library, Gansevoort-Lansing Collection.

12. *Walks about Jerusalem*, pp. iv, viii.

Though in *Clarel* Melville largely followed his own experience and the symbolical pattern of the poem in describing his hero's rambles about the city and its environs— the "New Jerusalem," Bethlehem, is at the end of Clarel's journey, not at the beginning, as in Bartlett—he clearly made use of Bartlett's illustrated "Views."

The most conspicuous example is "In the Glen," a canto by that name in Part I of *Clarel,* which describes a site outside the walls of Jerusalem on the banks of the Kidron, where Clarel's friend, the Italian nobleman Celio, "made his den." The exact location of Celio's "den" is plainly visible in Bartlett's illustration of "Tombs in the Valley of Jehoshaphat," which shows the three tombs exactly as described by Melville:

> A point there is where Kedron's shore,
> Narrowing, deepening, steepening more,
> Shrinks to an adamantine pass
> Flanked by three tombs, from base to head
> Hewn from the cliff in cubic mass,
> One quite cut off and islanded,
> And one presents in Petra row
> Pillars in hanging portico
> Or balcony, here looking down
> Vacantly on the vacant town.[13]

The heading of the canto, for example, echoes Bartlett's arrangement in "Walk II," in which the "way up the glen" leads the walker "along the brink of the Kidron" (Melville's spelling, "Kedron," is from Stanley's *Sinai and Palestine*) and brings him to the three tombs, "the most remarkable group of tombs around Jerusalem."[14] Clarel's and Celio's walks about Jerusalem may be traced with accuracy in Bartlett, and so may some of the historical reflections,

13. See plate in *Walks about Jerusalem,* facing p. 114 (my Fig. 1).
14. Ibid., p. 114.

1. Tombs in the Valley of Jehoshaphat.

e.g. the allusion to the seven-branched candelabrum of the
Jews on the triumphal arch of Titus which, in Bartlett, is
described and illustrated from a sketch by Melville's favorite artist, Piranesi.[15]

Melville's markings in Bartlett's *The Nile-Boat; or,
Glimpses of the Land of Egypt* are few, but this book, too,
made its contribution to *Clarel*. He was arrested by a passage on the Giza pyramids, by descriptions of dancing girls
watched by oriental officials with cold and sensual faces,
and by a vivid account of Egyptian slave-dealing which
Bartlett witnessed and found humane as compared with the
horrors of slavery in America.[16] Not only Bartlett's material but his artistic sensitiveness struck a deep chord of
sympathy in Melville, for he also marked a sentence in
which Bartlett speaks of the profound happiness we feel
"when a new page of the endless variety of creation lies
open before us."[17] A phrase in *The Nile-Boat* on "the desert of the Exodus," which Melville marked, evidently re-
minded him of Palmer's book of that title which he later
acquired.[18] Specifically, Melville's perusal of *The Nile-Boat*
had something to do with the "linked analogy" of Christ
and Osiris, which, in *Clarel*, strikes Rolfe, the much traveled American pilgrim in whom there is something of
Melville himself. Bartlett, at Philae, the "sacred" burial
place of Osiris, reflects on the remarkable analogy presented
by the Egyptian god who fell a sacrifice to the evil principle,
rose again to a new life, and became the judge of mankind
in a future state.[19]

15. *Clarel, 1,* 49–50. *Walks about Jerusalem,* p. 49.
16. See Melville's annotated copy of Bartlett's *The Nile-Boat* (5th
ed. New York, Scribner) in the New York Public Library (Gansevoort-
Lansing Collection), pp. 97, 113, 133.
17. *The Nile-Boat,* p. 116.
18. Ibid., p. 100.
19. Ibid., pp. 209–10.

But the book of greatest significance to Melville was
Bartlett's *Forty Days in the Desert* in which his markings
amount to almost seventy lines and checks. Most of the
words and passages marked, and many unmarked ones, are
clearly reflected in *Clarel,* often to the point of outright
borrowing in Melville's usual manner. The most noticeable
influence is in the first volume of the poem, in the canto
"Clarel," in Part I and in "Of Deserts," "Of Petra," and
"The Inscription" in Part II. But there are many traces of
the book throughout the poem often blended with similar
descriptions drawn from his own observation and other
writers, e.g. the striking juxtaposition of church and minaret which Rolfe contemplates in Jerusalem, a phenomenon
Melville noted in his journal, which Bartlett observed in
the convent of St. Catherine in the Sinai desert and Stanley mentioned in his description of the Church of the Holy
Sepulchre, two passages which Melville scored in both authors.[20]

The visions which pass before our pilgrim, Clarel, whose
sojourn in the Holy City has intensified his brooding on
"the intersympathy of creeds," present him the pageant of
the Meccan pilgrimage as it starts from Damascus Gate in
Jerusalem. In his mind's eye he sees the festive departure
of the Mahmal, the magnificent litter which contains the
Koran. It is borne by an

> *Elected* camel, king of all,
> In mystic housings draped in flow,
> *Silk-fringed,* with many a silver ball,
> Worked *ciphers* on the Koran's car
> And *Sultan's* cloth. He hears the jar

20. *Clarel, 1,* 123. Horsford, *Journal,* p. 142. Melville's annotated
copy of *Forty Days in the Desert* (5th ed. New York, Scribner) in the
New York Public Library, p. 78. Melville's annotated copy of Stanley,
in the New York Public Library, p. 455.

Of janizaries armed, a throng
Which *drum barbaric,* shout and gong
Invest. And camels—robe and shawl
Of *riders* which they bear along—
Each sheik a pagod on his tower,
Cross-legged and dusky. Therewithal,
In affluence of the opal hour,
Curveting troops of Moslem peers
And *flash* of scimetars and *spears*
In *groves* of grass-green pennons fair,
(Like *Feiran's palms* in fanning air),
Wherefrom the crescent silvery soars.
Then crowds pell-mell, a concourse wild,
Convergings from Levantine shores;
On foot, on donkeys; litters rare—
Whole families; twin panniers piled;
Rich men and beggars—all beguiled
To cheerful trust in Allah's care

. . . .
But long the way. And when they note,
. . . .
Some camp in field, nor far remote,
. . . .
Some child shall leap, and thrill in glee
'Mecca, 'tis Mecca, mother—see!'[21]

Melville must have read many descriptions of the Meccan
pilgrimage. In these lines, however, he borrowed details in
phrasing and arrangement from Bartlett, who described
the caravan of Mecca pilgrims as he had met them starting
from Cairo, on their way to Aqaba. Bartlett tells us that he
had timed his departure from Petra so as to meet the pilgrimage in the desert coming from the opposite direction.

21. *Clarel, I,* 26. The words in italics indicate Melville's borrowings, to be compared with the following passages from Bartlett.

His description of this caravan is one of the highlights of his book and is accompanied by a vivid illustration.[22]

Bartlett's account of the Mahmal evidently aroused Melville's particular interest, for he marked the sentence describing its contents: "the Mahmal contains nothing, besides two mus-hafs, or copies of the Koran, one on a scroll, and the other in the usual form of a little book, and each enclosed in a case of gilt silver, attached externally at the top."[23] He did not make any detailed use of this particular passage, but he appropriated many words and phrases from other passages that he did not mark.

The description of the Mahmal is introduced by Bartlett in the following manner:

> A burst of *tom-tom,* a rude sort of Arab *drum,* and a denser crowd, now indicated the approach of the central and most important part of the procession, viz., the Mahmal, or *camel selected* to carry, under a costly canopy, the copy of the Koran sent to Mecca. . . .
>
> The Mahmal, (seen in the centre of our view,) borne on the back of a fine camel, *selected* for the purpose, and exempted for the rest of its life from ordinary labour, consists of a square wooden frame, terminating in a pyramidal form, covered with dark brocade, and highly ornamented with gilt *fringes* and tassels. Mr. Lane [Edward William Lane, author of *Modern Egyptians,* translator of the *Arabian Nights*] states that in every cover he has seen, was worked a view of the Temple of Mecca, and over it the *Sultan's cypher.*[24]

This is how Bartlett describes the outriders of the caravan who were mounted on camels: "Their *riders,* gaily dressed

22. See plate in *Forty Days in the Desert,* facing p. 152 (my Fig. 2).
23. *Forty Days in the Desert,* p. 158.
24. Ibid., pp. 156–58.

2. The Mecca Caravan.

in long *silk* tunics . . . and splendid bernous adorned with golden *fringes,* were raised high on their saddle-bags, their *spears* glittering and *flashing* in the sun." The body of the caravan were "stragglers, who seemed as if they had been suddenly wafted from the suburbs of Cairo without note or preparation; a large proportion of them were tattered ragamuffins . . . some plodding *on foot,* others mounted *on donkeys;* women even bearing their children on their shoulders." He speaks of the pilgrims' *"blind reliance on the providence of Allah"* and contrasts the "deplorable rabble" with the groups of well-mounted gentlemen, some of whom "proud of their own gallant appearance . . . pranced and *curvetted."*[25]

Melville's striking comparison of the "groves" of pennons formed by the spears of the curvetting outriders to "Feiran's palms in fanning air," derives from Bartlett's previous description of the palm-groves of Wady Feiran in which he encamped and of which he included an illustration.[26] The change of Bartlett's "selected" camel into Clarel's "elected" camel clearly illustrates how Melville's source, in spite of literal borrowings, inevitably underwent an intrinsic artistic transmutation. In the hands of Melville, the Mahmal-carrying camel is suddenly transformed into a "chosen" incarnation of divine grace.

The terrible vision of the desert which follows the evocation of the Meccan pilgrimage in the canto "Clarel" was also drawn from *Forty Days in the Desert.* The Moslem mother in the caravan

> thinks upon the waste
> Whither the *Simoom* maketh haste;
> Where baskets of the white-ribbed dead
> Sift the fine sand, while dim ahead

25. Ibid., pp. 152–55.
26. See plate, ibid., facing p. 52 (my Fig. 3).

> In long, long line, their way to tell,
> The bones of camels *bleaching* dwell,
> With skeletons but part interred—
> Relics of men which friendless fell;
> Whose own hands, in last office, scooped
> Over their limbs the sand, but drooped:
> Worse than the desert of the Word,
> *El Tih, the great,* the *terrible.*[27]

Most of the passages in Bartlett which suggest these lines were marked by Melville, e.g.:

> The long procession, with its face set towards distant Mecca, defiled slowly away, the most advanced portion disappearing over the sandy swell, where we had first encountered it. I could not but follow it in imagination to its destined bourne, through the many perils which hovered about its painful track,—the Bedouins of the Great Desert, the fearful *Simoom,* the terrible destitution of water, and often of necessary food, under which many . . . must sink; I thought too, of the fate which, even now, might be hovering over the gayest and best furnished of these splendid pavilions, whose delicate tenants . . . must then be committed to their last homes in the wilderness, to form a fellowship in the grave with the broken-down straggler, whom the departing host has heartlessly left behind to perish, to dig with his expiring strength his own shallow grave in the sand, and await the passing of the angel of death. . . .
> . . . the high western Desert expands in endless prospect,—a vast plain of fine gravel, covered with small pebbles, varied by a long perspective of *camels' bones, bleached* perfectly white, pointing out the track of the pilgrims across its boundless level . . .[28]

27. *Clarel, I,* 27.
28. *Forty Days in the Desert,* pp. 149, 161.

Bartlett's account of El Tih, the northern tableland of the Sinai peninsula known as the Desert of the Wanderings (Tih), was not marked by Melville, but he followed Bartlett in his spelling and description of El Tih, the "great and terrible wilderness," and his knowledge of the terrain "which entombed an entire generation of the Israelites" must have been very thorough, drawn as it was not only from Bartlett but also from Stanley's *Sinai and Palestine*, where he did mark the passage on the Tih plateau, and Palmer's *The Desert of the Exodus* (in Palmer's correct spelling "Et Tih").[29]

Melville's description of the wilderness in his canto "Of Deserts" opens by reflecting the feeling of exhilaration which Bartlett experienced when walking at dawn in the desert air: "The sun is not yet up, though there is a glorious radiance through the vast opal concave of the sky . . . What most surprised me was the elasticity of spirits I generally experienced in the wilderness. The dry pure air probably had much to do with this. Sometimes the sense of free movement over the boundless expanse was indescribably and wildly ecstatic. . . ." The passage was marked by Melville, and so was the following, which describes the distress and listlessness suffered by man and beast as the sun rose higher and higher. In his opening lines Melville appropriated Bartlett's experience:

> Tho' frequent in the Arabian waste
> The pilgrim, up ere dawn of day,
> Inhale thy wafted musk, Cathay;
> And Adam's primal joy may taste,
>
> . . . .
>
> Tho' brisk at morn the pilgrim start,
> Ere long he'll know in weary hour

29. Ibid., pp. 64–65. Stanley, p. 7. E. H. Palmer, *The Desert of the Exodus* (New York, 1872), p. 232.

> Small love of deserts, if their power
> Make to retreat upon the heart
> Their own forsakenness.[30]

The desert in the canto extends as Bartlett described it, "Direct from Cairo by the Gate / Of Victors." Bartlett's statement that he joined his caravan in "the cemetery outside the Bab-en-Nusr, or Gate of Victory" was marked by Melville with his characteristic triple check.[31]

Melville's obsessive preoccupation with the pyramids and the vast shadow which they cast over the desert also appears in this canto. The secrets of these tombs loomed in Melville's imagination since his earliest writings. When he finally came face to face with the pyramids in December 1856, he was quite overwhelmed by their sinister influence—"vast, undefiled, incomprehensible, and aweful."[32] The passages on the pyramids in his *Journal* were reworked and revised many times. It was, therefore, a shock of recognition not a new discovery which prompted him to mark, both in *Forty Days in the Desert* and *The Nile-Boat,* for use in *Clarel* Bartlett's description of the pyramids of Giza casting, in the rising sun, immense and majestic shadows across the boundless and desolate Libyan desert:[33]

> When comes the sun up over Nile
> In cloudlessness, what cloud is cast
> O'er Libya? Thou shadow vast
> Of Cheops' indissoluble pile. . . .
>
> (*Clarel,* "Of Deserts")

In *Clarel,* the desert also encircles Petra, the petrified sym-

---

30. *Forty Days in the Desert,* p. 9. *Clarel, 1,* 215.
31. *Clarel, 1,* 216. *Forty Days in the Desert,* p. 5.
32. Horsford, *Journal,* p. 119.
33. *Forty Days in the Desert,* p. 196. *The Nile-Boat,* p. 97.

bol of man's heavenly city which in its phosphorescent gloom and desolation strikes terror in man's heart.

The rediscovery of Petra, the capital of Arabia Petraea of classical times, was one of the most famous feats of the nineteenth century. The Rock City, situated in the arid wasteland of the Dead Sea, was first visited by John Lewis Burckhardt (1784–1817), a Swiss by birth, who became a legendary figure to Melville's contemporaries owing to his unsurpassed knowledge of the Islamic way of life which he acquired in eight years of travel in Syria, Palestine, Egypt, the Arabian Peninsula, and the Hedjaz. Burckhardt's description of the holy cities of Mecca and Medina was the most accurate and complete account which had even been received in Europe up to that time. Adopting the name of Sheik Ibrahim and clad in the garb of a poor Arab—as Melville read in Bartlett—he was the first to explore the wonders of Petra, and his involuntary surprise and curiosity nearly led to the discovery of his assumed character as a Moslem.[34] Melville's interest in Petra first appears in 1853, three years before his Near Eastern journey, when Wall Street on a Sunday is described in "Bartleby" as "deserted as Petra." "New Petra" is also the residence of the meddling insensitive architect who explores Melville's symbolical chimney in the story "I and My Chimney" (1855). Burckhardt's reports were published in several volumes after his death, and Melville may have come across them in his voluminous reading of travel literature.[35] The books were

34. See "Preface of the Editor" to *Travels in Arabia* by the late John Lewis Burckhardt (London, 1829) and "Memoir on the Life and Travels of John Lewis Burckhardt" by H. Salt prefaced to Burckhardt's *Travels in Nubia*, 2d ed. London, 1822. Henry Salt (1780–1827) was appointed British consul-general in Egypt in 1815.

35. *Travels in Nubia*, London, 1819; *Travels in Syria and the Holy Land*, London, 1822; *Travels in Arabia*, 2 vols. London, 1829; *Notes on the Bedouins and Wahabys*, 2 vols. London, 1831.

available at the New York Society Library and were well
known from frequent references in periodical publications
and other contemporary writings. A portrait of the famous
"turbaned Swiss, Sheik Ibrahim" in his Arab burnous
served as a frontispiece to Bayard Taylor's *Cyclopaedia of
Modern Travel* (1856).

The story of Burckhardt's lonely death as a Moslem in
Cairo particularly affected Melville, for in his copy of *Forty
Days in the Desert* he marked Bartlett's reference to "poor
Burckhardt's grave." In *Clarel* he described the death and
Moslem funeral rites of the "blameless simulator"[36] of
which an eye-witness account by the British Consul in
Cairo had been reprinted in Taylor's *Cyclopaedia*.

Melville himself had not visited Petra, though he had met
a "Petra Party" at Jaffa, and he relied on other writers to
provide him with the material for scenes and sites which he
had not seen. The canto "Of Petra" thus naturally shows
heavy borrowing both from *Forty Days in the Desert* and
Arthur Penrhyn Stanley's *Sinai and Palestine*. As his numerous markings show, Melville read Stanley as thoroughly as
he read Bartlett, borrowing heavily from the text and scor-
ing references to other works, e.g. to an essay "Sacred Geography" in the *Quarterly Review* for March 1854, to the
famous *Biblical Researches* of Dr. Robinson, and to the
account of Dr. Clarke, the defender of Bruce and friend of
Burckhardt.[37]

Melville bought *Sinai and Palestine* in April 1870, about
two months after his purchase of Bartlett, and he read
Stanley with Bartlett's account in mind. "Dean Stanley," as
Melville knew him (and wrote on the title page of the book
below the author's name), was Canon of Canterbury and
Professor of Ecclesiastical History at Oxford when he pub-

36. *Forty Days in the Desert*, p. 6. *Clarel*, *1*, 156.
37. Melville's copy of Stanley's *Sinai and Palestine*, pp. ix, 453.

3. Encampment in Wady Feiran.

lished *Sinai and Palestine* in 1863. He was an acknowledged scholar in the field of "sacred geography" where Bartlett was a respected amateur. Stanley's purpose, as proclaimed in his work, has a direct bearing on the leitmotif in *Clarel:* the clash between the ideal and the real. "Much has been written, and still remains to be written, both on the History and the Geography of the Chosen People," writes Stanley. "But there have been comparatively few attempts to illustrate the relation in which each stands to the other. To bring the recollections of my own journey to bear on this question,—to point out how much or how little the Bible gains by being seen, so to speak, through the eyes of the country, or the country by being seen through the eyes of the Bible, —to exhibit the effect of the 'Holy Land' on the course of 'the Holy History,'—seemed to be a task not hitherto fully accomplished."[38]

In *Clarel* the canto "Of Petra" opens with a vision of a Red City found by a new Jason:

> 'The City Red in cloud-land lies
> Yonder'. . . .
>   'With dragons guarded round about
> 'Twas a new Jason found her out—
> Burckhardt . . .' 'The flume
> Or mountain corridor profound
> Whereby ye win the inner ground
> Petraean; this, from purple gloom
> Of cliffs—whose tops the suns illume
> Where oleanders wave the flag—
> Winds out upon the rosy stain,
> Warm colour of the natural vein,
> Of porch and pediment in crag.
> One starts. In Esau's waste are blent
> Ionian form, Venetian tint.

38. Stanley, "Advertisement," pp. vii–viii.

Statues salute ye from that fane,
The warders of the Horite lane.
They welcome, seem to point ye on
Where sequels which transcend them dwell;
But tarry, for just here is won
Happy suspension of the spell.'
                    'But expectation's raised.'[39]

The name of Petra, "The Red City," is given by Stanley and
associated with the red color of Petraean rock and the explanation that the Hebrew "Edom" means "Red." The
"purple gloom" of Petra's cliffs is also derived from Stanley,
for Melville especially marked Stanley's account of the city's
coloring.[40]
    In following Stanley, he was obviously particularly con-
cerned—as Nathalia Wright has pointed out[41]—with de-
picting Petra, the cloudland city, as encircled by dark hues
of gloom, not light. For Stanley especially criticized the descriptions of Petra colors by previous observers, including
Burckhardt, Dr. Robinson, and Harriet Martineau. "All
the describers have spoken of bright hues," writes Stanley.
"Had they taken courage to say instead, '*dull* crimson,
indigo, yellow, and purple,' their account would have lost
something in effect, but gained much in truth."[42] The word
"purple" is continuously stressed by Stanley throughout his
account, while Bartlett does not use it at all, referring to the
color as "crimson."[43] On the other hand, Stanley liked the
comparison of "that extraordinary veining and intermix-
ture of colours" in the rocks to "watered silk" which we find

39. *Clarel*, *1*, 298.
40. Stanley, pp. 88–89.
41. Nathalia Wright, "A Source for Melville's *Clarel:* Dean Stanley's
Sinai and Palestine," *Modern Language Notes*, *62* (1947), 110–16.
42. Stanley, p. 88.
43. Cf. *Forty Days in the Desert*, p. 128.

in Bartlett. A sentence in *Forty Days in the Desert* describes
the surface of the rocks as "veined after the manner of
watered silk"—the word "veined" singled out by Melville.[44] From Bartlett he also borrowed the following words,
which he marked: *the crimson-flowered oleander, rosy-*
coloured rock, pediment and *statues*. Bartlett, too, thought
of Venice when viewing the landscape from the top of
Mount Hor—though not, like Melville, of the "Venetian
tint" of Edomite rock, but of Venetian canals which, like
the clefts in Edomite rock, are concealed from the view of a
spectator who looks at the city from an elevated point.[45]

Stanley's reference to the wild tribes of Esau who hunted
on the mountains of Edom—also found in Harriet Martineau—probably inspired Melville's designation "Esau's
waste."[46] The image of the statues hewn into the rock as
"warders of the Horite lane" derives from Stanley's reference to Edomite or Horite habitations, underlined by Melville, and Stanley's note, also underlined, in which the
Hebrew name of the "Horim," who preceded the Edomites,
is explained as "dwellers in caves."[47] There is also Melville's
poetic transmutation of a prosaic comment to which Walter
Bezanson has drawn attention. Stanley says that "any one . . .
with highly-raised expectations" will feel disappointed at
the mere site of Petra. In the canto, the statement is transformed into a universal feeling that the vision of beauty is
more beautiful than the thing itself, challenged by the voice

44. Ibid., p. 134.
45. Ibid., pp. 121, 128, 129. The "Ionic" form of El Deir columns
(cf. Melville's "Ionian form") is pointed out by Harriet Martineau
(*Eastern Life*, Philadelphia, 1848, p. 357). See also colored plate of El
Deir in Vol. 1 of David Roberts, *The Holy Land, Syria, Idumea,
Arabia, Egypt and Nubia, from Drawings Made on the Spot*, 3 vols.
London, 1842.
46. Stanley, p. 87.
47. Ibid., p. 89.

of the optimist: "But expectation's raised."[48] The center of
the vision of Petra, as seen by Rolfe, is the "prospect from
Mount Hor" with a view of El Deir, "the convent," and
its portal:

> Imagine us now quite at home
> Taking the prospect from Mount Hor.
> Good. Eastward turn thee—skipping o'er
> The intervening craggy blight;
> Mark'st thou the face of yon slabbed height
> Shouldered about by heights? What Door
> Is that, sculptured in elfin freak?
> The portal of the Prince o' the Air?
> Thence will the god emerge, and speak?
> *El Deir* it is; and Petra's there,
> Down in her cleft. Mid such a scene
> Of Nature's terror; how serene
> That ordered form. Nor less 'tis cut
> Out of that terror—does abut
> Thereon: there's Art.[49]

It is precisely the "View from Mount Hor" that Melville
triple-checked in Bartlett's "List of Illustrations" in *Forty
Days in the Desert*. All of Petra that can be seen from Mount
Hor is the portal of El Deir, as Rolfe says, and it is clear that
the illustration itself, whose page number Melville marked,
provided the basis for the view in the canto. In approaching
El Deir, of which there is a separate illustration, Melville
also followed the arrangement of Bartlett, who announced
that true to his plan of "pictorial description," he would
"endeavour to give a more general idea of the entire site,

---

48. See Walter Bezanson, "Herman Melville's *Clarel*" (doctoral
dissertation, Yale University, 1943), p. 119. Stanley, p. 89. Bezanson's
edition of *Clarel* (New York, Hendricks House, 1960) appeared after
this book was in proof.

49. *Clarel, 1,* 299.

and then take the various monuments one by one in their natural order of succession from a given point."[50]

A close comparison of Melville's description with both Stanley and Bartlett and Melville's markings in both books reveals that in the actual wording of his lines Melville borrowed heavily from both.

Stanley's description of the Sīk, or "cleft" in which Petra —known among the Arabs as Wady Mousa—is situated prompted Melville's vision of Petra "down in her cleft."[51] Stanley, too, describing a "green platform" before El Deir, inspired the transmutation of the plateau on which El Deir stands into "Puck's platform." The ascent to the plateau in the canto is derived from marked passages in both books:[52]

> Of these flights of steps, that which conducts to El Deir is . . . one of the most remarkable works in the place . . . and nothing can well surpass the picturesque beauty of the ascent it affords to the upper region of the mountain—the ravine would have been impracticable without its assistance. The carved way is of unusual dimensions . . . sometimes cut on an inclined plane, and elsewhere fashioned into steps; it is now much injured by the action of the torrents, which occasionally pour down these ravines in a succession of waterfalls. [Bartlett]

> You turn up a torrent-bed . . . for torrent-beds from all sides pour down into this area . . . but soon leave it to ascend a staircase hewn out of the rock . . . High up in these rocks . . . with a green platform before it, is another temple . . . El Deir. [Stanley]

50. *Forty Days in the Desert*, p. 126: "List of Illustrations," "30-Mount Hor," "31-View from Mount Hor"; see plate facing p. 121 (my Fig. 4).

51. Stanley, p. 89.

52. *Forty Days in the Desert*, p. 136. *Stanley*, p. 92. *Clarel*, *1*, 299.

We should wind
Along ravine by mountain-stair—
Down which in season torrents sweep—
Up, slant by sepulchres in steep,
Grotto and porch, and so get near
Puck's platform, and thereby El Deir. [*Clarel*]

"The intervening craggy flight" between Mount Hor and
El Deir which Melville mentions echoes Stanley's words
"the intervening rocks," and is clearly seen in Bartlett's
illustration.[53] It is thus described in Bartlett's text: "Of this
wilderness of craggy summits, some are sharp and jagged . . .
others are buttressed and built up as if by art." This, combined with another passage describing two tombs cut out of
the rock, which Melville marked, is discernible in the most
significant lines of Melville's portrayal of El Deir:

Mid such a scene
Of Nature's terror; how serene
That ordered form. Nor less 'tis cut
Out of that terror—does abut
Thereon: there's Art.[54]

The canto entitled "The Inscription," which follows "Of
Petra," concerns a chalked message on a tablet found by
Derwent, the optimistic clergyman, on a rock in the wilderness of the Dead Sea. The inscription contains a symbolical—"mystical"—invocation to "the Slanting Cross." But

53. Stanley, p. 87.
54. *Forty Days in the Desert,* p. 121. *Clarel, 1,* 299. Walter Bezanson
regards these lines as a development of Stanley's comment on another
building in Petra, the Khasne or Treasury (Bezanson, "Herman Melville's *Clarel,*" p. 121). Cf. Stanley, p. 91: "One is more startled by
finding in these wild and impracticable mountains a production of
the last effort of a decaying and over-refined civilisation, than if it
were something which, by its better and simpler taste, mounted more
nearly to the source where Art and Nature were one."

4. View from Mount Hor.

before it is inspected and deciphered, Derwent wonders if
it is an "Inscription Sinaitic," and when the others leave,
one of the company of pilgrims, the Jewish geologist Margoth, lingers behind and scales the crag to add his heretical
signature to the tablet in the name of Science.[55]

The sequence in which "The Inscription" follows "Of
Petra" indicates the sources from which the idea of the
canto derived. Stanley ends his chapter on Petra with the
following observation: "The Arabic name, El Deir,—'the
Convent,'—implies their belief, that it was a Christian
church. Crosses are carved within it. The Sinaitic inscriptions are carved on the steps by which it is approached."[56]
In his account of Petra, Bartlett also refers "to a monument
with Sinaitic characters . . . which I did not see, but which,
if deciphered, may possibly throw light on many interesting questions connected with the former inhabitants of
Idumea."[57]

The circumstances under which the inscription is found
by Derwent and his companions show that Melville developed his theme from Bartlett's account of rocks "covered
with Sinaitic inscriptions" in the Sinai desert, in Wady
Maghara and Wady Mokatteb ("the Valley of the Inscriptions") and of his hunt for a hieroglyphic inscription which
he finally found on a tablet on the top of an almost inaccessible crag. Bartlett also reports how he found a Sinaitic inscription on the topmost block of granite, on the Serbal, the
highest crag in the Sinai desert, and added his signature on a
newspaper which he found folded between two fragments
in the rock and which bore the signatures of German scholars who had been there before him.[58]

Moreover, a section entitled "Encampment in Wady

55. *Clarel, 1,* 301–4.
56. Stanley, p. 92.
57. *Forty Days in the Desert,* p. 133.
58. Ibid., pp. 43, 45, 47, 63–64.

Feiran" immediately follows the account of "Sinaitic Writings" both in Bartlett's text and in the "List of Illustrations." It is therefore particularly striking to find the same arrangement in *Clarel:* "The Inscription" is followed by a canto entitled "The Encampment," in which Melville's Bethlehemites, like Bartlett's Bedouins "with Arab zest / ... spread the tent / And care for all."⁵⁹

The myths that had gathered around the Sinaitic Inscriptions began to evaporate in Melville's time, though to the present day their origins have not been fully clarified. The rock drawings and inscriptions, which date from the early Christian era, were first supposed to be records of the ancient Hebrews of the Exodus. By the time Melville was writing *Clarel* most of them had been deciphered as Aramaic, interspersed with Greek, Latin, and Arabic. Unlike other mystified travelers, Dean Stanley and E. H. Palmer (1840–82), a distinguished British Orientalist who was a member of the first Ordnance Survey of Sinai in 1869 and was later murdered by desert Bedouins, followed Niebuhr in adopting a firmly skeptical attitude. In a section entitled "Sinaitic Inscriptions" in *Sinai and Palestine* Stanley remarks that their numbers seemed to him to have been greatly exaggerated by previous travelers and that, in some instances, they had no "serious signification," having been cut by pilgrims or travelers who were visiting particular sacred localities. "Most of them could be written by any one, who, having bare legs and feet as all Arabs have, could take firm hold of the ledges, or by any active man even with shoes."⁶⁰ In the *Desert of the Exodus; Journeys on Foot in the Wilderness of the Forty Years' Wanderings*, which Melville bought on June 17, 1872, Palmer was even more emphatic:

59. *Clarel, 1,* 305. *Forty Days in the Desert,* p. 52.
60. Stanley, p. 60.

the 'Sinaitic inscriptions' are as worthless and unimpor-
tant as the Arab, Greek, and European *graffiti* with
which they are interspersed. . . . It is not true that they
are found in inaccessible places high up on the rock,
nor do we ever meet with them unless there is some
pleasant shade or a convenient camping ground close
by. In such places they exist in a confused jumble, re-
minding one forcibly of those spots which tourist
Cockneyism has marked for its own. . . . The instrument used appears to have been a sharp stone, by which
they were dotted in; a single glance is sufficient to convince the inquirer that neither care nor uniformity has
been aimed at in their execution. They have been
attributed entirely to Christian pilgrims, but, although
some of them are undoubtedly their work, the other
localities in which they are found renders it extremely
improbable that they can be assigned exclusively to this
class.[61]

It is obvious that Melville bore these accounts in mind
when he described his "Inscription Sinaitic" as "accessible"
and as a possible "crazy freak" of Mortmain, the melancholy
Swedish pilgrim in *Clarel*. The legend that the geologist
Margoth "rudely scores" into the rock acquires a particularly striking significance in relation to Melville's reading
of his scholarly sources:

> I, Science, I whose gain's thy loss,
> I slanted thee, thou Slanting Cross.[62]

It was Stanley's and Palmer's intrepid scholarship which
"slanted" the mystery of the Sinaitic Inscriptions, just as
Barthold Niebuhr's historical "science," which Melville

61. Palmer, *The Desert of the Exodus*, p. 160.
62. *Clarel, 1,* 304.

also condemned, deprived Roman history of both faith and myth.

Besides identifying sites, searching for inscriptions, and collecting place-names from the Sinai Bedouins, Palmer and a companion had the distinction of being the first to explore the Wilderness of the Wanderings, Et-Tih, the symbolical significance of which dominates Melville's landscape in the first volume of *Clarel*. Melville specifically relied on Palmer for the description of the Chapel of the Burning Bush in the Convent of St. Catherine on Mount Sinai in the second volume of *Clarel*:

> Where silence and the legend dwell,
> A cleft in Horeb is, they tell,
> Through which upon one happy day
> .   .   .   .
> .   .   .   .
> A sunbeam darts, which slants away
> Through ancient carven oriel
> Or window in the Convent there,
> Illuming so with annual flush
> The sombre vaulted chamber spare
> Of Catherine's Chapel of the Bush—
> The Burning Bush. Brief visitant,
> It makes no lasting covenant;
> It brings, but cannot leave, the ray.[63]

The lines, which seem a poetic paraphrase of Palmer, echo, in reverse order, Palmer's words "cleft," "darts," and "ray," as will be seen from the following passage: "The great attraction . . . is the Chapel of the Burning Bush, a little oratory at the east of the building. . . . Over the altar is a little window, shedding a dim, mysterious light, that well

63. Ibid., 2, 20.

befits so solemn a spot. It is said that the sunlight only pen-
etrates it one day in the year, and then a solitary ray darts
through a cleft in the mountain above and falls upon the
chapel-floor."[64]

The above examples show that borrowings from Melville's sources are scattered throughout the two volumes of
Clarel. They are visible not only in wording and imagery
but in the creation of secondary characters, in references to
biblical and Islamic history and the history of the Crusades.
The prototype of Nehemiah, for instance, the tract-dispens-
ing American "votary" bent on the restoration of Zion and
the conversion of the Jews, was a familiar figure in the
streets of Jerusalem and was probably modeled on Melville's
own acquaintance with an old Connecticut missionary, Mr.
Roberts, whom he observed in Jerusalem wandering about
with tracts.[65] Yet the creation of the character is also connected with Bartlett's allusion to "a certain eccentric missionary" in *Forty Days in the Desert* (which Melville underlined) and the distribution of missionary tracts in Arabic,
French, and English "to such as could read" by John Macgregor, an enterprising contemporary Englishman who
achieved fame as "The Rob Roy" after the name of his
canoe in which he undertook solitary cruises on the water-
ways of Europe and the Near East.[66] Macgregor's *The Rob
Roy on the Jordan*, which Melville acquired in November
1870, described the most adventurous of his voyages,
through the Suez Canal, down the Red Sea, and on the Jordan and Lake Gennesareth—being particularly valuable in
its detailed account of biblical lakes and rivers.

64. Palmer, pp. 64–65.
65. Horsford, *Journal*, p. 142.
66. *Forty Days in the Desert*, p. 86. John Macgregor, *The Rob Roy
on the Jordan, Nile, Red Sea, and Gennesareth, &c. A Canoe Cruise
in Palestine and Egypt, and the Waters of Damascus* (New York, 1860),
p. 69.

Biblical references and allusions to Jewish, Christian, and Islamic history naturally permeate *Clarel* as they do any book on the subject of Syria and Palestine, not merely Melville's traceable sources. These sources, too, are closely interdependent. Bartlett, a popular writer famous for his illustrations, was, as we have seen, made use of by Thomson. Palmer and Macgregor often quote Stanley to establish topographical and etymological accuracy. In fact, *The Desert of the Exodus* opens with a tribute to Stanley's "masterly exposition of the connection between sacred history and sacred geography" which, says Palmer, "embodies the whole idea of those who conceived and matured the scheme for making an accurate survey of the Peninsula of Sinai."[67]

The relation between "sacred history" and "sacred geography" fascinated Melville, as it did all his contemporaries, though in *Clarel*, as well as in the *Journal*, it acquired a tension almost to a breaking point. Yet he was also anxious to turn his work into an accurate "travelogue," however symbolical, and the most famous travelers throughout the ages were allotted their rightful places in the poem.

In fact, Stanley's reference to an essay "Sacred Geography" in the *Quarterly Review* of March 1854, which he marked, led him to a classified list of travelers to Syria, Palestine, and Arabia through the ages, beginning with the religious pilgrims during the period of the Roman Empire and ending with the scientific and literary explorers in his own time. He followed the pattern in his canto "Night in Jericho," alluding, like the essay, to "the healthy pilgrims of times old" who saw ancient shrines which have since disappeared, and listing the Frenchmen Volney, Chateaubriand, and Lamartine, in succession, as recent pilgrims.[68] Volney (1757–1820), a savant dubbed a "pilgrim deist" in

67. Palmer, p. 17.
68. Stanley, p. ix. London *Quarterly Review*, *94* (1854), 357 f. *Clarel*, *1*, 234.

Clarel, was, in the words of the essay, "almost wholly indifferent, if not hostile, to the events that have invested Palestine with such transcendent interest. His book is chiefly important for its clear classification of the several populations which inhabit the country."[69] Volney's *Travels through Syria and Egypt* (published in English in 1788), and *A Pilgrimage to the Holy Land* by the poet and statesman Lamartine (1790–1869), appear to have been the main sources from which Melville drew his information on the Druzes.[70] Chateaubriand (1768–1848) visited the Near East in quest of imagery for *The Martyrs*. Appropriately, he is called "The Catholic pilgrim" in *Clarel*. His *Travels in Greece, Palestine, Egypt and Barbary during the Years 1806 and 1807* appeared in America in 1816 and was among the books owned by Evert Duyckinck.[71] Melville evidently consulted the book when he was writing his poem, for apart from the reference to Chateaubriand himself, the Arabic name of Jerusalem, El Cods, as Walter Bezanson first noted, appears in *Clarel* in Chateaubriand's French spelling.[72]

Another well-known contemporary "commentator on the East," with whose most famous book Melville was evidently familiar, is David Urquhart (1805–77), author of *The Spirit of the East* (1838). Urquhart, a British diplomat, was known as an extravagant Turkophile whose enthusiasm clouded his judgment, and Melville's reference to him as

69. London *Quarterly Review*, *94*, 362.

70. *Clarel*, *1*, 234; *2*, 76–77. A. M. L. de Lamartine, *Pilgrimage to the Holy Land* (2 vols. Philadelphia, 1835), *2*, 37, 49 f.

71. See "Catalogue of the Books of Evert A. Duyckinck in 1838," in the New York Public Library.

72. *Clarel*, *2*, 79. F. A. R. de Chateaubriand, *Travels* (Philadelphia, 1816), p. 258. "El Cods" is not "a peculiar misspelling of the Arabic for Jerusalem," as Bezanson suggests ("Herman Melville's *Clarel*," p. 150); the spelling represents a common French transliteration of the Arabic "K" or "Q" (al-Quds) by "C." The word is spelled "El-Kods" in the English version of Volney, *Travels* (2 vols. London, 1788), *2*, 304.

an "eccentric ideologist" accurately reflects the view of his
time.[73]

An indication of the books which Melville used as material for *Clarel* is important in understanding his workmanship and the background of the poem. Yet the poem
itself, like Melville's other work—an inexhaustible treasure house for the sub-sub-librarian—is deeply rooted in
Melville's own experience, not only spiritual but physical.
Clarel's excursions from Jerusalem, to Jericho, the Jordan,
Sodom, the Dead Sea, Mar Saba, and Bethlehem do not
range beyond Melville's own trips which he recorded in his
journal. The editor of Melville's *Journal of A Visit to
Europe and the Levant* has shown "the extreme closeness"
in narrative, characterization, scenes, sights, and incidents
with which he followed it in composing the poem *Clarel*.
He did not put the journal aside when he returned home in
1857, writes Howard C. Horsford: "the experiences of the
trip which the journal records were such a living and vital
part of his thinking that he read and reread, used and reused
it constantly throughout at least the next fourteen or fifteen
years." This is amply demonstrated by the evidence of
much revision and marking, particularly in the sections on
Constantinople, Egypt, and Palestine. "In ink, black lead
pencil, and a kind of red-brown drawing pencil, he repeatedly underscored interesting observations, marked them
with marginal lines or stars or asterisks or various other

73. *Clarel*, 2, 204. In *Clarel* Urquhart appears, "now obsolete," in
a discussion concerning the Turkish and Polish questions in which
he was deeply implicated. At the time of the Crimean War he rejected the principle which prompted English action, i.e. the substitu-
tion of a European protectorate over the Christian subjects of Turkey
for that exercised by Russia, and maintained that such a step constituted an interference into the internal affairs of Turkey and
violated the law of nations. In this connection he published "Appeal
of a Protestant to the Pope to restore the Law of Nations" (*DNB, 58,*
43–45).

symbols of his own invention, enclosed them in boxes, changed words, crossed out others, and added new comment."[74]

The central idea of *Clarel* is the experience of "sacred geography" both in its physical and metaphysical aspects, from several viewpoints, which resolve themselves in the hero's progress from religious disillusionment to a triumphant affirmation of the force of the human spirit that transcends the limitations of creed. In the treatment of its theme *Clarel,* like *Moby-Dick* and all of Melville's best work, follows a pattern which clearly arises from Melville's method in the use of his journal and of the books he bought while writing *Clarel.* The complex symbolic meaning is riveted to a solid foundation of realism that is shaped by the author's own experience but firmly established on an impressive structure of authoritative contemporary literature.

SAADI'S *GULISTAN*

It was not until the end of the eighteenth century that the West began to be really curious about the movement of Islamic mysticism known as Sufism, and the Sufi poets of medieval Persia. The fame of Hafiz (d. about 1390) in the West stemmed from a poem, "A Persian Song of Hafiz," which was included by Sir William Jones in his translations from Asiatic poetry, published at Oxford in 1772. This book, entitled *Poems, Consisting Chiefly of Translations from the Asiatick Languages,* contains the first English translation of a Persian poem. Its influence on the most famous nineteenth-century poets—Goethe, Byron, Southey, Moore, and, in America, Emerson—was prodigious and comparable only to the later influence of Fitzgerald's Omar Khayyam. Saadi (d. 1291) had become familiar in the West through the interest of Voltaire and Goethe and the speci-

74. Horsford, *Journal,* "Introduction," p. 32.

mens of his poetry that had appeared in Sir William Jones' *Asiatic Miscellany* of 1792.[1] As a Western scholar of Persian poetry has noted: "It was left to Jones to tell us that there was poetry in Shiraz." Also, "we may add to Jones's title to fame: *genuit Fitzgerald*."[2]

In America there is no indication of any general interest in Saadi until 1830, when the *American Quarterly Review* published as its main article a lengthy and learned review of a French translation of the *Gulistan*. There it is stated that, in America, the Persian writings have "not yet begun to be in vogue."[3] They were so, however, a decade later, when Emerson published his poem "Saadi" in the *Dial* in 1842 and the Orientalism of the Transcendentalists had popularized the Sufi mystics. The work of the Persian poets, says Emerson in his preface to the *Gulistan*, "must draw the curiosity of good readers. It is provincial to ignore them."[4]

Melville had come across them by the time he was writing *Mardi*, where there is a reference to Hafiz, and Yoomy, the poet—apparently named after Jami (d. 1492)—addresses the dawn "with a Persian air."[5] He was well aware of the Persian connotations of rose and wine imagery long before he read Saadi's *Gulistan* and the *Rubaiyat of Omar Khayyam*.

1. See *Oeuvres complètes de Voltaire* (ed. Moland, 52 vols. Paris, 1877–85), *12*, 62 f.; *20*, 617; *24*, 30. Goethe, *West-Oestlicher Divan*, 3 vols.; Vol. 2, *Noten und Abhandlungen* (ed. Ernst Grumach, Berlin, 1952), p. 49. *Asiatic Miscellany* (Calcutta, 1792), p. 95.

2. R. M. Hewitt, "Harmonious Jones," in *Reginald Mainwaring Hewitt* (Oxford, 1955), pp. 47, 54. Arberry, *Asiatic Jones* (above, p. 44, n. 5), p. 33.

3. *American Quarterly Review, 8* (1830), 1.

4. *The Gulistan or Rose Garden. By Musle-Huddeen Sheik Saadi, of Shiraz. Translated from the Original by Francis Gladwin. With an Essay on Saadi's Life and Genius, by James Ross, and a Preface, by R. W. Emerson* (Boston, Ticknor and Fields, 1865), p. vi.

5. *Mardi*, 2, 54, 188.

Melville bought the *Gulistan* in September 1868, when he was writing *Clarel*.[6] Significantly, the second volume is permeated with the rose and grape imagery associated with the Sufi poets, and also has a reference to "Saadi's wit."[7] Melville's copy of the *Gulistan*, in the classical translation of Francis Gladwin (first published in Calcutta in 1806), has come down to us, with his markings and one annotation. But it is the London edition of 1822 which he bought, not the first American edition of 1865 to which Emerson wrote his famous preface. Yet the date of the purchase makes it likely that Melville's interest was stimulated by Emerson's enthusiasm for the author of the *Gulistan* which, in itself, is not a mystical but a didactical work, a typically Oriental collection of anecdotes and maxims, written in a mixture of verse and prose.

The *Gulistan* has left no direct imitations or verbal correspondences in *Clarel*, unlike the other books which were bought and read about the same time, though the mystical perfume of the Persian rose garden pervades the second volume of *Clarel* in the same measure as the aridity of the biblical wilderness corrodes the first. It is clear that his perusal of the *Gulistan* impressed Melville with "Saadi's wit" rather than with his saintliness or his mystic apprehension of the divine; this is evident from the poem "The Rose Farmer," which the Persian author of the "Rose-Garden" inspired.[8]

The overt significance of Melville's reading of the *Gulistan* lies somewhere else. By revealing the profound differ-

6. The book is in the possession of the Yale University Library (Yale Collection of American Literature). *The Gûlistân, or Rose-Garden; by Musle-Huddeen Shaik Sâdy, of Sheeraz. Translated from the Original, by Francis Gladwin, Esq., New Edition,* London, 1822. "H. Melville Sep. 29, 1868, N.Y."

7. *Clarel*, 2, 227.

8. See below, pp. 258 f.

ence with which he and Emerson regarded Saadi, his markings in the book provide additional evidence for the extreme divergence in the spiritual outlook of the two men.

To Emerson, Saadi was primarily a "fortunate" man, i.e. "a happy nature, to which victory is habitual, easily shedding mishaps, with sensibility to pleasure, and with resources against pain." The nature of such a man "results from the habitual perception of the beneficent laws that control the world." According to Emerson's preface to the *Gulistan,* Saadi "inspires in the reader a good hope. . . . He asserts the universality of moral laws, and the perpetual retributions. He celebrates the omnipotence of a virtuous soul." Emerson cannot help exclaiming: "What a contrast between the cynical tone of Byron and the benevolent wisdom of Saadi!" The side of Saadi which does not conform with this view is blurred over by Emerson: "With the exception of a few passages, of which we need not stop to give account, the morality of the *Gulistan* . . . is pure."[9]

A very different picture emerges from the pattern formed by Melville's markings in Saadi. So far from ignoring Saadi's moral lapses, of which Emerson did not "stop to give account," Melville marked a chapter on homosexuality which even after the attempted "purification" of the translator has still to be faced by the reader as an integral part of Saadi's moral code.[10] The other passages singled out by Melville

9. Preface to *Gulistan,* pp. vii, viii, x.

10. Melville's copy of the *Gulistan,* Tale IV, p. 179. On this passage there is the following comment by James Ross, reprinted in the American edition of the *Gulistan:* "I put my translation of the Gulistan into the hands of my friend Mr. Gladwin, wishing to have his opinion of it, when he told me, that he had also projected a translation of it, and meant to obviate another indelicate allusion, particularly in the fifth chapter, by changing the male for the female character. That I see he has done; and he has otherwise endeavoured by castrating the English of it, to purify Gentius's text." Gentius was the first translator of the *Gulistan* (1651), on whose Latin work Gladwin's Calcutta edition was based.

contradict Emerson's view of Saadi's "benevolent" wisdom and his belief in the omnipotence of good. They deal with evil in the world: fear, envy, malignity, ingratitude, false friends, hypocrisy, loneliness, the abuse of power, frustrated hopes, death, and, above all, poverty. The most heavily marked passage of all inspires the reader not with "good hope" but with pity and terror, and the frustration of Ecclesiastes: "Whosoever stretcheth out his neck claiming consequence, is beset by enemies from all quarters. Sâdy lies prostrate, freed from worldly desires; no man attempteth to combat with one who is down on the ground."[11] This passage is singled out by Melville in two ways: it is heavily underscored and also marked by triple marginal lines—the sign of utmost stress in Melville's system of marking.[12] The passage that is most conspicuously marked after that is equally tortured; it can hardly be said to reveal Saadi's "fortunate" nature: "Many a person has slept an[d] hungered without any one knowing who it was: many a vital spirit has departed, over which no one has wept."[13]

The only penciled annotation in Melville's copy of the *Gulistan* concerns the statement that a man's enemies often inherit his estate: "This good news concerns not *me* but *mine enemies; that is, those who shall succeed to my kingdom.*" Melville's footnote to this passage expresses a revealing bitterness of feeling about family relationships. It consists of two words: "His family?" he asks.[14]

There are mere glimpses of Saadi's perception of the beneficent laws of the universe in the following markings: "Rectitude is the means of conciliating the divine favour. I

11. *Gulistan*, p. xx.
12. On Melville's manner of marking his books see William Braswell, "Melville as a Critic of Emerson," *American Literature*, *9* (1937), 317–34; W. E. Bezanson, "Melville's Reading of Arnold's Poetry," *PMLA*, *69* (1954), 367.
13. *Gulistan*, pp. 27–28.
14. Ibid., p. 18.

never saw any one lost on a straight road"; or, "Sugar obtains not its value from the cane, but from its innate quality." The passages on this theme are few. Their culmination is reached in an Emersonian cry for self-reliance as a defense against evil: "A great river is not made turbid by a stone; the religious man who is hurt at injuries, is as yet but shallow water." But the perception of truth can only be achieved in solitude: "Though you possess riches, rank, lands, and chattels, if your heart is with God you are a recluse," is marked by Melville. But he also marks: "It is contrary to reason and to the counsel of the wise, to take medicine without confidence, or to travel an unknown road without accompanying the caravan."[15]

There is only one trait that Melville and Emerson have in common in their reading of Saadi. Both were attracted by the Persian's "sensibility to pleasure."[16] In Melville this attraction expresses itself in his markings of Saadi's nostalgic descriptions of spring: "O the season when verdure bedecked the garden, then how blithe was my heart. Wait, my friend, until the return of spring, when you will behold grass growing out of my clay." In another sentence the word "midspring" caught Melville's attention. He underlined it, as if to bring out its virginal voluptuousness which Saadi, in the same sentence, caught in the image of "the rose decked with pearly dew, like blushes on the cheek of a chiding mistress." Both Melville and Emerson called attention to Saadi's ardor for beauty: "for whosoever has beauty, wherever he puts his foot, doth not every one receive him with respect?" is marked by Melville. But he also marked what Emerson passed over, the defeat of beauty by ugliness: "for the sound of the harp cannot overpower the noise of the drum, and the fragrance of ambergris is overcome by

15. Ibid., pp. 29, 93, 113, 281, 289.
16. Emerson, preface to *Gulistan*, p. viii.

fetid garlic." It is in the perception of evil and the maleficent
laws of the universe that Melville found an affinity with
Saadi. Also, unlike Emerson, he recognized the predominance of the practical moralist over the mystic. He checked:
"Tranquility of mind requires a fixed income."[17]

It is curious to find, on the evidence of modern scholars,
that it was Melville, not Emerson, who appears to have "got
at" Saadi more closely. In considering the Sufi attitude to
the problem of Good and Evil the following conclusion is
reached in the *Legacy of Persia:*

> The great body of Muslims . . . incline to the belief
> that Creation is wholly good, the extremist view being
> that what seems to be evil comes from God too, and
> must therefore be good. . . . This attitude alone could
> not satisfy the Sufis, however; they saw Good and Evil
> as inevitably and intimately linked in manifest Crea-
> tion. . . . Like many Christians, numbers of them were
> ultimately drawn into . . . holding Creation itself as
> the Supreme Evil.[18]

As to the predominance of the moralist over the mystic in
Saadi, we have the authoritative testimony of E. G. Browne:
"In the main it may be said without hesitation," he says in
his *Literary History of Persia,* "that worldly wisdom rather
than mysticism is his chief characteristic, and that the *Gulistan* in particular is one of the most Machiavellian works
in the Persian language. Pious sentiments, and aspirations,
indeed, abound; but they are, as a rule, eminently practical,
and almost devoid of that visionary quality which is so characteristic of the essentially mystical writers."[19] But he

17. *Gulistan,* pp. xv, 152, 240, 249, 280.
18. G. M. Wickens, "Religion" in *Legacy of Persia* (Oxford, 1953),
pp. 162 f.
19. E. G. Browne, *Literary History of Persia* (4 vols. Cambridge,
1928), 2, 526.

sensed Saadi's worldliness. The figures of the Persian gentleman rose-farmer in Melville's rose poems and of the poet
Zardi in the unpublished "Rammon," which Saadi inspired,
are "unconsciously pledged to avert themselves from entire
segments of life and thought."[20]

To Melville there was only one remedy against evil:
goodness—man's humanity to man. Again and again he
marked passages in the *Gulistan* which refer to benevolence and kindness. *"Enjoy and bestow"* is underlined as
a motto for the rich man. "If you eat colocynth from the
hand of a kind man, it is preferable to a sweetmeat given
by one who has a crabbed countenance." It is man's *"duty
to look kindly on any one"* (underlined). Benevolence
should include the wicked. *"O man of prudence, do thou
good to the wicked"* is also underlined. But he also scores:
"Die, thou envious wretch!" and even "whosoever killeth
a wicked man, relieveth the world from his injuries and de-
livereth himself from the wrath of God." The wicked man
cannot help being evil, slanderous words "will" issue from
his lips.[21] The manner in which Melville marked this passage shows his power as a reader who probes "at the very
axis of reality." His line under "will" has the effect of a
flash which suddenly illumines the impersonal power of
evil and the helplessness of the wicked man entangled in the
ropes of his own nature as Fedallah is in the whale-line of
Moby-Dick. Melville's pencil probed into a depth that Saadi
himself never reached. But Saadi's humanity ties him to
Melville: "The children of Adam are limbs of one another,
and are all produced from the same substance: when the
world gives pain to one member, the others also suffer un-
easiness. Thou who art indifferent to the sufferings of

20. On "Zardi" see Eleanor M. Tilton, "Melville's 'Rammon': A
Text and Commentary," *Harvard Library Bulletin, 13* (winter 1959),
69, 74. Cf. the discussion of "The Rose Farmer" below, p. 258.

21. *Gulistan,* pp. 13, 44, 131, 252, 258, 265, 299.

others, deservest not to be called a man."[22] This passage
was marked by Melville along the margin. Saadi's humanity
is recognized by scholars and critics of Persian literature:
"As the chief virtue he seems to regard 'goodness,' great
sympathy for our fellow-creatures without any egotistic
view. He that obtains the qualification of good is really immortal."[23]

In his copy of Emerson, Melville heavily marked a Persian saying praised by Emerson in *The Conduct of Life:*

> Fooled thou must be, though wisest of the wise;
> Then be the fool of virtue, not of vice.[24]

Melville's heroes are "fools of virtue." Pierre is "the fool
of Truth, the fool of Virtue, the fool of Fate."[25] This points
to another aspect in considering Melville's reading of Saadi,
namely its relation to his own work.

We do not know whether Melville's purchase of the
Gulistan in 1868 was the beginning or the culmination of
his interest in this particular work. It should be pointed
out, however, that there is a striking parallel in Tale VII
of the *Gulistan* with the story of Pip, "The Castaway" in
Moby-Dick.[26] In Melville's copy of the *Gulistan* this tale
is marked with three interlocked checks:

> A King was sitting in a vessel with a Persian slave. The
> boy having never before seen the sea, nor experienced
> the inconvenience of a ship, began to cry and lament,
> and his whole body was in a tremor. Notwithstanding

22. Ibid., p. 20. Cf. W. M. Thackeray, *Notes of a Journey from
Cornhill to Cairo* (London, 1846), p. 64: "The Maker has linked together the whole race of man with His chain of love. I like to think
that there is no man but has kindly feelings for some other, and he
for his neighbour, until we bind together the whole family of Adam."

23. *Encyclopaedia of Islam* (4 vols. Leyden, 1913–34), *4, 38.*

24. "Illusions," in *The Conduct of Life.*

25. *Pierre,* Bk. XXVI, p. iv.

26. *Moby-Dick,* chap. 93.

all the soothings that were offered, he would not be pacified. The King's diversion was interrupted, and no remedy could be found. A philosopher who was in the ship said, "If you will command me, I will silence him." The king replied, "It will be an act of great kindness." The philosopher ordered them to throw the boy into the sea, and after several plunges, they laid hold of the hair of his head, and dragging him towards the ship, he clang to the rudder with both his hands. When he got out of the water, he sat down quietly in a corner of the vessel.[27]

Pip, too, is a boy. When Stubb "lowered with him," Pip "evinced much nervousness" and was afraid of the whale. To teach him a lesson in "courageousness," Pip "was left behind in the sea" by Stubb when he jumped from the boat in his terror at the whale. When he was finally rescued, Pip "went about the deck an idiot" with "passive eyes."

Melville's markings of passages with sea imagery in the *Gulistan* also echo his own novels: "Why should he dread the waves of the sea who hath Noah for his pilot?" is checked. Saadi's symbolical use of "diving" and of the dualism of sea and shore attracted Melville's attention: "If the diver were to think of the jaw of the crocodile, he would never get in his possession precious pearls." Or, "the sages have remarked, that in the sea there are good things innumerable; but that if you wish for safety, you must seek it on the shore."[28]

In his vision of death Melville felt a kinship with Saadi. *"Life is snow and the summer sun advanceth,"* is marked and underlined. The anguish he suffered at his public failure as a writer is revealed by a heavy marginal line against the following passage, doubled at the first sentence: "Shame

27. *Gulistan*, p. 16.
28. Ibid., pp. vii, 30, 162.

on that man who departed without finishing his work; who, when the drum was beating for marching, had not made up his burthen." And "for the last time come before me, O my friends! my days have been spent in ignorance; I have not performed my duty: shun my example."[29]

Saadi's sense of *"the desert of Jerusalem"*[30] is underlined, for it reflects Melville's own experience of the Judean desert on his trip of 1856–57 which was transmuted in the symbolism of *Clarel*. Of similar interest in relation to this poem are Saadi's reflections on the necessity of restraint in speech and the wisdom of silence. They are echoed in the character of Rolfe in *Clarel*. Rolfe's characteristic tendency is to "say so." But his frankness in expressing his inmost thoughts has brought so many rebuffs that he distrusts his impulse to be "indiscreet in honesty."[31] The conclusion "that we have here a projection of Melville's own problem" at the time[32] is confirmed by the passages on speech and silence which Melville underlined in the *Gulistan,* e.g. "How then could I venture to make my appearance in the assembly of grandees of sovereignty, the confluence of men of piety and the center of profound scholars; where, *if in the course of conversation I shall feel animated, I might be presumptuous?"*[33] Other marked passages show that Melville was particularly preoccupied with the problem of silence versus speech, its expediency, but, above all, as a defense against a hostile environment: "Whilst you are silent, no one has any business with you . . ." is checked by a triple marginal line.[34] Emerson praised Saadi for his

29. Ibid., pp. xii, 19.
30. Ibid., p. 100.
31. *Clarel, 1,* 121, 300; 2, 4 f. The theme is repeated in the posthumously published tale "Under the Rose."
32. Bezanson, p. 175.
33. *Gulistan,* p. xx.
34. Ibid., p. 168.

"splendor of expression," his "large utterance" which he considered to be the poet's "royal trait." He extolled "the fluent mind in which every thought and feeling came readily to the lips."[35] But the author of *Moby-Dick* had been crushed into silence by public indifference to what he felt most moved to write when he was reading the *Gulistan* and was composing his "Poem and Pilgrimage." To him "large utterance" was for those who had finished with the world. There is a check against the following sentence: "Whosoever washeth his hand of life, uttereth whatever is in his heart."[36]

OMAR KHAYYAM

Melville's reading of Omar Khayyam's *Rubaiyat* in Fitzgerald's translation is attested only after the publication of *Clarel*. There were three copies of the Persian poet in Melville's library: the first American edition published at Boston in 1878, which is extant with Melville's markings; another American edition of 1886, with drawings by Elihu Vedder; and an unidentified edition which Melville received from James Billson, an English admirer, in February, 1886.[1]

35. Essay, "Persian Poetry."
36. *Gulistan*, p. 1.
1. The only trace of a "semi-manuscript 'Omar'" in Fitzgerald's translation is found in a vague reference contained in W. F. Prideaux, *Notes for a Bibliography of Edward FitzGerald* (London, 1901), pp. 28 f. In discussing Fitzgerald's translation of Jami's *Salaman and Absal*—the first fruit of Fitzgerald's Persian studies—Colonel Prideaux writes: "Salámán & Absál. An Allegory. From the Persian of Jámi. Ipswich: Cowell's Steam Printing Works, Butter Market. . . . 1871. . . . This volume seems to have been privately printed in a very limited issue. . . . As the only copies of the edition which have come under my notice contain alterations and corrections in FitzGerald's handwriting, there can be little doubt that it was printed with his sanction, and probably by his instructions . . . A copy of this edition, bound up with the third edition of the "Rubáiyát," and containing

When James Billson sent Melville a "semi-manuscript 'Omar,' " he evidently contributed to an interest that was already there. Melville's acknowledgment of the gift in a letter to Billson stated that the text "coming in that unique form" had "imparted yet added significance to that sublime old infidel."[2] Melville had written the poet's name—"by Edward Fitzgerald (Omar Khayyam)"—on a copy of Fitzgerald's *Polonius* which he had bought in January 1875. The preoccupation with the Persian poet and his translator was to last until the end of his life—Fitzgerald's works were among the last books he borrowed from the New York Society Library in April, 1890.[3]

The famous translation of the Rubaiyat or Quatrains of Omar Khayyam (d. about 1122), "the Astronomer-Poet of Persia," was originally published by its author in pamphlet form in 1858.[4] The first American edition, which Melville

MS notes by FitzGerald, sold . . . at Sotheby's." There was, however, an English verse translation of the Rubaiyat by E. H. Whinfield which may be described as "semi-manuscript." This edition represents indeed a "unique form," for it reproduces the original Persian text side by side with the English verse translation: *The Quatrains of Omar Khayyám. The Persian Text with an English Verse Translation, by E. H. Whinfield, M.A. Late of the Bengal Civil Service*, London, 1883. See A. G. Potter, *A Bibliography of the Rubáiyát of Omar Khayyám*, London, 1929.

2. Leyda, *Log*, p. 798.

3. *Works of Edward Fitzgerald*, 2 vols. New York and Boston, 1887.

4. The literary discoverer of the *Rubaiyat* was Charles Eliot Norton. "To Norton belonged the signal honour of being the first to accord public recognition to the Rubaiyat; a small second edition had been published by Quaritch in 1868, and on this, together with J. B. Nicolas' French edition and translation of Omar (Paris 1867), he had written a notice in the October 1869 issue of the *North American Review* . . . Not for the first nor the last time in English literary history, an English author had had to wait for his genius to be acclaimed on the other side of the Atlantic, before his fellow countrymen should muster the courage to acknowledge it themselves" (A. J. Arberry, *The Romance of the Rubáiyát*, London, 1959, p. 27).

owned, was reprinted from the third London edition, which appeared in 1872. Melville's markings in this edition show a particular interest in versification. "The original Rubáiyát . . . are independent Stanzas," says Fitzgerald, "consisting each of four Lines of equal, though varied, Prosody. . . . Something as in the Greek Alcaic, where the penultimate line seems to lift and suspend the Wave that falls over in the last."[5] Melville was obviously experimenting with verse forms at the time he read Omar Khayyam. But there is no trace of attempted versions from Persian poetry in Melville as there is in Emerson.[6]

In the preface, which Melville carefully read and marked, Fitzgerald takes pains to dissociate Omar from the Sufis "whose Practice he ridiculed." Omar's philosophy is interpreted as purely one of *carpe diem:* "Having failed (however mistakenly) of finding any Providence but Destiny, and any World but This, he set about making the most of it." Omar's "Epicurean Audacity of Thought and Speech," says Fitzgerald, caused him "to be regarded askance in his own Time and Country." The Sufi poets, including Hafiz, borrowed largely of Omar's material, but turned it "to a mystical Use more convenient to Themselves and the People they addressed." It is in their hands, not Omar's, that the traditional Persian imagery of wine, roses, and love became a code of mystical symbols. What they did was to create a poetry "in which they could float luxuriously between Heaven and Earth, and this World and the Next, on the wings of a poetical expression, that might serve indifferently for either." In Fitzgerald's words, "Omar was

5. See Melville's copy in the Houghton Library, Harvard University: *Rubáiyát of Omar Khayyám, the Astronomer-Poet of Persia. Rendered into English Verse. First American from the Third London Edition* (Boston, Houghton, Osgood, 1878), p. 18.

6. See Yohannan, "Emerson's Translations of Persian Poetry from German Sources," *American Literature, 14* (1943), 407–20.

too honest of Heart as well as of Head for this." His philosophy of life was dominated by "the very original *Irreligion of Thinking men from the first*"—a statement Melville characteristically underlined.[7] Fitzgerald's view of Omar's irreligion has been confirmed by modern scholarship on the authority of medieval Persian biographers who report "how he was accused of irreligion, and thereafter reined his tongue."[8] In view of all this the great attraction Omar exercised on Melville's mind is not surprising. The affinity Melville felt for the poet is evident in an implicit parallelism which he drew with his own fate: In Fitzgerald's preface a marginal line scores the passage that describes Omar's lack of popularity in his own country and the rarity and mutilation of his manuscripts.[9]

The most significant impact of Omar on Melville is seen in the symbolism of the posthumously published tale "Under the Rose." In the Constable edition of *Billy Budd*, "Under the Rose" is included among "the eight sketches surviving in manuscript, written, in all probability, after Melville's retirement in 1886, at the age of sixty-seven, from his post as Inspector of Customs in New York City."[10] Melville resigned his post on December 31, 1885, at the age of sixty-six and five months. The date of the tale may be conjectured from a reference with autobiographical overtones which describes the hero, an English ambassador to the Persian court, as a man who "the last Michaelmas, his birthday . . . was three score and three years old, and in growing fear . . . of a certain sudden malady whereof his father and grandfather before him had died about that age."[11]

7. *Rubaiyat,* pp. 12, 13, 22.

8. A. J. Arberry, *Omar Khayyám* (New Haven, 1952), p. 30.

9. *Rubaiyat,* p. 14.

10. Raymond W. Weaver, *Billy Budd and Other Prose Pieces* (Constable), "Introductory Note," p. v; "Under the Rose," pp. 339–45.

11. "Under the Rose," pp. 344–45.

The approximate date of the composition falls into the period of Melville's interest in Omar Khayyam, and the Persian character of the tale is clearly proof of that interest. The tale is called " 'Under the Rose' (Being an extract from an old MS. entitled 'Travels in Persia (Iran) by a servant of My Lord the Ambassador')." It is written in a mildly satirical vein, in imitation of seventeenth-century travel books on Persia, like the "Voyages into Asia and Africa" of Sir Thomas Herbert which is quoted in *Moby-Dick*. Melville's deliberate imitation of the stylistic peculiarities of this type of narrative is evident not only from the subtitle—"Travels in Persia"—but in the construction of the tale as a personal account of "a servant of My Lord the Ambassador," in his use of archaisms—withal, quoth, verily, meseems, in sooth, certes—and in the usual paraphernalia of British embassies to the Persian court which Sir Thomas Herbert also describes: My Lord the English Ambassador; an audience with the Shah or one of his grandees; a Greek interpreter; a court poet; an exchange of gifts; and the ceremonial imbibing of pipes and coffee.[12] But the main interest of the tale does not lie in the local color supplied by travel books and Melville's own experience of the Near East. It is in its allegorical meaning, which is drawn from the imagery of Persian poetry and the philosophy of Omar Khayyam.

The allegory is focused on an amber vase of exquisite workmanship and great beauty which an English lord (My

---

12. Cf. John Fryer, *A New Account of East-India and Persia. Being Nine Years of Travels, Begun in 1672. And Finished 1681 etc.*, London, 1698; *Sir Antony Sherley His Relation to His Travels into Persia*, London, 1613; James Morier, *A Journey through Persia*, Philadelphia, 1816. In a letter to his mother on his first trip to the East, Byron mentions that he has engaged a servant who, before entering his service, had accompanied his master to Persia (Moore, *Life of Byron*, London, 1851, p. 88).

Lord the Ambassador) tries to obtain from the "Azem," a Persian grandee. The value of the vase is enhanced by "certain little relics of perished insects" which "it held marvellously congealed within its substance." The vase is first noticed by the narrator, the Ambassador's servant. He sees it when, "at the Azem's bidding," it is filled with "roses of divers hues." When dropped into the vase, these roses "fell as of themselves into the attitude of young damsels leaning over the balustrade . . . so that the vase itself was all but hidden from view, at least, much of the upper part thereof." The part which was hidden from view by the roses contained "relievos . . . of a mystical type." When the vase which the "Azem" kept on a "marble buffet" was emptied of its roses, the narrator could distinguish a "round device of sculpture on one side . . . showing the figure of an angel with a spade under arm like a gardener, and bearing roses in a pot; and a like angel-figure, clad like a cellarer, and with a wine-jar on his shoulder; and the two angels, side by side, pacing toward a meagre wight, very doleful and Job-like, squatted hard by a sepulchre, as meditating thereon." Enchanted by his servant's description of the vase, the ambassador pays a visit to the Persian with the purpose "so to work on the Azem as that he . . . might be drawn to make a gift of it." But the "Azem" subtly refuses to part with the vase. It was the very vase "that being on a bridal festival filled with roses in the palace of the old Shaz[13] Gold-beak at Shiraz, had tempted their great poet, one Sugar Lips,[14] to

13. Melville's "Shaz" for "Shah" is a contraction of "Shazada," literally "son of the Shah," a title given the eldest son of the Mogul in Bengal.

14. Weaver's reading "Lugar Lips" is a mistake ("Under the Rose," pp. 343, 344, 345). The correct manuscript reading is "Sugar Lips." MS in Houghton Library, Harvard University. As Jay Leyda has noted, transcribers of Melville's manuscripts have trouble with his capital S's, writing "Lo" for "So" (Leyda, *Complete Stories*, p. xiv).

a closer inspection, when tenderly dividing the flowers one
from another, and noting the little anatomies congealed in
the amber, he was prompted to the inditing of certain
verses; for which case the vase was thenceforth forever in-
estimable." Instead, the Englishman was presented with
"a vellum book, about the bigness of a prayer-book for
church-going, but very rich with jewelled clasps, and writ
by some famous scribe in the fair Persian text." This book
contained the verses which the vase had inspired. At the
request of the ambassador they were translated into English
by a "Greek renegade . . . a polyglot infidel" who proceeded
to his task fortified with wine. The verses provide the key
to the vase as a symbol of man's destiny:

> Specks, tiny specks, in this translucent amber,
> Your leave, bride-roses, may one pry and see?
> How odd! a dainty little skeleton-chamber;
> And—odder yet—sealed walls but windows be!
> Death's open secret.—Well, we are;
> And here comes the jolly angel with the jar!

Man is caught in the grip of death like the tiny specks in
the amber of the vase, even though his transitory existence
is brightened by beauty and love—the "bride-roses" which
decorate the vase. There is no escape, for the chamber of
death has sealed walls instead of windows. The only allevia-
tion of man's tragic condition is the full enjoyment of life
while it lasts.

The extent to which Melville drew on his knowledge of
Sufism, Persian poetry, and particularly Omar Khayyam is
apparent from an analysis of the imagery and symbolism of
the tale. The master image, the rose-heaped amber vase, is
Melville's own but the allegorical interpretation to which
it is subject is modeled on the manner of the Sufi mystics
and the "philosophy" of Omar Khayyam. The flower-
heaped urn is one of those symbols which constantly recur

in Melville's writings. It establishes an organic connection between the imagery in *Mardi* and works like *Clarel* and "Under the Rose," which were composed several decades later.

In *Mardi* the image underlies the concept of Serenia. The people of Serenia welcome Taji and his companions with a song which is symmetrically grouped around the following vision of beatitude:

> Hail! voyagers, hail!
> Think not our groves will brood with gloom;
> In this, our isle,
> Bright flowers smile!
> Full urns, rose-heaped, there valleys bloom.

Death, which lurks beneath the roses, the theme of "Under the Rose," is ignored in the land of Serenia, where Babbalanja, the philosopher, parts company with Taji in order to accept "all which may be had."[15] Taji, who is not content to remain in Serenia, is confronted with the image of a flower-filled urn in another guise, the emblem of the sensuous delight offered by Hautia—the theme of Persian poetry in its literal interpretation: "Again the syrens came. They bore a large and stately urn-like flower, white as alabaster, and glowing, as if lit up within. From its calyx, flame-like, trembled forked and crimson stamens, burning with intensest odours. . . . Then it changed, and glowed like Persian dawns."[16]

In *Clarel* the symbolism of the urn is crystallized into its "original" meaning of a skull-shaped vessel which holds life but is at the same time a "funeral urn," a chamber of death.[17]

15. *Mardi*, 2, 380.
16. Ibid., p. 383.
17. *Clarel*, *1*, 71, 111; 2, 18.

In "Under the Rose," the vase is described as "delicate," imbedding in its amber substance the tiny specks of perished insects. This image first appears in *Mardi* and *Moby-Dick:* "Imbedded in amber, do we not find little fishes' fins, porpoise teeth, seagulls' beaks and claws . . .?"[18] We know that Melville was fascinated with the properties of amber "made waxy, then firm, by the action of the sea." Its connotations of embalmment are brought out in both novels. In "Under the Rose" the symbol reiterates the tragic predicament of mortal man trapped in an enigmatic substance which is both life-in-death and death-in-life.

The owner of the vase is called the "Azem." It is obvious that Melville knew the meaning and usage of the Arabic word al-'Azīm, the Great, as one of the attributes of God. The attributes of Allah must have come to Melville's attention in the *Poems* of Sir Edwin Arnold, which he is known to have read and marked.[19] The designation "al-'Azīm" was not included in Arnold's poems, but Arnold's "Pearls of the Faith," a string of verses modeled on the Moslem custom of repeating the "ninety-nine beautiful names of Allah" with the help of a rosary of ninety-nine beads, probably served to intensify his interest both in the Moslem titles of the Deity and in Moslem ritual. By giving the owner of the vase in his tale an Islamic appellation of God, Melville in a flash turned the "hidden significance" of the story into an "open secret."

The roses—"young damsels leaning over the balustrade" —were dropped in the vase "at the Azem's bidding." Their

---

18. *Mardi*, 2, 62. *Moby-Dick,* chap. 92.

19. Sealts, No. 15: Sir Edwin Arnold, *The Poems*, New York, Hurst, 1879. "Marked. (Examined by Raymond Weaver; present location unknown)." The term "El-Azeem" is listed as one of the ninety-nine "Beautiful Names of God" of Koranic tradition in John P. Brown, *The Dervishes: or Oriental Spiritualism* (Philadelphia, 1868), No. 34, p. 117.

function is to hide the sculptured design on the vase. The roses are "of divers hues, red, yellow, pink, and white"—an image which recalls Fitzgerald's note on the colors of roses common in Persia.[20] The "relievos" are on the "upper part" of the vase, and the craft of the artificer, says the narrator, had "right deftly" hidden any junction of two or more parts of which the vase was composed. The symbolical implications of this "junction" seem to correspond with a line in Fitzgerald's version of Jami's "Salaman and Absal," published in the *Works* of 1887, which speaks of "the Double world that is but One."[21]

The sculptured design on the vase is the size of "My Lord's seal" and represents two angels which approach the Joblike figure of man. Evidently, Melville was thinking of the stamp of death upon life in the shape of two angels of Islamic tradition, Munkar and Nakir, who are thought to examine the dead in their tombs and are mentioned in Edwin Arnold's *Poems*.[22] One of the angels in the tale, the "gardener" with the spade and the pot of roses, suggests a grave-digger. The other, the "cellarer" carrying a wine-jar on his shoulder, is modeled on the image of the wine-bearer or saqi in Persian poetry. The figure of the first angel with the roses also appears in a poem, "The Rose Window," which Melville included in "A Rose or Two," a series of poems dated February 13, 1890:

> I saw an Angel with a Rose
> Come out of Morning's garden gate,
> And lamp-like hold the Rose aloft;
> He entered a sepulchral Strait,

20. Melville's copy of the *Rubaiyat*, p. 71, n. 6.
21. *Works of Edward Fitzgerald, 1*, 110.
22. "Monker and Nakir" in "Notes to Pearls of the Faith," Arnold, *Poems*, p. 323.

I followed. And I saw the Rose
Shed dappled down upon the dead;
The shrouds and mort-cloths all were lit
The plaids and chequered tartans red.[23]

The image was probably directly inspired by a remark in Fitzgerald's preface in which one of Omar's disciples describes the poet's death: "My tomb shall be in a spot where the north wind may scatter roses over it," Omar is reported as saying to Nizami. Fitzgerald also mentions Thorvaldsen, the nineteenth-century sculptor, who "desired to have roses grow over him." The second angel is a replica of the first—"a like angel-figure." He, too, in the final analysis, represents death, as is seen from Quatrain 43 of the Rubaiyat, which Melville checked:

So when the Angel of the darker Drink
At last shall find you by the river-brink,
And, offering his Cup, invite your Soul
Forth to your Lips to quaff—you shall not shrink.[24]

The "darker Drink" is the juice of the "black grape"—another Melvillean symbol of great importance.

23. *Collected Poems*, p. 299.
24. Melville's copy of the *Rubaiyat*, p. 45. Cf. Quatrain 58:

And lately, by the Tavern Door agape,
Came shining through the Dusk an Angel Shape
Bearing a Vessel on his Shoulder; and
He bid me taste of it; and 'twas—the Grape!

Professor Arberry has used this quatrain—"one of Fitzgerald's most suggestive stanzas"—to show how freely Fitzgerald adapted the Persian original text. "There is nothing in the original about an Angel Shape, and the whole ghostly atmosphere of Fitzgerald's version is completely at variance with the dissolute scene as pictured by Omar" (*Omar Khayyām*, p. 24).

In *Clarel* the "black grape" is associated with Vine, Melville's "fictive presentment of Hawthorne."[25] Derwent, the optimistic parson, characterizes Vine as a black but juicy grape—a quality linked with Melville's feeling for Hawthorne: "Now, it is that blackness in Hawthorne, of which I have spoken, that so fixes and fascinates me."[26] A preoccupation with "the bitter cup" is also the characteristic of Mortmain, the self-annihilating Swedish revolutionary who drinks the bitter waters of the Dead Sea.[27] In "Under the Rose," the meaning of the verses on the vase is distilled from "the black grape." The "black grape," then, represents both the recognition of evil and death as the bitter essence of life which Melville admired in Hawthorne, and the overruling element of evil and death in life itself, which is the theme of "Under the Rose."

Fitzgerald constantly refers to Omar's verses as "the Juice of the Grape." When the Greek interpreter, "one long dwelling in Persia," is asked to translate Sugar Lips' verses on the Azem's vase into English rhyme, he first demands "the juice of the grape," for "this same Sugar Lips' verses being all grapes, or veritably saturated with the ripe juice thereof, there is no properly rendering them without a cup or two of the same."

The name which Melville gave to his Persian poet, Sugar Lips, was obviously coined on the model of "Coral Lips" in the *Arabian Nights* and "Rubylips" in Disraeli's *Tancred*.[28] The poet's "intoxication" before composing poetry represents the concept of poetic inspiration in the

25. Bezanson, "Herman Melville's *Clarel*."

26. *Clarel*, 2, 69. "Hawthorne and His Mosses," *Literary World, 6,* 126.

27. *Clarel, 1,* 181, 184.

28. "The Story of the Sleeper Awakened," *Arabian Nights. Tancred*, Bk. VI, chap. 1.

mystical connotation of Persian poetry. The poet as the interpreter of the mystery of existence—the verses on the
vase—must first enter into a state of ecstatic obsession, like
Taji in his quest for Yillah, before he is able to grasp the
essence of reality. The poet's supreme function is intensified
by a double interpretation like that of Fitzgerald in relation to Omar Khayyam: Sugar Lips, the Oriental, is the
original composer and interpreter of the verses; the Greek
reinterprets them to the West.

The religious connotations of the verses are clear from
the fact that they have been entered in "a vellum book,
about the bigness of a prayer-book for church-going . . .
illuminated withal like . . . great Popish parchment folios."
The "mystical type" of the design which they describe resembles "pictures in the great Dutch Bible in a library at
Oxon, setting forth the enigmas of the Song of the Wise
Man, to wit, King Solomon." While interpreting them into
English, the Greek is in a state of religious ecstasy, "hum-
ming and hooing to himself—and swaying his body, like
the dervishes." The tale, like Fitzgerald's translation of
Omar Khayyam, thus links the religions of Persia and
Greece, Islam and Christianity, East and West, in the quest
for the meaning of existence. But when the verses are
finally interpreted, the essence of the mystery beneath the
roses stands revealed as the "open secret" of Death.

> "And is that all?" said My Lord, composedly, but scarce
> cheerfully, when the renegado had made an end; "and
> is that all? And call you that a crushing from the grape?
> the black grape, I wis"; there checking himself, as a
> wise man will do, catching himself tripping in an in-
> discreet sincerity; which to cover, peradventure, he,
> suddenly rising, retired to his chamber, and though
> commanding his visage somewhat, yet in pace and fig-
> ure showing the spirit within sadly distraught.

The appeal which Fitzgerald's description of Omar as a free-thinker had for Melville is evident in the ambassador's reaction to "the interpreted verses." Owing to the animosity of the Sufis who attacked his irreligion, Omar had to control his tongue. But his poetry, says Fitzgerald, presents us "Omar himself, with all his Humours and Passions, as frankly before us as if we were really at Table with him, after the Wine had gone round"—a statement which Melville, inevitably, marked.[29]

The direct connection with Omar is made particularly clear in the concluding remarks of the narrator: "But for my part I always esteemed it a mighty weakness in so great a man to let the ribald wit of a vain ballader, and he a heathen, make heavy his heart." The "hidden" meaning of the "vain ballader" exactly corresponds to that of Omar Khayyam in the interpretation of Fitzgerald. Omar was "saddest perhaps when most ostentatiously merry."[30] Under Omar's wine and roses, the theme of the Rubaiyat is Death. Again and again Melville marked Omar's death images in the poems: Man goes from sleep to sleep; life flies; spring vanishes like the rose; man goes through the door of darkness. Fitzgerald's remark about the literal and mystical interpretation of Omar's poetry, which Melville marked,[31] is reflected in the narrator's own reaction to "the interpreted verses" which conclude the tale: "I was in secret pleased with the lax pleasantry of this Sugar Lips, but in such sort as one is tickled with the profane capering of a mountebank. . . . Howbeit, had I been, God knows, of equal reverend years with my master, and subject by probable inheritance to the like sudden malady, peradventure I myself in

29. Melville's copy of the *Rubaiyat,* p. 25. Cf. Melville's own comment on "the great Art of Telling the Truth" in "Hawthorne and His Mosses," *Literary World, 6,* 126.

30. Melville's copy of the *Rubaiyat,* p. 19.

31. Ibid., p. 23.

that case might have waxed sorrowful, doubting whether the grape was not indeed the black grape, as he phrased it, wherefrom that vain balladry had been distilled."

In "Under the Rose" the ambassador's sadness stems from his secret conviction that the poet's wine, i.e. the joy of life which he celebrates, is crushed from "the black grape" (death and annihilation), not divine love. But "as a wise man will do" he checks his "indiscreet sincerity" and keeps silent. This revelation—like the allusions to insanity in the ambassador's family and the premonitions of death— is evidently a projection of the personal problem which dominated Melville's life and work and which he communicated to Hawthorne at their last meeting in Liverpool in 1856 when he said that "he had pretty much made up his mind to be annihilated"—there was no life after death. The inhibition to voice his unbelief in the face of a thoughtlessly complacent world which, like Omar's Sufis, conveniently believed in an afterlife, presented the special kind of problem, of silence versus speech, which, as we have seen, is reflected in Melville's markings in the *Gulistan*, in the "indiscreet honesty" of Rolfe in *Clarel*, and finally in the "indiscreet sincerity" of the ambassador in "Under the Rose." In the tale this fear is given a special kind of poignancy by the Persian poet, whose poetry has been called "the voice of the great defeated."[32]

32. Arberry, *Omar Khayyām*, p. 27.

PART TWO: *Oriental "Polysensua"*

"The leaves, I repeat, are uncut—let them remain so—
and let me supplementarily hint, that a bit of old parchment
(from some old Arabic M.S.S. on Astrology) tied round each volume,
& sealed on the back with a Sphynx, & never to be broken till
the aloe flowers—would not be an unsuitable device for the
bookbinders of 'Mardi.'"

MELVILLE TO EVERT DUYCKINCK

4. Explorers of the Ancient East

In a letter to Can Grande della Scala, Dante defined the subject of his *Divine Comedy* in the following words: "Be it known that the sense of this work is not simple, but on the contrary it may be called polysemous, that is to say, of more senses than one; for it is one sense which we get through the letter, and another which we get through the thing the letter signifies: and the first is called literal but the second allegorical or mystic."[1]

In the works of Melville, the designation "polysensuum" is used by Babbalanja, the philosopher in *Mardi,* to indicate the multiplicity of meaning latent in the contemplation of an ancient tree-trunk: "an immense wild banian-tree . . . so vast, and its fabric so complex."[2] The full significance of the term in Melville is crystallized in the words of Cassirer about Goethe: "The contemplation of the totality of being has ceased to be an aim but has become a starting-point. The whole is no longer reached in a gradual progression from the particular but exists and is compressed as it were, in one point, in one concrete symbol."[3]

The contemplation of totality as a polysensuous complex which characterizes Melville is inseparable from a special

1. *Dantis Alighierii Epistolae,* ed. Arnaldo Monti (Milan, 1921), p. 337. Flanders Dunbar, *Symbolism in Medieval Thought* (New Haven, 1929), p. ix.
2. *Mardi,* 2, 41, 42.
3. Ernst Cassirer, *Freiheit und Form* (Berlin, 1918), p. 315: "Dieses Ganze wird nicht mehr im allmaehlichen Fortschritt vom Besonderen aus erreicht, sondern es besteht und draengt sich gleichsam in einen Punkt, in ein konkretes Symbol zusammen."

kind of historical intuition which experiences history as symbol and myth. Historical personages and happenings are intuitively apprehended as archetypal controlling images which, in the language of Carlyle about symbols, present "some embodiment and revelation of the Infinite; the Infinite is made to blend itself with the Finite, to stand visible, and, as it were, attainable there."[4] Melville echoed these words in *Mardi* when he spoke of "things infinite in the finite; and dualities in unities."[5] He also shared with Carlyle his basic philosophical premise: his sense of the eternal mystery of the Infinite and of its finite intimations in the personality of the hero and the heroic deed.

"Universal History, the history of what man has accomplished in this world, is at bottom the History of the Great Men who have worked here," wrote Carlyle in his lectures *On Heroes, Hero-Worship and the Heroic in History,* which Melville borrowed from Evert Duyckinck. "Could we see *them* well, we should get some glimpses into the very marrow of the world's history." World history, in its turn, is "a window through which we may look into Infinitude itself," and the distinction of the Carlylean hero is "that he looks through the show of things into things."[6] This process is the Alpha and Omega of heroism. The Hero as Explorer is, then, as it were, The hero of heroes, for he is totally dedicated to penetrating the mysteries of the unknown.

The Hero as Explorer is the Melvillean hero par excellence. It is his image that is reflected in Melville's preoccupation with the explorers, prophets, and conquerors of the ancient Near East—the inevitable focus of a vision in which

4. *Sartor Resartus,* Bk. III, chap. 3.
5. *Mardi,* 2, 328.
6. *On Heroes, Hero-Worship and the Heroic in History,* Lecture I, "The Hero as Divinity"; Lecture II, "The Hero as Prophet. Mahomet: Islam."

the totality of being is apprehended at its "original" historical source. To Byron and Moore and other nineteenth-century writers the East was a romantic literary attitude, an exotic masquerade. But to Goethe and Melville, concerned as they were with the uses of the past in relation to the deepest meanings of existence, the East was the "Ur" of world history, the original location of man's window to the unknown. Just as the artistic form of the "West-East Divan" is not decoration or a distinctively literary device but is woven into the very texture of Goethe's feeling and thought, the significance of Melville's Near Eastern images is deeply embedded in the total content of his work as a "polysensuum" of the human condition.

BELZONI AND ANCIENT EGYPT

Melville's use of ancient Egypt in his imagery is an outstanding example of what Cassirer calls the process of "historical palingenesis," in which the historical and the poetic are fused into a new contemporary existence. In frequency and importance the references to Egyptian history and mythology are only secondary to the allusions to Polynesia in Melville's works. But while Polynesia is the ideal, the symbol of man's primordial yearning for paradise, ancient Egypt and ancient Assyria are the real—the tangible usable past buried under layer upon layer of lived human experience which man, the explorer, has to penetrate in order to reach the bedrock of truth. The monuments of ancient Egypt, particularly the pyramids, pervade Melville's consciousness of the artist's mission—to teach mankind a due reverence for its "mummies"—and of the symbolic significance of structure and form—in Carlyle's words, visible and attainable—in which the sacred mysteries of existence are encased and enwrapped.

The image of Belzoni, "worming himself" through the subterranean passages of Egyptian tombs is the apotheosis of the Melvillean hero. Belzoni is mentioned by name in *Typee,* where he is the prototype of the narrator and Toby, travelers encountering impediments in their progress to their destined goal. "The topography of *Typee,*" says Charles Feidelson, "is metaphoric. Certainly the book is primarily a travelogue; its scene is the solid earth; and the language does not often *invite* a symbolistic interpretation. Yet here, at the beginning of Melville's literary career, the stuff of his experience seems to hover on the verge of the symbolic expansion it was to undergo in *Mardi* and *Moby-Dick.*"[7] Significantly, the image of Belzoni, though pervasive in Melville's works, undergoes its fullest symbolic expansion in "I and My Chimney," the Kafkaesque story about himself published four years after *Pierre,* the heroic epic of tragic moral idealism.

Giovanni Battista Belzoni (1778–1823) was a famous nineteenth-century explorer of Egyptian antiquities who was born in Padua and for a time was employed by a circus in England. The purpose of his journey to Egypt in 1815 was to promote a hydraulic machine he had invented which was to regulate the waters of the Nile. But the project was soon abandoned for a search of antiquities in pursuit of which he traveled in Egypt and Nubia until 1819—the year of Melville's birth. Belzoni is not described as an Egyptologist, for his methods bore closer resemblance to those of the California gold-rush than of respectable investigation. Also, his discoveries predated Champollion's deciphering of the hieroglyphs in 1821—which initiated Egyptological studies. But he was widely known as a traveler and explorer whose outstanding achievements as de-

7. Feidelson, *Symbolism and American Literature* (Chicago, 1953), p. 165.

scribed by himself and discussed in the periodical literature
of the time were the opening of the second pyramid of
Giza and the pyramid of Khefren, the transportation from
Upper Egypt to the British Museum of the bust of "Memnon" (Ramses II), which intrigued and mystified his contemporaries, and the penetration of the tombs of the kings
at Thebes, among which that of Seti I is still known as
"Belzoni's Tomb."[8] His *Travels in Egypt* was standard
reading, particularly since, showman that he was, he had
arranged an exhibition of his treasures in the famous "Egyptian Hall" in London in 1820, when the book was published. The full title is *Narrative of the Operations and
Recent Discoveries within the Pyramids, Temples, Tombs,
and Excavations, in Egypt and Nubia, and of a Journey to
the Coast of the Red Sea . . . and Another to the Oasis of
Jupiter Ammon.* The book was not reprinted in America,
but a popular American account for children by one Sarah
Atkins entitled characteristically *Fruits of Enterprise Exhibited in the Adventures of Belzoni in Egypt and Nubia*
was published in 1824 with a reproduction of "Memnon"
on its title page. The catalogue of the Albany Library, of
which Melville's uncle, Peter Gansevoort, was a member,
shows that "Belzoni's Travels in Egypt" was included
among the library's books, though the library of the Albany
Young Men's Association, Melville's own library, had no
copy. At any rate, Sarah Atkins' version achieved sufficient
popularity in America to be republished in 1846 in the
"Library for school districts and families."[9]

Melville's allusion to Belzoni by name in *Typee* may

8. For an autobiographical account see Belzoni's *Narrative of the
Operations and Discoveries in Egypt and Nubia* (2d ed. London,
1821), pp. v–viii. Cf. H. Beston, *The Book of Gallant Vagabonds* (New
York, 1925), pp. 57–92; C. W. Ceram, *Gods, Graves, and Scholars*
(New York, 1951), pp. 116–20.

9. *Catalogue of Books in the Albany Library* (July 1828), No. 750.

stem from reading about him in general accounts, though
there are curious traces of similarities between Belzoni's
Narrative and a chapter in which Melville describes the
perilous passage of a ravine which "Tom" and Toby had to
undertake before their descent into the valley of Typee:
"Belzoni, worming himself through the subterranean passages of the Egyptian catacombs, could not have met with
greater impediments than those we have encountered,"
writes Melville. Evidently he was thinking of Belzoni's
progress in the tombs of Kurnah ("Gournou") in Upper
Egypt. This tomb, which Belzoni describes as his most important discovery, was situated in the basin of a waterfall
at the foot of a steep hill "under a torrent, which, when it
rains in the desert, pours a great quantity of water over the
very spot I have caused to be dug." In *Typee* the narrator
and Toby, comparing themselves to Belzoni, make their
difficult way through the bed of a watercourse that "was
covered with fragments of broken rocks, which had fallen
from above, offering so many obstructions to the course of
the rapid stream." A similar impediment is described by
Belzoni: "The valley is so much raised by the rubbish,
which the water carries down from the upper parts, that
the entrance into these tombs is become much lower than
the torrents."

Belzoni's account of a night's lodging in the entrance of
a tomb has its counterpart in the nights which the narrator
and Toby spent in the ravine; another parallel experience
is the manner in which the narrator and Toby pacified the
gnawings of hunger "by chewing the tender bark of roots
and twigs, which . . . were at least sweet and pleasant to the
taste." Belzoni, in a similar emergency, resorted to the
chewing of sugar cane which he, with less enthusiasm than
Melville, described as "pleasant at the first taste."

Significantly, there is a heading "The First Cataract" in
the chapter on the ravine. Perhaps Melville remembered

Belzoni's table of contents with "the first cataract" as a subheading. Be that as it may, there is no doubt that he was thinking of the cataracts of the Nile.[10]

Belzoni is next mentioned in *Mardi* in a chapter entitled "They Go Down into the Catacombs." In Padulla the hero Taji and his four companions descend into a vault in order to view the collection of antiquities of one Oh-Oh, "famous as a venerable antiquarian" whose expletory name was bestowed on him "by reason of the delighted interjections with which he welcomed all accessions to his museum." The descent into the vault is obviously a piece inspired by the exploration of Egyptian tombs: "Upon gaining the vault, forth flew a score or two of bats, extinguishing the flambeau, and leaving us in darkness, like Belzoni deserted by his Arabs in the heart of a pyramid. The torch at last relumed, we entered a tomb-like excavation at every step raising clouds of dust; and at last stood before long rows of musty, mummyish parcels."[11] The name Padulla with which the reference to Belzoni is here connected may recall the fact that Belzoni was a native of Padua. In fact, the whole passage seems partly modeled on Belzoni's entry into a tomb at Kurnah in the course of which he lost an interpreter and one Arab, having entered the tomb with several candle-carrying companions.[12]

An incident of bats and extinguished torches much like the one in Oh-Oh's "vault" is described in a descent into the heart of a pyramid not by Belzoni but by Dr. E. D. Clarke in his famous *Travels in Various Countries of Europe, Asia and Africa* (1818). Clarke was mentioned in an article in the *Penny Magazine* of April 12, 1834, from which, as we know, Melville drew his first information on

10. *Typee*, chap. 9. Belzoni, *Narrative*, pp. xii, 181, 233.
11. *Mardi*, 2, 67, 72.
12. Belzoni, pp. 51–53, 239 f.

Pompey's Pillar.[13] In *Moby-Dick* a reference to "the vignettes and other embellishments of some ancient books"
seems to echo a "List of Embellishments and Vignettes" in
the *Travels* of Clarke. Much later, as we have seen, Melville
underlined Clarke's name in his copy of Stanley's *Sinai and
Palestine*.[14]

Describing the descent into the heart of the pyramid of
Cheops, Clarke writes: "The difficulty too was increased by
the necessity of bearing lighted tapers in our hands which
were liable to be extinguished at every instant in the efforts made to advance. As we continued to struggle in this
manner, one after another, fearful of being at last jammed
between the stones, or suffocated by heat and want of air,
a number of bats, alarmed by our intrusion, endeavoured to
make their escape. . . . Flying against our hands and faces,
they presently extinguished some of our tapers."[15]

The symbolic significance of the descent into "the heart"
of the pyramid is evident in Melville's intense preoccupation with the hidden mysteries of mummies and tombs.
Like the mystic in the *Confidence-Man,* Melville made it
part of his own mission "to teach mankind a due reverence
for mummies." In *Mardi* Samoa's arm is bandaged over and
over in cerements. Old women are compared to mummies
in *Redburn*. In *Moby-Dick* Starbuck, "prepared to endure
for long ages to come," looks like a mummy: "His pure
tight skin was an excellent fit and closely wrapped up in it,
and embalmed with inner health and strength, like a re-

13. *Redburn,* chap. 41. On Melville's fascination with Pompey's
Pillar see Horsford, *Journal,* p. 122.

14. Melville's copy of *Sinai and Palestine,* p. 454.

15. Clarke, *Travels* (London, 1818), 5, xxvii, 194. The book, in five
parts, was first published in London in six volumes (1811–23) and in
Philadelphia in two volumes (1811–13). The fourth edition (London,
1816–24), a completed account including Clarke's travels in Scandi-
navia, was published in eleven volumes.

vivified Egyptian." Finally, in *Pierre,* "Ten million things were as yet uncovered to Pierre. The old mummy lies buried in cloth on cloth; it takes time to unwrap the Egyptian king."[16]

Melville's tomb images are mostly connected with Thebes, though they are not limited to ancient Egypt. The nineteenth-century New York prison "The Tombs," in which Bartleby the Scrivener was confined, was part of the Egyptian revival in American architecture and "the Egyptian character of the masonry" lent itself particularly to Melville's artistic purpose. In *Israel Potter* "the walls of the Thebes of the oppressor" embody the pervasive idea of bondage as encasement, linked to an invisible tyranny. Like all Egyptian monuments in Melville's imagery, the Theban tomb is the "original" emblem of both majesty and ruin, life and death. The contemporary descriptions of royal Egyptian tombs plundered by grave robbers, resounding with the yell of jackals, and filled with houseless Arab squatters, haunted Melville's imagination with "unspeakable meanings."

But even the gloom of mummies and tombs is frequently lightened by Melville's humor. Thus the mummification of the ibis by the ancient Egyptians is turned into a juicy exotic feast. The cult was described by Denon and Clarke; Beloe, in his notes to *Herodotus* speaks of "earthen pots" and "burnt cinders" found in the ibis pits; there is a reference to the ibis in the *Confessions of an Opium Eater,* which Melville read in London in December 1849; finally, Belzoni describes a mummified ibis looking "like a fowl ready to be cooked." All these in conjunction must have supplied the ingredients for the Egyptian banquet in *Moby-Dick:* "it is out of the idolatrous dotings of the old Egyp-

16. *Confidence-Man,* chap. 36. *Mardi, 1,* 89. *Redburn,* chap. 38. *Moby-Dick,* chap. 26. *Pierre,* Bk. XXI.

tians upon broiled ibis and roasted river horse, that you see the mummies of those creatures in their huge bake-houses the pyramids."[17]

The contents of Oh-Oh's vault comprise "long rows of musty, mummyish parcels" of which the most ancient and treasured possession is "a hieroglyphical 'Elegy on the Dumps' consisting of one thousand and one lines." When Taji and his companions reach the Isle of Fossils, they find more "Egyptian" treasures—another caricature of the "fossils" and "petrifications" found among the ruins of the pyramids that Clarke depicted and of the contents of Egyptian tombs that Belzoni described: "Luxor marks, Tadmor ciphers, Palenque inscriptions. In long lines, as on Denderah's architraves, were bas-reliefs of beetles, turtles, ant-eaters, armadilloes, guanos, serpents, tongueless crocodiles."

The allusion to Denderah is particularly interesting as it recurs in *Moby-Dick* in a strikingly similar context:

> But not alone has this Leviathan left his preadamite traces in the stereotype plates of nature, and in lime-stone and mark bequeathed his ancient bust; but upon Egyptian tablets, whose antiquity seems to claim for them an almost fossiliferous character, we find the unmistakable print of his fin. In an apartment of the great temple of Denderah, some fifty years ago, there was discovered upon the granite ceiling a sculptured and painted planisphere, abounding in centaurs, griffins, and dolphins, similar to the grotesque figures on the celestial globe of the moderns. Gliding among them, old Leviathan swam as of yore; was there swim-

17. Vivant Denon, *Travels in Upper and Lower Egypt* (2 vols. New York, 1803), *1*, 296. Clarke, *5*, 233–36. *Herodotus* (Philadelphia, 1814), *1*, 358, n. 124. De Quincey, *Opium-Eater* (Boston, 1841), p. 158. Belzoni, p. 169. *Moby-Dick*, chap. 1.

ming in that planisphere, centuries before Solomon
was cradled.[18]

The passage, with its description of the planisphere discovered "some fifty years ago," indicates the source from
which Melville drew his information on Denderah: Vivant
Denon's *Travels in Upper and Lower Egypt, in Company
with Several Divisions of the French Army, during the Campaigns of General Bonaparte,* published in London and
New York in 1803. To Melville, Denon—one of the famous
savants who accompanied Napoleon's expedition to Egypt
—must have been what he was to Thomas Moore: an "old
acquaintance . . . whose drawings of Egypt . . . I frequently
consulted."[19] Denon's work, with its original illustrations,
was the first authoritative account of the antiquities of
Egypt that had reached the West. It had caused a sensation
on its appearance and even inspired Egyptian forms in
American architecture.[20]

Among Denon's drawings of various parts of the Denderah temple there is the "Inner Door of the Sanctuary"
which shows an architrave of the type to which Melville
alludes in *Mardi*. Melville's description of the Denderah
planisphere derives from one of Denon's plates of the "planisphere" and a plan of the "apartment" in which the planisphere was found. The grouping of a griffin and dolphin in
close proximity with a centaur is clearly visible in this

18. *Moby-Dick,* chap. 104.
19. See Moore's "Preface" to *The Loves of the Angels.* Belzoni
mentions Denon as an authority on Denderah (*Narrative,* pp. vi, 35).
Cf. also Beloe's translation of *Herodotus, 1,* 360, n. 126.
20. An extreme example was "Trollope's Folly," the Bazaar built
by Mrs. Trollope in Cincinnati in 1828 which advertised an Egyptian
colonnade as its chief architectural attraction, constructed after "the
temple of Appolinopolis at Etfou, as exhibited in Denon's Egypt"
(Clay Lancaster, "The Egyptian Hall and Mrs. Trollope's Bazaar,"
Magazine of Art, March 1950, 94–99).

illustration. Among the mythological signs of the zodiac are the two fishes and another fish—Melville's "leviathan."[21]

A combination of Denon and Belzoni evidently inspired Melville's idea of "Dolzono," a Mardian islet situated in the lake of Yammo—obviously from "yam," the Hebrew for lake. Dolzono is modeled on the islands of Philae and Elephantine in the Nile, satirically considered. It is the site of a mighty temple, with "lines of sphinxes and griffins" like the avenues of sphinxes at the temples of Edfu, Karnak, and Luxor. Belzoni's description of the goddess Isis, who was covered with a hieroglyphically inscribed net, is a traceable pattern in "the divers bit of tappa, hieroglyphically stamped" which are deposited on the altar of the gods on Dolzono. But the dominant image in the great gallery of Dolzono gods—whose images were "more or less defaced"— was an "obelisk-idol, so towering, that gazing at it, we were fain to throw back our heads."[22]

The supreme symbolical importance that Melville's vision attached to towering shapes which enclose a hidden vacancy found its objective correlative in the monuments of ancient Egypt. The image of the obelisk and the pyramid expands in symbolic significance until the identification of man with a pyramidal shape, the "I" in "I and My Chimney," is complete: "The architect of the chimney must have had the pyramid of Cheops before him; for after that famous structure it seems modeled."[23]

21. Denon, 2, plate XIX facing p. 70; plate LVIII facing p. 316. Other nineteenth-century accounts of the famous zodiac lacked Denon's detailed description. Cf. Belzoni, pp. 34 f.; "A Journey in Egypt by M. Lelorrain, and Observations on the Circular Zodiac of Denderah by M. Saulnier" in *New Voyages and Travels, 8,* London, 1822; "The Zodiac of Denderah," *North American Review, 8* (1823), 233-42.

22. *Mardi, 2,* 26–27, 35.

23. On the identification of the chimney with Melville's own personality see M. Sealts, "Herman Melville's 'I and My Chimney,'" *American Literature, 13* (1941), 142–54.

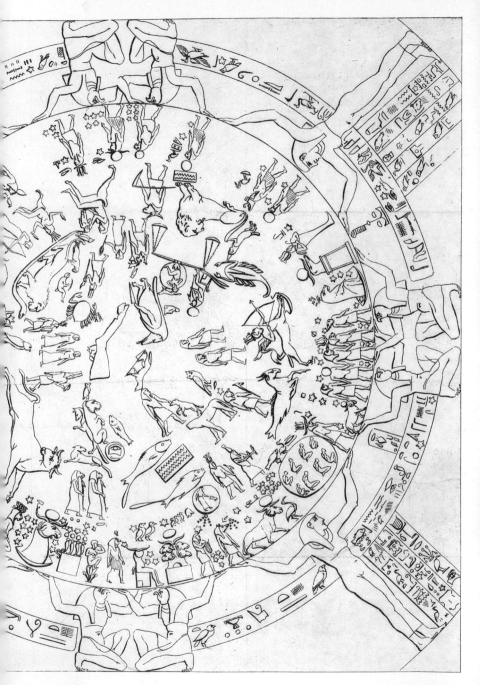

5. Plan of the Small Apartment. Section of the Denderah Planisphere.

In *Typee* and *Redburn,* where the scene is still solid earth, the pyramids and obelisks of Egypt are metaphors of grandeur, antiquity, and human vanity. The "hermit" obelisks of Luxor are "idle towers of stone; which, useless to the world in themselves, vainly hope to eternize a name, by having it carved, solitary and alone, in their granite."[24]

The celebrated column called Pompey's pillar, which Melville likened to a "long stick of candy, well sucked" when he finally saw it for himself in Alexandria, is a favorite image in his earlier work. Melville first learned of the pillar from an illustrated article in the *Penny Magazine,* as he says in *Redburn,* comparing two smokestacks on the outskirts of Liverpool to two Pompey's pillars, perhaps through an association with Cleopatra's Needles, two granite obelisks that Melville also saw in 1856 before they were removed to London and New York, in his own lifetime. Clarke fully described these columns as he had seen them in Alexandria in 1801, enlarging on the hieroglyphs cut in their granite[25] —an idea of immortality which to Melville epitomized the vanity of human wishes hovering on the verge of the mysterious unknown.

For centuries the hieroglyphs had been used in literature as a metaphor to designate symbolic forms of divine mysteries. They were finally deciphered, while Melville was still alive, but the Renaissance conception of them as unlinguistic symbols of ideas still prevailed.[26] To Melville, as to Schlegel and other romantic writers, the hieroglyphs remained a "mystic" reflection of the mystery of the universe—the chiseled features of the White Whale. In *Typee* an old sailor's tattoo is compared with hieroglyphs on a sarcophagus. In *Mardi* Aleema, the priest, "was like a

24. *Redburn,* chap. 32. Cf. Denon, 2, 263.
25. Clarke, 5, 345 f.
26. See L. Dieckmann, "The Metaphor of Hieroglyphics in German Romanticism," *Comparative Literature,* 7 (1955), 306–12.

scroll of old parchment, covered all over with hieroglyphical devices"; the wrinkles on his brow "were characters still more mysterious, which no Champollion nor gypsy could have deciphered." Stones are covered with "hieroglyphical inscriptions," and the names of idols are "carved on their foreheads" like the hieroglyphs on the heads of statues of Egyptian kings and gods. In *Moby-Dick* whales have "mystic hieroglyphics" upon their backs, like Egyptian scarabs. Finally, all mankind is a mysterious and undecipherable Egypt: "Champollion deciphered the wrinkled granite hieroglyphics. But there is no Champollion to decipher the Egypt of every man's and every being's face."[27]

The inscrutable darkness in the hieroglyphical mysteries exercised a peculiar fascination on Melville's mind and was embodied for him in the image of the Egyptian priesthood. The "supernatural" spirit of the Egyptian priests permeated his impression of the pyramids when he saw them in 1856. The priests of ancient Egypt, like the idea of the god they conceived, were a "terrible mixture of the cunning and the awful." Melville recorded in his journal that he shuddered at the thought of the ancient Egyptians: "They must needs have been terrible inventors, these Egyptian wise men."[28] The idea obsessed him even before his journey to Egypt. In the *Confidence-Man* "chemical practitioners, who have sought out so many inventions," are compared to the Egyptian priests. "For what do their inventions indicate, unless it be that kind and degree of pride in human skill, which seems scarce compatible with reverential dependence upon the power above? Try to rid my mind of it as I may, yet still these chemical practitioners with their tinctures, and fumes, and braziers, and occult incantations, seem to me like Pharaoh's sorcerers, trying to beat down the will of

27. *Typee*, chap. 1. *Mardi*, *1*, 151; 2, 17, 26. *Moby-Dick*, chaps. 45, 68, 79.

28. Horsford, *Journal*, pp. 118, 123–24.

heaven."[29] In "Benito Cereno," submitted for publication about the time of the *Confidence-Man,* the old Spanish sailor who makes the emblematic knot for Captain Delano in the hope that he would guess the true state of affairs on the ship, "looked like an Egyptian priest, making Gordian knots for the temple of Ammon."

Melville's concept of the Egyptian priesthood derived from his reading of classical writers—Herodotus, Plutarch, and Pliny—during whose time the Theban priests were regarded as sages and magicians and were much sought after by travelers, including Alexander the Great. Manetho, the first Egyptian priest known to history, who is mentioned in Plutarch's *Morals,* appears in *Mardi* in the important chapter on "Faith and Knowledge' 'in which the narrator identifies himself with characters and incidents of the historical past. In *Redburn,* the walls of "Aladdin's Palace" are hung with "such pictures as the high priests, for a bribe, showed to Alexander in the innermost shrine of the white temple in the Libyan oasis."[30] In Melville's time the oracle of Jupiter Ammon was explored and described by Belzoni. Melville read Plutarch in Holland's translations, as we know from the "Extracts" in *Moby-Dick.* Plutarch apparently was also responsible for the curious image of whaling as "that Egyp-

29. *Confidence-Man,* chap. 16.
30. *Redburn,* chap. 46; cf. Plutarch's *Lives,* "Alexander." Melville's interest in Alexander the Great is also reflected in *Mardi* and *White Jacket* (see reference to Alexander's horse Bucephalus in *Mardi, 1,* 110; cf. Pliny, *Natural History,* trans. P. Holland, 2, Bk. VIII, chap. 42). In *White Jacket* (chap. 18) Melville speaks of the founding of Alexandria: "Wrecked on a desert shore, a man-of-war's crew could quickly found an Alexandria by themselves, and fill it with all the things which go to make up a capital." Cf. the description in Denon, *1,* 76: "I saw art triumph over nature and the genius of Alexander employ the active medium of commerce, to lay on a barren soil the foundations of a superb city, which he selected to be the depository of the trophies of the conquest of the universe."

tian mother, who bore offspring themselves pregnant from her womb." Isis and Osiris, according to the tradition reported by Plutarch, "were in love with one another before they were born, and enjoyed each other in the dark before they came into the world."[31] The son of Isis, Horus, was thus begotten in the womb of his mother while she herself was in her mother's womb.

The expansion of the pyramid from image to symbol can be traced almost chronologically in Melville's works. In *Typee* and *Redburn,* and even in *Mardi,* the metaphorical use of the pyramids is centered on their own physical identity as monumental phenomena of human toil and vanity like the obelisks of Luxor. But "more enduring monuments are built in the closet with the letters of the alphabet than even Cheops himself could have founded, with all Egypt and Nubia for his quarry."[32] The relationship established between the pyramid and the image of man is visible and concrete: "like a pyramid, a great man stands on a broad base."[33] In *Moby-Dick* the image has begun to emanate transcendental connotations: the sperm whale is connected with "the elemental pyramids," and the purpose of the pyramids is linked to "the mast-head standers of the land." The historical information about the pyramids which Melville acquired from Beloe's *Herodotus* and probably from Denon, Belzoni, and Clarke has undergone a sea-change: "I

31. Plutarch, *Morals,* "Of Isis and Osiris" (ed. Godwin, *4, 75*). Melville's favorite image of dawn drawing near in a boat was, of course, inspired by the belief of the ancient Egyptians that the sun and moon, both gods, traveled about the world in boats (*Mardi, 1,* 193; *2,* 129; Plutarch, ed. Godwin, *4,* 94). Other mythological figures drawn from ancient Egypt are Apo, the god of Yillah in Ardair, probably modeled on Apis; Serapis, "the Egyptian symbol of death," the name of a warship in *Israel Potter* (chap. 19), and Sesostris, the mythical conqueror of the world (*Mardi, 1,* 17; *Herodotus,* ed. Beloe, 2, 1 f.).

32. *Redburn,* chap. 32; cf. *Israel Potter,* chap. 15.

33. *Redburn,* chap. 56.

take it, that the earliest standers of mast-heads were the old
Egyptians. . . . And that the Egyptians were a nation of
masthead standers is an assertion based upon the general
belief among archaeologists, that the first pyramids were
founded for astronomical purposes; a theory singularly sup-
ported by the peculiar stair-like formation of all four sides
of those edifices."[34]

A further development, linking the pyramid to the
perennial ritual of the buried corn as a symbol of spiritual
resurrection reveals itself in the well-known letter to Hawthorne written shortly before the publication of *Moby-
Dick:* "I am like one of those seeds taken out of the Egyptian Pyramids, which, after being three thousand years a
seed and nothing but a seed, being planted in English soil,
it developed itself, grew to greenness, and then fell to
mould."[35] The image recurs in "Bartleby" two years later:
"The Egyptian character of the masonry weighed upon me
with its gloom. But a soft imprisoned turf grew under foot.
The heart of the eternal pyramids, it seemed, wherein by
some strange magic, through the clefts, grass-seed, dropped
by birds, had sprung."[36] The monumental rigidity of the

34. *Moby-Dick,* chaps. 35, 68. Belzoni discusses the "astronomical
purposes" of the pyramids, though he does not agree with this theory;
Clarke speaks of a "staircase" in describing his ascent of the pyramid
of Cheops (Belzoni, p. 278; Clarke, 5, 173).

35. Letter to Hawthorne, June 1851, in *Letters,* p. 130. According
to an account of Charles L. James, son of the novelist G. P. R. James,
the James family, who lived at Stockbridge and were neighbors of the
Melvilles at Arrowhead, Pittsfield, had received and planted some
Egyptian wheat taken from the inside of a mummy cave. The wheat
came up and was seen growing. See S. M. Ellis, *The Solitary Horseman* (Kensington, 1927), p. 164. The idea of wheat in the pyramids
was inspired by the common notion that they had served as "Joseph's
Granaries" in time of famine. See extract from John Mandeville in
J. Bonwick, *Pyramid Facts and Fancies* (London, 1877), pp. 112–13.

36. Leyda, *Complete Stories,* p. 45.

pyramids has thus been transmuted into a living organism which, in *Pierre*, is vibrant with deep mystical meaning. In the pyramid Melville's idea of truth—man's heroic attempt to see into the essence of things through an absolute knowledge of self—has achieved a living visible habitation: "By vast pains we mine into the pyramids, by horrible gropings we come to the central room; with joy we espy the sarcophagus; but we lift the lid—and no body is there!—appallingly vacant as vast is the soul of a man."[37]

The above passage reflects Belzoni's description of his entry into the pyramid of Khefren "after thirty days' exertion" and the discovery of a "half open" sarcophagus in the "central chamber."[38] But Melville has turned Belzoni's "operations and discoveries" into a mystical experience, the archetypal search for one's own soul.

The pyramidal shapes of Melville's concept of human being are crystallized in another key symbol in *Pierre:* the statue of Memnon. "Memnon" dominates the imagination of the youthful Pierre. In the woods near his home, in the intermediate period between the first and second meetings with Isabel, he discovers a rock formation. This rock has never been found by the villagers, and Pierre christens it "the Memnon Stone." The stone is wedge-shaped, like a lengthened egg, and seems precariously balanced on a hidden lateral ridge, like an inverted pyramid. Pierre also calls the stone Terror Stone because of its "Mute Massiveness" and "pondrous inscrutableness" which, in its "eternally immovable balancings," threatens to crush him. "A fitting conceit has often crossed him, that he would like nothing better for a head-stone than the same imposing pile; in which, at times, during the soft swayings of the surrounding foliage, there seemed to lurk some mournful and lamenting

37. *Pierre*, Bk. XXI, sec. i.
38. Belzoni, pp. 270–71.

plaint, as for some sweet boy long since departed in the antediluvian time."[39]

Memnon, the post-Homeric hero of Greek mythology with his Egyptian associations, exercised a peculiar magnetism on nineteenth-century writers, on Byron and De Quincey, Disraeli and Carlyle. Referring to "the head of Memnon in the British Museum," apparently the head of Ramses II which Belzoni had brought, De Quincey says that it is "the most diffusive and pathetically divine that the hand of man has created."[40] Carlyle was deeply moved by the "solemn and dirge-like" sound which the Egyptian statue of Memnon, on the authority of ancient tradition, was believed to have uttered at sunrise.[41] The phenomenon was described by the writers of classical antiquity. Strabo believed it to have been an ingenious trick of the priests; modern scholars explain it by the effect of the sun's rays striking the chilled damp granite of the statue.[42] In Egypt the name of Memnon was connected with the colossal statues of Amenhotep III near Thebes; but the hero of Greek mythology was an Ethiopian prince, son of the Dawn, Eos-Aurora, a nephew of Priam, on whose account he fought and perished at Troy. His mother wept bitterly for him, and his subjects erected a statue on the western bank of the Nile which, in Melville's words in *Pierre*, "touched by the breath of the bereaved Aurora . . . gave forth a mournful broken sound, as of a harp-string suddenly sundered."[43] Denon and

39. *Pierre*, Bk. VII, sec. iv. See also *Confidence-Man*, chap. 37; *Collected Poems*, "At the Hostelry," p. 333.

40. See Henry A. Murray, "Explanatory Notes," in *Pierre* (New York, 1949, Hendricks House), p. 464; De Quincey, "The Affliction of Childhood," in *Autobiographical Sketches*. Cf. *Gallery of Antiquities Selected from the British Museum* (London, 1842), plate 39.

41. *Sartor Resartus*, Bk. II, chap. 5.

42. Strabo, *Geography* 17.1.46.

43. *Pierre*, Bk. VII, sec. vi.

Belzoni had a discussion of the Memnonium and its statues at Thebes, debating the claim of the various statues of Egyptian kings to be the true Memnon.[44] Curtis, whose *Nile Notes* were published four years after *Pierre*, felt the presence of Memnon "darling of the dawn, marvellous, but melodious no longer."[45]

The popular story of Memnon was retold by Melville from Bacon's "Memnon, or a Youth too forward" in *The Wisdom of the Ancients*.[46] But the deep Melvillean significance of the image reveals itself in its association with the stone which characterizes Pierre's growth from youthfulness to maturity:

> When in his imaginative ruminating moods of early youth, Pierre had christened the wonderful stone by the old resounding name of Memnon, he had done so merely from certain associative remembrances of that Egyptian marvel, of which all Eastern travellers speak. . . . But, if after-times, when placed in far different circumstances . . . Pierre pondered on the stone . . . then an immense significance came to him. . . . For, not to speak of the other and subtler meanings which lie crouching behind the colossal haunches of this stone, regarded as the menacingly impending Terror Stone —hidden to all the simple cottagers, but revealed to Pierre—consider its aspect as the Memnon Stone. For Memnon was that dewy, royal boy, son of Aurora, and born King of Egypt, who, with enthusiastic rashness flinging himself on another's account into a rightful

44. Denon, *Travels in Upper and Lower Egypt*, *3*, 81; Belzoni, p. 39; cf. Pococke, "Travels in Egypt," in *Voyages and Travels*, *15*, 249.
45. *Nile Notes of a Howadji* (New York, 1856), p. 104.
46. See Murray's introduction to *Pierre*, p. xcvii; Francis Bacon, *Essays and the Wisdom of the Ancients* (London, 1696), p. 50.

quarrel, fought hand to hand with his overmatch, and met his boyish and most dolorous death beneath the walls of Troy.

The myth of Memnon, like the story of Hamlet, is the key not only to Pierre's personality but to the "unsummed world of grief" in Melville's work. "For in this plaintive fable," says Melville, "we find embodied the Hamletism of the antique world; the Hamletism of three thousand years ago: 'The flower of virtue cropped by a too rare mischance.'" Hamlet is "but Egyptian Memnon, Montaignized and modernized." Memnon is the timeless historical embodiment of "that nobly-striving but ever-shipwrecked character in some royal youths" which is the theme of both *Hamlet* and *Pierre*.

The sound which the statue of Memnon emitted at dawn is related to another dominant theme in Melville's writings, the barrenness of the age he lived in: "But Memnon's sculptured woes did once melodiously resound; now all is mute. . . . Aurora's music-moan is lost among our drifting sands, which whelm alike the monument and the dirge."[47]

The full implications of the Memnon image come to the surface when we consider that the hero himself is "stone"— pierre. The Memnon Stone is therefore a symbolic projection of the hero's own personality—a crystallization of his endless probings into the mysteries of his own soul like the architectonic images of the tower, the pyramid, and the chimney, which, in Melville, become an American manifestation of the universal myth of The Sacred Mountain, the archetypal center, "the meeting point of the three cosmic regions: heaven, earth, and hell."[48]

The significance of the etymological identity of Pierre's name and the stone which he is the first and only one to dis-

47. *Pierre,* Bk. VII, sec. vi.
48. Mircea Eliade, *Cosmos and History* (New York, 1954), p. 12.

cover is fully laid bare in the light of "I and My Chimney."
The chimney "has a druidical look, away down in the um-
brageous cellar there, whose numerous vaulted passages,
and far glens of gloom, resemble dark, damp depths of primeval woods."[49] This is an echo from *Pierre,* where the
Memnon Stone is hidden, "belted and topped by the dense
deep luxuriance of the aboriginal forest." The stone revealed itself to Pierre and to Pierre alone after he had
"plunged deep into the woods." Like the chimney, it contained a vacancy "convenient to admit a crawling man, yet
no mortal being had ever been known to have the intrepid
heart to crawl there." Pierre explores the stone and ponders
on it as the narrator explores and ponders the chimney. The
narrator's wife, on the other hand, who wants the chimney
removed, is one of the simple cottagers to whom the Memnon Stone could be "nothing but a huge stumbling-block,
deeply to be regretted as a vast prospective obstacle in the
way of running a handy little cross-road through the wild
part of the manor."

The Memnon Stone is as typical of Melville's content and
method as the White Whale of the Pacific. Like the whale,
it is "simultaneously the most solid of physical things and
the most meaningful of symbols."[50] The stone in *Pierre* was
actually modeled on Balance Rock, a boulder in the neigh-
borhood of Pittsfield where Melville lived, yet it embodies
all the complexities of Melville's vision of man and the universe. In Melville's mythical landscape its situation in the
dark forest relates it to the prehistoric primitive altars of
Polynesia;[51] but its shape and name proclaim it as one of
the historical monuments of civilization in its original setting of the ancient Near East.

49. Leyda, *Complete Stories,* p. 380.
50. Feidelson, p. 184.
51. Baird, pp. 284 f.

The Egyptian pyramid and its explorer Belzoni finally control the story of "I and My Chimney," where the identification of "I" with the pyramid is complete. Like the Memnon Stone, the chimney is structurally related to the pyramid, "it pyramidically diminished as it ascended." The analogy between the narrator's exploration of his chimney and Belzoni's operations and discoveries is consistently maintained throughout the tale. The narrator digs around the foundation of the chimney "obscurely prompted by ideas of striking upon some old, earthern-worn memorial of that by-gone day when, into all this gloom, the light of heaven entered, as the masons laid the foundation-stones." His neighbor promptly suspects him of gold-digging, like the Turkish Aga of Thebes who was convinced that Belzoni was digging for treasure.

The narrator's wife conceives the idea of a tunnel which was to penetrate the chimney at some convenient point and was to conduct the traveler from the front door to the dining room in the rear of the mansion. If the project had been accomplished, says Melville, "some Belzoni or other might have succeeded in future ages in penetrating through the masonry, and actually emerging into the dining-room." This passage, too, suggests Belzoni's penetration of the pyramid of Khefren and the opening of the tomb in the ravine at Thebes, which are first alluded to in *Typee*. Belzoni describes the entry through an aperture into a hall and various chambers, one of which he christened "drawing-room." There seems to be another allusion to that particular passage when the narrator descends into the shaft of the chimney with Scribe, the architect, who is called at the wife's request: "We seemed in the pyramids; and I, with one hand holding my lamp over head, and with the other pointing out, in the obscurity, the hoar mass of the chimney, seemed some Arab guide, showing the cobwebbed mausoleum of the great god Apis." Scribe's activity in determining the situation of a supposed secret closet in the chimney through measurements may have been inspired by Belzoni's measurements and computations to determine the entrance into the Khefren pyramid.

Because of the chimney, the complex structure of the narrator's house was such that guests would stay with him several weeks "and every now and then, be anew astounded at some unforeseen apartment." Again, Belzoni had guests stay with him in his tent at Giza to watch the opening of the pyramid and the entry into unexpected apartments.[52]

The correspondence is so close and so consistent as to give the impression of an obsessive interest in Belzoni on Melville's part. Indeed, Jay Leyda has found "the true direction" of "I and My Chimney" in a journal entry on Belzoni in Taylor's *Life of Benjamin Robert Haydon* that Melville bought in April 1854.[53] It would also seem that Melville's story entitled "The Happy Failure," which three months later appeared in *Harper's Magazine,* had something to do with Belzoni.[54] For the unsuccessful invention in the tale is a "Great Hydraulitic-Hydrostatic Apparatus" like Belzoni's hydraulic machine for the water of the Nile which was never used.

However that may be, there can be no doubt that Melville fully agreed with Haydon's estimate of Belzoni and probably applied it to himself:

> In every sense Belzoni is a grand fellow. He suffered in his progress, as all suffer who dash at once upon great undertakings which thousands have feared to touch. The attempt alone is an insult to the under-

52. Belzoni, pp. 265, 268.
53. Leyda, ed., *Complete Stories,* p. xxv.
54. "The Happy Failure, a Story of the River Hudson," *Harper's New Monthly Magazine,* July 1, 1854 (Leyda, *Complete Stories,* p. 467).

standing of all those who have never attempted and
would never attempt such a bold attack. When a great
undertaking is accomplished it is "opportunity" and
"luck." When it was undertaken it was "insanity!"
They first endeavor to hinder a man from all attempts
beyond the ordinary course, by asserting the impossi-
bility of success, and when he proves them in error,
they charitably attribute his success to "happy chance,"
to anything in short but a combined action of his own
understanding and will.

How strange it is that the very people who make a
man celebrated by talking of his name (which they
cannot avoid) revenge themselves by attaching everything to it that can bring him down to their own
level.[55]

"I and My Chimney" appeared in *Putnam's Monthly
Magazine* in March 1856. In October of that year Melville
embarked on the Mediterranean journey which finally
brought him face to face with the pyramids. The passages
describing them are the most moving and tortured in his
Journal. In 1849 he had looked forward to seeing them with
exuberant glee when he planned a Near Eastern tour with
his traveling companions to Europe. In his letter to Hawthorne he drew hope from the seed that had fallen from the
eternal pyramids and, "by some strange magic," had developed into greenness. But this hope was blighted when he
looked at the pyramids on December 31, 1856: "Color of
pyramids same as desert. . . . No vestige of moss upon them.
Not the least. Other ruins ivied. Dry as tinder. No speck of
green. . . . Grass near the pyramids, but will not touch
them—as if in fear or awe of them."

The terrible significance of vastness, of truncated and
mutilated shapes, colored the whole landscape at Giza:

55. *Life of Benjamin Robert Haydon* (London, 1853), 2, 14–15.

Pyramids from distance purple like mountains. Seem
high & pointed, but flatten & depress as you approach.
. . . Pyramids still loom before me—something vast,
undefiled, incomprehensible, and aweful. . . . The lines
of stone look less like courses of masonry, than like
strata of rocks. . . . It is not the sense of height, or
breadth or length or depth that is stirred, but the sense
of immensity that is stirred. . . . The tearing away of
the casing, though it removed enough stone to build a
walled-town, has not subtracted from its apparent mag-
nitude. . . . To the imagination Man seems to have had
as little to do with it as Nature. . . . It was in these pyramids that was conceived the idea of Jehovah. Terrible
mixture of the cunning and the awful.[56]

The passages on the pyramids in the *Journal* were reworked and revised many times; descriptions of the pyramids were marked by Melville in the books he subsequently read; but only two short poems, "The Great
Pyramid" and "In the Desert," express something of the
feeling recorded in the *Journal*. In *Clarel* the pyramids
appear in a flash—a darkly looming landmark thrown
across a desert.[57]

LAYARD AND ANCIENT ASSYRIA

The use that Melville made of Babylonian material is
charged with the traditional prophetic experience. Most of
his Assyro-Babylonian images were drawn from the Bible,
the Book of Jonah and the Book of Daniel,[1] and present
man's iniquity embodied in the kings of Babylon and the

56. Horsford, *Journal*, pp. 117, 118–19, 122, 123–24.
57. *Clarel*, *1*, 70, 216.
1. See Nathalia Wright, *Melville's Use of the Bible* (Durham, 1949),
pp. 36–38, 147–48.

splendors of Nineveh and man's effort to penetrate the mysteries of the universe personified in the Chaldean magi. Like the historical material in his hands, the Babylonian scenery of the Bible is transmuted into a new presentness: the gourd which God prepared "to come up over Jonah" becomes a familiar suburban sight in local Ninevehs on the American continent, and "the thing" that was "fulfilled upon Nebuchadnezzar" ("and he was driven from men, and did eat grass as oxen, and his body was wet with the dew of heaven, till his hair was grown like eagles' *feathers,* and his nails like birds' *claws*") is divested of its biblical grimness by a Falstaffian twist: "Folly and foolishness!" exclaims Redburn, "to think that a gentleman is known by his finger-nails, like Nebuchadnezzar, when his grew long in the pasture."[2] A cube of salt beef tastes delicious to Omoo after "the Nebuchadnezzar fare of the valley."[3] Finally, in "I and My Chimney," the narrator's parched and insensitive wife raves after "all sorts of salads and spinaches, and more particularly green cucumbers," a psychologically revealing vegetarian diet, "as if she were own daughter of Nebuchadnezzar."[4]

Significantly, the play of Melville's comic spirit did not touch the image of the Babylonian wise men. To White Jacket "to study the stars upon the wide, boundless sea, is divine as it was to the Chaldean Magi, who observed their revolutions from the plains."[5] Melville's interest in ancient Babylonia and Assyria was not confined to biblical sources, however. Like his preoccupation with ancient Egypt it was fostered by the archaeological discoveries of the time, specimens of which he saw for himself at the British Museum on his visit to London in 1849.[6]

2. *Redburn,* chap. 56.
3. *Omoo,* chap. 1.
4. *Complete Stories,* p. 386.
5. *White Jacket,* chap. 19.
6. Metcalf, *Journal,* p. 33.

The glimpse of "Nineveh sculptures" which Melville caught at the British Museum is hardly sufficient to provide much guidance to what he knew of Assyrian antiquities. But in *White Jacket,* which he took with him to London for publication, he mentions the foremost contemporary authority on the subject, the famous British traveler Sir Austen Henry Layard, who excavated Nineveh in 1846 and 1847. Layard's account of his expedition appeared in two volumes in 1848–49. It was entitled *Nineveh and Its Remains; with an Account of a Visit to the Chaldean Christians of Kurdistan and the Yezids, or Devil-Worshippers; and an Enquiry into the Manners and Arts of the Ancient Assyrians* followed, in 1849, by *The Monuments of Nineveh, Illustrating Mr. Layard's First Expedition to Assyria, from Drawings made on the Spot.*[7]

The image of Nineveh in *Mardi,* written before the publication of Layard's drawings, seems to reflect an illustration of Nineveh, with birds flying over it, in Kitto's *Cyclopaedia of Biblical Literature.* "In the distance what visions were spread!" writes Melville of a superb sunset. "The entire western horizon high piled with gold and crimson clouds; airy arches, domes, and minarets; as if the yellow, Moorish sun were setting behind some vast Alhambra. Vistas seemed leading to worlds beyond. To and fro, and all over the towers of this Nineveh in the sky, flew troops of birds."[8]

But in *White Jacket,* which Melville completed in Au-

---

7. Charles Knight, the London publisher, has recorded that Wordsworth, whom he met through Harriet Martineau in 1849 when the poet was seventy-nine years old, "told me that he felt no interest in any modern book except in Mr. Layard's Nineveh, which had then been recently published" (*Passages from the Life of Charles Knight,* New York, 1874, p. 437).

8. *Mardi, 1,* 8. Cf. John Kitto, *Cyclopaedia of Biblical Literature* (Edinburgh, 1848), p. 620.

gust 1849, the sailors on the *Neversink* who objected to the captain's orders to have their hair and beards trimmed are figures straight from *The Monuments of Nineveh:* "and the old tars who still sported their beards stood up, grim, defying, and motionless, as the rows of sculptured Assyrian kings, who, with their magnificent beards, have recently been exhumed by Layard."[9]

A plate of a bearded and grim-looking Assyrian king from *Nineveh and Its Remains* was also reproduced in an article on Layard in the *Quarterly Review* of December 1848, which, in its turn, was discussed in Dr. Robinson's preface to the American edition of the book reprinted in the *Literary World* in March 1849. The article in the *Quarterly Review* describes Nineveh as the archetypal City of Cities:

> Still there seems no doubt from Mr. Layard's . . . successful excavation . . . that each or all of these places, . . . where the same great mounds appear, were, if not parts of one vast city, the successive localities occupied or comprehended by *Nineveh* under its successive dynasties. As . . . Babylon, Seleucia, Ctesiphon, Bagdad, succeeded each other on sites at no considerable distance, so as to be loosely described as the same city; in like manner, from that imperial caprice which seems almost to be a characteristic of great eastern sovereigns, each proud of being the founder of his own capital, the temples or palaces which it is manifest stood on every one of these sites, differing as they apparently do in age, and to a certain extent in the character of their art, may each have been the *Nineveh* of its day.[10]

In *Redburn,* which Melville was writing at a time when *Nineveh and Its Remains* was discussed far and wide, the

---

9. *White Jacket,* chap. 86.
10. *Quarterly Review, 84* (1849) 111–12.

future inhabitants of New York are described as regarding
their Broadways and Bowerys "as but the paltry nucleus to
their Nineveh."[11] The picture of the Babylonian City is
intensified in *Pierre,* which abounds in Babylonian imagery,
particularly in the description of Pierre's morning ride
with Lucy. Pierre is mounted on a gray-haired steed like "an
old Chaldean,"[12] He seems "a youthful Magian" in a mystical mood. But the mood alternates with a mad unbridled
merriment which releases itself in "Chaldaic improvisations." The scenery through which Pierre and Lucy take
their morning ride resolves itself into a panorama of a Babylonian city:

> Soon the swift horses drew this fair god and goddess
> nigh the wooded hills, whose distant blue, now
> changed into a variously-shaded green, stood before
> them like old Babylonian walls, overgrown with ver-
> dure; while here and there, at regular intervals, the
> scattered peaks seemed mural towers; and the clumped
> pines surmounting them, as lofty archers, and vast, out-
> looking watchers of the glorious Babylonian City of
> the Day.[13]

In the characteristic conception of Melville, the wooded
hills of an American landscape are filled with the souls of
past civilizations and represent the total historical experience of man. As Pierre and Lucy, in their archetypal significance, become the incarnations of a god and goddess of
past mythologies, the wooded hills near Pierre's home trans-
form themselves into the mounds of "the glorious Babylonian City of the Day," i.e. they become a contemporary

11. *Redburn,* chap. 30.
12. *Pierre,* Bk. II, sec. iii. For an illustration of an Assyrian horseman see *Nineveh and Its Remains,* 2, 28.
13. *Pierre,* Bk. II, p. v. In Jonah 3:4 Nineveh is "the city of three
days' journey" into which Jonah entered "a day's journey."

Nineveh comprising a historical succession of cities, each of which, in the words of the *Quarterly Review*, was "the Nineveh of its day."

Another matter of topical interest to the nineteenth century was the word "Chaldean," which Melville especially liked. In fact, in a letter on Layard to the *Literary World* Dr. Robinson objected to Layard's use of the term to designate the Nestorian Christians of Syria.[14] In the Book of Daniel and Herodotus "Chaldeans" denote "Babylonians" and, in a secondary meaning, "astrologers, astronomers, wise men." Melville uses the term in the biblical sense of both Babylonian and sage. His other favorite term for a wise man, astrologer, and diviner of the will of heaven, is "magian," properly a fire-worshiper. The "Chaldean Magi," who observed the revolutions of the stars from the plains, stem from both biblical and classical sources. In speaking of "the awful Chaldee of the sperm whale's brow" and the "Chaldaic improvisations" which burst from Pierre to convey "unspeakable meanings," Melville has merged the term with the romantic metaphor of hieroglyphics to denote the mysteries of the divine.[15]

There were various theories concerning the origin of the Chaldeans and the accurate application of the term in Melville's time. James B. Fraser, author of a popular history of Persia as well as one of Mesopotamia and Assyria that was published in Harper's Family Library in New York in 1845, states the general view of the time that "there is no doubt that the Chaldeans, as the dominant people in ancient Babylon, possessed all power and learning as well as the influence which belonged to the priesthood."[16]

14. E. Robinson, "The Discoveries at Nineveh," *Literary World*, 4 (1849), 243.

15. *Moby-Dick*, chap. 79. *Pierre*, Bk. II, sec. iv.

16. J. B. Fraser, *Mesopotamia and Assyria* (New York, 1845), pp. 84–85.

This idea, with its overtones of "philosopher," permeates
Melville's image of Queequeg: "No dying Chaldee or Greek
had higher and holier thoughts than those, whose mysterious shades you saw creeping over the face of poor Queequeg."[17] Zoroaster, with whom the dying savage is identified, was also believed to have been a Chaldean by Melville's
contemporaries, for according to *Purchas His Pilgrimage*
the Persian magi were derived from the Chaldeans.[18]

Melville perhaps had some acquaintance with Fraser's
Mesopotamia and Assyria, for his comparison of the whalemen on the *Pequod* to an old Mesopotamian family seems
to recall a statement in that book. In *Moby-Dick* he describes the class consciousness of the whalemen and the
rigorous discipline which obtained on board from a sense of
rank: "the punctilious externals . . . of the quarter-deck are
materially relaxed, and in no instance done away," even
though "in some primitive instances" the whalemen live
together "like an old Mesopotamian family."[19] In contrast
to Fraser, the image of the Mesopotamian family is here
used to indicate a relaxation of discipline. Nevertheless it is
set in a context that is curiously reminiscent of Fraser's description of Mesopotamian family life. "In a community so
closely resembling that of the Highland families," writes
Fraser of the Mesopotamian Arabs, "it was interesting to
notice the demeanour observed towards relatives and
friends, and to trace the respective degrees of estimation
assigned to the various grades of kindred or connexions.
The mode of reception to each was varied and accurately
defined."[20]

Like the Egyptian imagery, Melville's Babylonian allusions persist throughout his writings. In fact, an echo of

17. *Moby-Dick,* chap. 110.
18. *Purchas His Pilgrimage* (London, 1613), 5, 55.
19. *Moby-Dick,* chap. 33.
20. Fraser, *Mesopotamia and Assyria,* p. 271.

Assyria is the only Near Eastern reference to recur in his last work, *Billy Budd*. At the beginning of the story the Handsome Sailor is linked both to primitive Africa and the historical bull worship of Assyrian priests:

> With no perceptible trace of the vainglorious about him, rather with the offhand unaffectedness of natural regality, he seemed to accept the spontaneous homage of his shipmates . . . a common sailor, so intensely black that he must needs have been a native African of the unadulterate blood of Ham. A symmetric figure much above the average height . . . he rollicked along, the centre of a company of his shipmates. These were made up of such an assortment of tribes and complexions as would have well fitted them to be marched up . . . as Representatives of the Human Race. At each spontaneous tribute rendered by the wayfarers to this black pagoda of a fellow . . . the motley retinue showed that they took that sort of pride in the evoker of it which the Assyrian priests doubtless showed for their grand sculptured Bull when the faithful prostrated themselves.

Like the Memnon Stone in *Pierre,* the symbol of both the human identity and the human condition, the godlike figure of Melville's *Puer Aeternus* thus arises both from man's primitivist experience and from his historical consciousness.

5. Prophets and Conquerors

ZOROASTER AND ANCIENT PERSIA

In the chapter entitled "The Candles" in *Moby-Dick* "when God's burning finger has been laid on the ship," when His "Mene, Mene, Tekel Upharsin" has been woven into the shrouds and cordage, Ahab, the "grand, ungodly, godlike man," throws his fatal defiance in the face of heaven: "In the midst of the personified impersonal, a personality stands here."

Ahab, captain of the *Pequod,* is the Carlylean Hero, both as Prophet and as Conqueror. In Carlyle's definition, "Ever, to the true instinct of men, there is something god-like in him. . . . I should say, *sincerity,* a deep, great, genuine sincerity, is the first characteristic of all men in any way heroic. . . . Such a man is what we call an *original* man; he comes to us at first-hand."[1] The American whaling captain is Melville's incarnation of the prophets and conquerors of the ancient Near East created in the image of Milton's Satan and cast in the grandiose proportions of an archetypal "Ecce Homo." He is the biblical Ahab but also Zoroaster and Mohammed, preaching a new creed of man's "queenly personality" flinging "her royal rights" at the powers above; he is Tamerlane and Suleiman the Magnificent, Commander over Men, subordinating the wills of his loyal, sur-

1. *On Heroes,* Lecture II.

rendering subjects to the relentless pursuit of the enemy—
the White Whale.

The clash of good and evil as coexistent universal forces
is the central theme in Melville's work. "Moby Dick," in
the words of Newton Arvin, "does not, reassuringly and
finally symbolize the Christian God, transcendent and absolute, and, however mysterious in His workings, a God of
absolute love and justice and truth. A cosmic scene lorded
over by the White Whale is one from which the soul-freez-
ing possibility of an ultimate atheism is never wholly absent,
and of course it was terribly present to Melville's spirit
when he wrote the book."[2] In creating his grandiose sce-
nario of universal ambiguities Melville transmuted what he
knew of the Oriental dualism of Persian creeds, fire worship, Gnosticism, Manichaeism, and Zoroastrianism, into a
philosophy of a "depravity according to nature" in which
evil is realized as a godlike flame, an implacable natural
force.

Ahab, turned heathen by his hatred of the White Whale,
rejects the orthodox Christian belief in the goodness of the
universe. He worships fire and is guided by Fedallah, a
Parsee—the diabolic alter ego of the Quaker captain from
Nantucket. "Ahab has sold his soul to the fire-worshipping
Parsee, the Parsee who, in this case, worships fire not as a
symbol of light and truth but as a symbol of raging and de-
structive Evil. Moby Dick, however, is indestructible, and
the upshot of their impious onslaught upon him is not his
but their destruction."[3] As in *Vathek,* the heathen connotations of the fire symbolism in *Moby-Dick* are crucial to its
essence as a "wicked book," though the heroic grandeur of
Ahab's quarrel with God, infinitely more profound and
ennobling than Vathek's, lends the satanic flames and their

2. Newton Arvin, *Herman Melville* (New York, 1957), p. 188.
3. Ibid., p. 192.

faithful servant Fedallah a tragic dignity and piety of their own.

The symbolic use to which Melville put Zoroastrianism and the older Persian cult of the elements is entirely his own. But again, his preoccupation with the religions of ancient Persia was a phenomenon of the age he lived in. On a metaphorical level it may be traced with equal strength in nineteenth-century literature and thought in England and America, ranging from Thomas Moore's *Lalla Rookh* and the *Penny Magazine* to Emerson and Hawthorne. Melville used Zoroastrianism and fire worship as he used other Oriental creeds and rituals—to add a layer of timeless universal significance to his themes and characters. But the fire symbolism in *Moby-Dick* is related to the central meaning of the book and thus lends special importance to what Melville knew of ancient Persia.

His acquaintance with the more common aspects of ancient Persian history, the stories of Darius, Cyrus, Cambyses, Artaxerxes, and Xerxes, stemmed from classical sources, mainly Herodotus.[4] The image of Xerxes and his Persian host recurs in his works with great frequency in connotations of vastness, multitudes, and military pomp. Significantly, the Xerxes images cluster around the period when Melville bought Herodotus. They appear in *Mardi, Redburn, White Jacket,* and *Moby-Dick,* but less frequently in his later works. Beloe's translation of Herodotus, which Melville acquired in March 1849, belonged to a set of thirty-

---

4. Melville could not have known of the identification of the biblical Ahasuerus with Xerxes, son of Darius (see Nathalia Wright, *Melville's Use of the Bible,* p. 22). In Melville's time the Ahasuerus of Scripture was assumed to have been Cambyses, who succeeded Cyrus, or Darius I. The identification with Xerxes dates from the end of the nineteenth century. See J. B. Fraser, *Historical and Descriptive Account of Persia* (New York, 1841), p. 108; James Hastings, *Dictionary of the Bible, 4,* 958.

seven volumes of Harper's Classical Library including *Xenophon's History of Cyrus's Expedition into Persia and The Retreat of the Ten Thousand Greeks* in Spelman's translation, to which reference is made in the chapter on "Dreams" in *Mardi*. In Herodotus, Melville seems mainly to have drawn on the account of the campaigns of Xerxes. The profound impression which Herodotus' description of Xerxes' cavalry made on him may be gauged from *Redburn:* "Me thinks I am Xerxes, the nucleus of the martial neigh of all the Persian studs. Like gilded damask-flies thick clustering on some lofty bough, my satraps swarm around me."[5] The following description is given by Herodotus:

> A thousand of the first and noblest Persians attended his person, bearing their spears according to the custom of their country; and a thousand horse, selected like the former, immediately succeeded. A body of ten thousand chosen infantry came next; a thousand of these had at the extremity of their spears a pomegranate of gold, the remaining nine thousand, whom the former enclosed, had in the same manner pomegranates of silver. They who preceded Xerxes, and trailed their spears, had their arms decorated with gold; they who followed him had, as we have described, golden pomegranates: these ten thousand foot were followed by an equal number of Persian cavalry.

A majestic image of the approaching dawn in *Mardi* evokes the splendor of Xerxes' army:

> But now, a bright mustering is seen among the myriad white Tartar tents in the orient; like lines of spears defiling upon some upland plain, the sunbeams thwart the sky. And see! amid the blaze of banners, and the

5. *Redburn*, chap. 49.

pawings of ten thousand golden hoofs, day's mounted
Sultan, Xerxes-like, moves on; the Dawn his standard,
East and West his cymbals.[6]

In *Clarel* a similar image of dawn has fused the noble res-
tiveness of Xerxes' cavalry with the pomp of the Sultan of
the Saracens in Scott's *Tales of the Crusaders* and William
Bartlett's portrayal of the Meccan pilgrimage, which was
transmuted into poetry in an earlier canto:

> The startled East a tremor knows—
> Flushes—anon superb appears
> In state of housings, shawls and spears,
> Such as the Sultan's vanguard shows.
>   Preceded thus, in pomp the sun
> August from Persia draweth on,
> Waited by groups upon the wall
> Of Judah's upland capital.[7]

Some elements in Melville's historical knowledge of pre-
Islamic Persia may be traced to a book which has been
established as one of the sources for *Moby-Dick*. His de-
scription of the fishlike incarnation of the Hindu goddess
Vishnu, "the Matse Avatar," has been shown to stem from
Thomas Maurice's *Indian Antiquities*.[8] A discussion of the
Persian fire-worshipers precedes the comment on the Matse
Avatar in Maurice's preface. Similarly, an engraving of the
Matse Avatar is preceded by a plate representing the sacred
fire of the Persians on an altar.[9] This plate, as Maurice

6. *Mardi*, 2, 188. Herodotus, 3.403.
7. *Clarel*, *1*, 59. Cf. *The Talisman*, chap. 6. Bartlett, *Forty Days in
the Desert*, p. 152. See above, p. 68.
8. H. O. Vincent, *The Trying-Out of Moby Dick* (Boston, 1949),
pp. 278–80.
9. Thomas Maurice, *Indian Antiquities* (London, 1800), *1*, 101–2;
2, plate facing p. 90.

indicates, is drawn from Thomas Hyde's *Veterum Persarum Religionis Historia,* the standard work on the subject in the eighteenth and nineteenth centuries. Hyde is also extensively quoted in an article on Zoroaster in Pierre Bayle's *Historical and Critical Dictionary,* which Melville bought in 1849 and is known to have consulted for *Moby-Dick.*[10] The Zoroastrian Bible, the Zend-Avesta, is mentioned in *Pierre* in a list of books some of which Melville had probably read,[11] though the standard version of the work was a three-volume translation into French by Anquetil-Duperron published in Paris in 1771. Extracts from it, however, are found in John Malcolm's well-known *History of Persia* (1829); in Fraser's *Historical and Descriptive Account of Persia* (1834), an American edition of which appeared in Harper's Family Library in 1841; and in popular periodicals, for example, the New York *American Review* of September 1848.

Actually Melville did not incorporate much historical material on Zoroaster or Zoroastrianism.

Bayle says that "the followers of the ancient religion of the Persians . . . maintain that they do not adore the sun, but only turn toward it when they pray to God." This statement, it has been pointed out, is reflected in Melville's comparison of the phenomenon of a large herd of whales, "all heading towards the sun and for a moment vibrating in concert with peaked flukes" to "the adoration of the gods" by Persian fire-worshipers.[12] Melville may also have drawn on his reading of Bayle in the picture of Zoroaster's death

10. Pierre Bayle, *The Dictionary Historical and Critical* (5 vols. 1734–38), 5, 633–34. Thomas Hyde, *Veterum Persarum et Parthorum et Medorum Religionis Historia,* 1st ed. Oxford, 1700.

11. *Pierre,* Bk. XXI, sec. iii. Melville is known to have read "Abraham Tucker" (*An Abridgement of The Light of Nature Pursued,* London, 1807): see Leyda, *Log,* pp. 479, 606.

12. See Vincent, p. 298; *Moby-Dick,* chap. 86; and Bayle, 5, 637.

which is visualized by Ishmael when he watches his apparently dying friend Queequeg: "An awe that cannot be named would steal over you as you sat by the side of this waning savage, and saw as strange things in his face as any beheld who were bystanders when Zoroaster died. For whatever is truly wondrous, and fearful in man, never yet was put into words or books."[13] According to Greek and Latin tradition as reported by Bayle, Zoroaster "wished to be struck with thunder and consumed by fire from Heaven." He "ordered the Persians to collect his bones after he was burnt in this manner, and to keep and venerate them. . . ."[14] The "waning" Queequeg is a heathen holy man consumed by flames. There is also an Iranian tradition of Zoroaster's death which is not mentioned by Bayle. It derives from the Shahnameh, or Book of Kings, the celebrated Persian epic by Firdausi, which comprises the whole mythical and legendary history of Persia down to the Arab conquest and the introduction of Islam. There it is stated that Zoroaster, together with eighty priests, was slain in the presence of the sacred fire in the sanctuary of the fire-worshipers in the city of Balkh in the province of Bactria—"and the brilliant Fire has been extinguished by their blood."[15] This scene of Zoroaster's death appears in the Latin prose version of the Shahnameh given by Hyde. In view of Melville's not infrequent Latin quotations there is no reason to assume that he would have hesitated to look at Hyde's learned opus.[16] Overtones of the Iranian version of Zoroaster's death are reflected in the chapter "The Candles" in *Moby-Dick:* "Aye, aye, men!" cried Ahab. "Look up at it, mark it well, the white flame

13. *Moby-Dick,* chap. 110.
14. Bayle, 5, 632.
15. A. V. W. Jackson, *Zoroaster* (London, 1899), p. 130.
16. Hyde, p. 329; cf. Latin quotation from Henry de Bracton, *De Legibus et Consuetudinibus Angliae,* at the head of *Moby-Dick,* chap. 90.

but lights the way to the White Whale! Hand me those
main mast links there; I would fain feel this pulse, and let
mine beat against it, blood against fire! . . . Oh! thou clear
spirit of clear fire whom . . . I as Persian once did worship."
There is also an earlier allusion in *Mardi:* "Fire flames on
my tongue; and though of old the Bactrian prophets were
stoned, yet the stones in oblivion sleep."[17] Bayle describes
Zoroaster as "king of the Bactrians." But Melville refers to
the legend that the Bactrian prophets, who included Zoroaster, met a violent death, which is not mentioned in Bayle.

The rites of Persian fire worship, which predated the appearance of Zoroaster, were freely adapted by Melville to
his own symbolic purposes. Particularly interesting is the
statement in *Moby-Dick* that the white forked flame was
considered "the holiest on the altar" by the fire-worshipers.
The whiteness of the flames is consistently emphasized: the
white flame lights the way to the White Whale; the white
flame is contrasted with the "Satanic blue flames" of the
tattooing on Queequeg's body.[18] There is no description of
fire worship in Bayle, and it is at least conceivable that Melville's "researches up to the very springhead" had introduced him to the two authoritative works on the Parsi religion in his time: Hyde's Latin history with its interesting
plates of sacred fires, and a book published by the American
Mission Press in Bombay, John Wilson's *The Parsi Religion.*[19] The kind of fire which the Persians regarded as
holiest is described by Wilson in a note. He states that there
were "five great kinds of fire" and that the fire "was always
increasing in the presence of Hormazd," i.e. Ahmazd, the

17. *Mardi*, 2, 54.
18. *Moby-Dick*, chaps. 42, 119.
19. See, however, Vincent, *The Trying-Out of Moby-Dick*, p. 379,
n. 7. He considers it doubtful that Melville had seen Anquetil-Duperron's translation of the *Zend-Avesta*, or that he knew about Wilson's
Parsi Religion (n. 20 below).

god of light, the highest god of the Parsis and the rival of
Ahriman, the god of darkness.[20]

According to Firdausi, the author of the Shahnameh, as
quoted in Malcolm's *History of Persia*, the Devil spoke to
Zoroaster from the midst of a flame.[21] That the Persian fire-
worshipers held the color blue in abomination is stated by
Layard in his account of the devil-worshiping Yezidis, who,
as we know from Melville's markings in Hope's *Anastasius*,
aroused the particular interest of the author of *Moby-
Dick*.[22] Another important element in Ahab's adoration
of fire, the number of the flames, may be also connected
with the veneration of the number nine by Persian fire-
worshipers, of which Herodotus and Maurice's *Indian Antiquities* give examples.

Melville's use of the number nine, a fundamental symbol
of the Holy Trinity in Dante and Milton, was clearly a
deliberate perversion of Christian belief and sacrament.
Like his use of fire, the symbolism of nine in his work was
based on its anti-Christian connotations, and he must have
been aware from his reading of the special place this number held among the non-Christian peoples of the Near East.
The importance of the number first strikes one in *Mardi*.
Babbalanja tells a story of nine blind men setting out to
see the island where they were born; the remains of nine
swordfish are among the rare treasures of Oh-Oh's cave; and
there is Babbalanja's philosophical exposition of unity and
plurality in terms of nine as a triad of triads.[23]

In *Moby-Dick* the symbolical impact of the number is

20. John Wilson, *The Parsi Religion* (Bombay, 1843), p. 229.

21. J. Malcolm, *History of Persia* (2 vols. London, 1829), *1*, 45.

22. Cf. review of *Nineveh and Its Remains* in *Quarterly Review*,
84 (1849), 130. See Melville's copy of *Anastasius* (2 vols. London,
Murray, 1836), 2, chap. 4, p. 200 (Houghton Library, Harvard University).

23. *Mardi*, 2, 40, 69, 111.

highly significant. Ahab's invocation of fire centers around nine flames which leap lengthwise to thrice their previous height and form "a tri-pointed trinity of flames."[24] More important still, the *Pequod* has nine gams before the encounter with Moby Dick and the final catastrophe. In "I and My Chimney," the number is linked with the structure of the chimney: "The puzzling nature of the mansion, resulting from the chimney, is peculiarly noticeable in the dining-room which has no less than nine doors, opening in all directions and into all sorts of places."[25]

Melville may have been originally influenced by Milton in choosing the number nine to convey the heathen and Satanic associations of his theme. In *Paradise Lost* the fall of Satan and the other rebel angels into hell is made a matter of nine days; the gates of hell and the depth of the flames that encompass Pandemonium are also made ninefold.[26]

But Melville's interest in the properties of the number nine must have been greatly intensified by Persian and Tartar usage. Both Herodotus and Maurice mention the use of nine by the Persian fire-worshipers in selecting their victims for sacrifice.[27] As Purchas and Gibbon point out, the mysterious number was held in religious reverence by the Tartars and figured in the offerings which were given to Tartar Khans, including Ahab's prototype, Tamerlane.[28] The Tartar preference for nine was most emphatic, and

24. *Moby-Dick*, chap. 119, "The Candles."
25. Leyda, *Complete Stories*, p. 389.
26. *Paradise Lost*, 2, 436; 6, 871. On Milton's use of nine see James Curtis, *A Dissertation upon Odd Numbers, Particularly No. 7 and No. 9* (London, 1909), pp. 63, 72 f.
27. Herodotus, 7.114. *Indian Antiquities*, 2, 55, 57–58.
28. Purchas, 5, 419. Gibbon (6 vols. Dublin, 1788–89), 5, 311, n. 14; 333. Also see J. Richardson, *A Dissertation on the Languages, Literature and Manners of Eastern Nations* (Oxford, 1788), p. 159; and Malcolm, *1*, 292.

the number also had special significance in the eyes of the Greeks, the Hindus, and the Mohammedans.[29]

In *Moby-Dick* Melville refers to the ancient Persian cult of water. "Why did the old Persians hold the sea holy?" asks Ishmael.[30] The reverence in which the ancient Persians held both fire and water is pointed out by Herodotus, Wilson, Hyde, and Bayle, but without any particular reference to the sea.[31] On the other hand, it is stated in Fraser's *Account of Persia* that "the Parsees and Ghebers never willingly throw filth either into fire or water. ... This reverence for the elements prevents them from being sailors, as in a long voyage they might be forced to defile the sea."[32]

At times the absence of a particular allusion in Melville is almost as puzzling as its presence. The well-known Persian legend of Rustam's fight with the White Demon, of which there is no trace in *Moby-Dick* among the great number of references to Persia, is an instance of this kind. This famous combat is described in the Shahnameh and frequently referred to in the literature of the time—for example, in Moore's notes to *Lalla Rookh*.[33] Moore explains that Rustam is the Hercules of the Persians and refers to an account of the legend in the *Oriental Collections* and Ouseley's *Persian Miscellanies*, both of which were favorite source books of Oriental material. There Rustam is described as fighting against "an imaginary being endued with preternatural qualities; which, in some respects, may be found to correspond with the Demigods of Greece."[34] Rustam arrives at the combat in seven stages which are part of

29. Cf. Curtis, *The Howadji in Syria*, p. 54.

30. *Moby-Dick*, chap. 1.

31. Cf. *Lalla Rookh*, "The Fire-Worshippers."

32. Fraser, *Persia*, p. 120.

33. See section prefaced to the "Veiled Prophet of Khorassan."

34. Ed. W. Ouseley, *Oriental Collections* (2 vols. London, 1797–99), *3, 45. Persian Miscellanies* (London, 1795), pp. 94–95.

the rhythmical and structural pattern of the story in the same way as the nine gams in *Moby-Dick*. A plate in the *Oriental Collections* depicts the extraordinary fight in which the White Giant is seen clasping Rustam's left leg.[35]

Melville's knowledge of the Shahnameh is attested much later, when he read Matthew Arnold's "Sohrab and Rustum" in *New Poems*, which he acquired and annotated in 1871.[36] It seems unlikely that he was unaware of the Persian epic at the time he wrote *Moby-Dick*, when extracts from the poem and a biography of Firdausi, its author, appeared in popular magazines like the *American Review*. He certainly knew of another hero of the Shahnameh, Jamshid, who is listed among "the deified heroes of the remotest antiquity" in John Kitto's *Cyclopaedia of Biblical Literature* (1845), which he consulted for his chapter "The Honour and Glory of Whaling."[37] Jamshid is also mentioned in *Vathek*, for like Beckford's hero he "became intoxicated with his greatness . . . and arrogated to himself divine honours; but the Almighty raised up even in his own house, a terrible instrument to abase his pride."[38]

The White Whale represents the mythological dragons of both Western and Eastern tradition. It seems strange that in the parade of all his reading Melville should have overlooked the story which accurately reflects the theme of *Moby-Dick* and was thus rendered by the *American Review* in a translation from the Persian:

Hadst thou not heard of the White Demon's power
Of him who, from the gorgeous vault of heaven

---

35. *Oriental Collections*, 2, plate 53.

36. Melville noted under the title of Arnold's poem: "from the 'Shah Nameh' of Firdausi." See Melville's copy of *New Poems* (Boston, 1867), in Houghton Library, Harvard University.

37. See Vincent, p. 282.

38. *Vathek* (Bentley, Standard Novels), p. 105.

Can charm the stars? From this mad enterprise
Others have wisely shrunk—and what hast thou
Accomplished by a more ambitious course?[39]

MOHAMMED AND THE ARABS

In *Conversations with Eckermann,* a book which is quoted in the preface to *Moby-Dick,* Goethe characterized the
driving passion of the prophet of Islam as "the categorical
imperative of faith"—a pure singleness of mind which is
also the driving passion of the Carlylean hero.[1] About the
same time Melville read Carlyle's lectures on *Heroes, Hero-
Worship, and the Heroic in History* which, disregarding
Goethe's reservations, glorified Mohammed—"The Hero
as Prophet." The central feature in Carlyle's portrait of
Mohammed is reflected in Melville's characterization of
Ahab: "this wild man of the Desert, with his wild sincere
heart, earnest as death and life, with his great flashing natural eyesight, had seen into the kernel of the matter."[2] Melville acquired Goethe's *Truth and Poetry* in London in
1849 and, like Carlyle, was acquainted with Goethe's concept of the Moslem prophet: "The plan occurred to me of
taking the life of Mahomet, whom I had never been able
to think an impostor," writes Goethe in his autobiography,
"for a dramatic exhibition of those courses which in actual
life, I was strongly convinced, invariably lead to ruin much
more than to good."[3]

Yet, if we examine Melville's references to Mohammed
throughout the body of his work, we find that the stature of
the prophet is overshadowed by the impact of a sensuous
personality—a feature of Mohammed's character which is

39. *American Review, 9,* 64.
1. S. M. Fuller, *Conversations with Goethe* (Boston, 1839), p. 361.
2. *On Heroes,* Lecture II.
3. *Truth and Poetry* (London, Bohn, 1848–49), 2, 30.

touched on by Goethe in the Notes to the *West-East Divan* but wholly ignored by Carlyle. Apart from the heroic characteristics which left their traces in Ahab, there is no allusion to Mohammed as a spiritual hero in Melville's works, while the image of Mohammed as an "exquisite" appears both in *White Jacket* and *Pierre*.

In *Mardi*, where the founder of Islam is first mentioned, the reference relates to a more commonly known tradition, the story of the prophet's nocturnal journey to Jerusalem and the ascent to afterlife through the seven heavens—a legend which has left its mark on the *Divine Comedy*.[4] "For the Immeasurable's altitude," says Melville, "is not heightened by the arches of Mohomet's heavens." The religious discussion in Maramma prompts Mohi, the historian, to exclaim in defense of pilgrimages: "But Alma is also quoted by others, in vindication of the pilgrimages to Ofo. Many declare that the prophet himself was the first pilgrim that thitherward journeyed: that from thence he departed to the skies."[5]

In *White Jacket*, however, Melville speaks of "that old exquisite, Mohammed, who so much loved to snuff perfumes and essences, and used to lounge out of the conservatories of Khadija, his wife, to give battle to the robust sons of Koriesh." More important, the Oriental streak of a feminine voluptuousness, somewhat unusual to Western eyes in a prophet, recurs as a characteristic of Pierre: "it was one of his own little femininenesses—of the sort sometimes curiously observable in very robust-bodied and big-souled men, as Mohammed, for example—to be very partial to all pleasant essences."[6]

4. *Mardi, 1,* 268, 284; cf. Miguel Asin, *Islam and the Divine Comedy* (London, 1926), Pt. I.

5. *Mardi,* 2, 2.

6. *White Jacket,* chap. 65. Note Melville's spelling "Koriesh" for "Koreish." *Pierre,* Bk. V, sec. iii.

The standard American "Life" of Mohammed in the first half of the nineteenth century was by the Reverend George Bush and appeared in Harper's Family Library in 1830.[7] An elaborate description of Mohammed's journey from Mecca to Jerusalem and "from thence to heaven" was found in popular earlier accounts—for example, Ockley's *History of the Saracens,* which was read by Emerson, and the *Universal History,* a widely used work of historical reference from which Moore drew material for *Lalla Rookh.*[8] In the tradition of earlier biographies Bush treated Mohammed as an impostor. He was following in the footsteps of the seventeenth-century biographer Humphrey Prideaux, whose "Life" was entitled: "The true nature of imposture fully display'd in the life of Mahomet."[9] Prideaux and Bush are the only biographies of Mohammed to be listed in the catalogue of the New York Society Library in 1850, when Melville was a member. Washington Irving's *Mahomet and His Successors,* which treated Mohammed with greater tolerance, did not appear till 1850 and is listed in the supplement to the catalogue.[10]

To Melville the traditional Christian view of the Moslem prophet as an impostor suggested the character of Foni, the upstart prophet in *Mardi.* Nevertheless it is clear that he

7. Harper's Family Library, No. 10: *Bush's Life of Mohammed,* New York, 1830.

8. Ockley, *History of the Saracens* (London, 1847), pp. 20 f. *Universal History* (23 vols. Dublin, 1744–65), *1,* 39. Bush drew on the *Universal History* for his description of Mohammed's personal appearance.

9. The second edition of Prideaux's *Life* appeared in London in 1697. His chief Arab source was Abulfeda's *Moslem Annals,* translated by J. Gagnier, Oxford, 1723.

10. See Stanley T. Williams and Mary Allen Edgar, *A Bibliography of the Writings of Washington Irving* (New York, 1936), p. 93. *Alphabetical and Analytical Catalogue of the New York Society Library* (New York, 1850), pp. 68, 607, 608; cf. also *Catalogue of 1838,* p. 413.

inclined toward the more balanced historical assessment of Mohammed found in Edward Gibbon.

In considering Mohammed as an enthusiast rather than an impostor, Gibbon was following the eighteenth-century account of Boulainvilliers, the first of Mohammed's Western biographers to attack the prejudices of Prideaux.[11] In the creation of Foni, Melville, it seems, conveniently combined Gibbon's account of Mohammed with the popular idea of him as a charlatan. There can be no doubt that Gibbon furnished Melville with the description of his phony prophet as "a personage distinguished for the uncommon beauty of his person," for Melville's phrase echoes Gibbon's statement in the fiftieth chapter of the *Decline and Fall* (which is entirely devoted to Mohammed) that "Mahomet was distinguished by the beauty of his person."[12]

A reference to Mohammed's love of perfumes, which Melville transferred to Pierre, is also found in the *Decline and Fall*. The peculiar trait does not appear in Bush or the *Universal History,* though it is mentioned by Ockley and Washington Irving.[13] In view of the borrowed phrase about Mohammed's beauty, Gibbon seems the most likely source of Melville's "exquisite." There is another aspect of the prophetic personality in Gibbon which Melville also used in *Pierre:* "Mohammed hath his own dispensation," says Plinlimmon, the philosopher.[14] Gibbon refers to the prophet's conviction that "a special revelation dispensed him from the laws which he had imposed on his nation." Adopting this statement, Bush naturally enlarged upon the theme of

11. Boulainvillier, *The Life of Mahomet. Translated from the French Original,* London, 1731; Gibbon, chap. 50, n. 71.

12. *Mardi,* 2, 24. On Melville's reading of Gibbon see Sealts, No. 223b.

13. Ockley, "Life of Mohammed," *History of the Saracens.* Irving, *Mahomet and His Successors, 1,* chap. 39.

14. *Pierre,* Bk. XXI, sec. iii.

the prophet's laxity in obeying his own rules.[15] The article
on "Mahomet" in Bayle's dictionary refers to Mohammed's
incontinence and describes the special privilege of the practice of incest which the prophet allotted to himself;[16] but
it does not mention the other features of Mohammed which
Melville used, all of which are found together in Gibbon.

Other references to Mohammed in Melville's works do
not reflect any information which need be attributed to
special reading on the subject. In *White Jacket,* the captain, with his disciplinary measures, is "an undignified
parody upon Mohammed enforcing Moslemism with the
sword and the Koran."[17] The popular image of the proselyt-
izing prophet recurs in a posthumously published fragment about a hero of the American revolution: "shot and
shell and spelling-books were to be distributed broadcast
and gratis, a sort of Mohammed, sir, of the Malthusian
sort."[18] In *Moby-Dick* Mohammed is only mentioned once,
in a quotation from Leo Africanus. In Melville's quotation
of "John Leo, the old Barbary traveller," evidently taken
from John Harris' *Collection of Voyages,* it is affirmed on
the authority of Arab historians that "a Prophet who
prophesy'd of Mahomet" came forth from a Berber temple
on the North African coast, the "Afric Temple of the
Whale."[19] In the original text of Leo Africanus, it is stated
on the authority of Arab historiographers, with less chron-
ological accuracy, that "the same Prophet, of whom their
great Mahomet foretold" would proceed from that temple. The reference to the future prophet is connected with
the story of the Prophet Jonah, incidentally the only one of

15. Bush, p. 162.
16. Bayle, Vol. 3 (1710), 2092–2112.
17. *White Jacket,* chap. 72.
18. "Major Gentian and Colonel J. Bunkum" in *Billy Budd and
Other Prose Pieces.*
19. *Moby-Dick,* chap. 104.

the major and minor prophets mentioned in the Koran and whom Mohammed numbers among the apostles of God.[20]

While the reader gains the impression that Melville had read a "Life" of Mohammed, one feels certain that he did not take the trouble to read the Koran. Even Carlyle, who tolerantly defined Islam as "a confused form of Christianity," felt that "nothing but a sense of duty could carry any European through the Koran."[21] The standard English version (first published in 1734) was by George Sale, whose "Preliminary Discourse" on the history and ritual of Islam had wide literary ramifications. The only significant feature that Melville associates with the Koran is the prohibition of wine to Moslems, which is alluded to in the *Confidence-Man* and *Clarel*.[22] Another vague reference in *Clarel* pertains to the injunction to treat all men as equals; otherwise the Koran does not figure in Melville's imagery.[23]

But Melville's familiarity with the general features of Moslem belief and practice is readily apparent. His frequent references to the Moslem paradise are in tune with the romantic tradition. One of the chapters in *Omoo* is entitled "The Hegira, or Flight." The hero's escape from one of the Polynesian islands dates subsequent events like the original hegira, which marks the beginning of the Moslem era from Mohammed's flight in A.D. 622. In *Moby-Dick* there is a chapter called "The Ramadan" and a reference to the Meccan pilgrimage.[24] In the *Piazza Tales* we have the image of the Kaaba, the Holy Black Stone of Mecca.[25] In *Pierre* there even seem to be allusions to the "Golden

20. J. Horowitz, *Koranische Untersuchungen* (Berlin und Leipzig, 1926), p. 155.
21. *On Heroes*, Lecture II.
22. *Confidence-Man*, chap. 24. *Clarel*, 2, 70.
23. *Clarel*, 2, 203 f.
24. *Moby-Dick*, chaps. 17, 92.
25. "The Piazza," *Complete Stories*, p. 437.

Verses" that were suspended from the Kaaba in pre-Islamic
times.[26] The Islamic imagery naturally multiplies in *Clarel*. Features of Moslem ritual which Melville mentions are
the use of the color green to designate a descendant of the
prophet, the cry of the Muezzin—"Prayer is more [better]
than sleep," the custom of making ablutions with sand in
the absence of water, the departure of the Mahmal for
Mecca, the direction toward Mecca in time of prayer and
death, and the habit of telling beads on a rosary.[27] Melville's knowledge of the terminology and postures of Moslem prayer, as described in *Clarel*, derived from his reading
rather than personal observation, for there is little evidence
of it in the *Journal* of his Near Eastern tour beyond the
note that he saw a Moslem facing Mecca in prayer in the
hills of Bethlehem.[28] The ritual of Moslem prayer was
elaborately explained and illustrated in Lane's *Account of
the Manners and Customs of the Modern Egyptians*, which,
with Lane's notes to the *Arabian Nights*, served as a handbook on Moslem customs to Melville's contemporaries. The
description of the blind Muezzin calling from his minaret in
Clarel recalls Lane's statement that blind men were generally preferred for that office, "that the hareems and ter-
races of surrounding houses may not be overlooked" from
the minarets.[29] Melville makes a direct reference to the
fatalism of Islam but concludes that "we are all Fatalists
at bottom."[30] He is thoroughly familiar with the signifi-

26. The Moallakat were described in Jones' essay on "The Poetry of
the Eastern Nations". They "were transcribed in characters of gold
upon Egyptian paper, and hung up in the temple, whence they were
named Modhahabat, or Golden" (Jones, *Works, 10, 341*). Beckford
refers to these verses in a note to *Vathek*.

27. *Clarel, 1, 26, 61, 80, 82, 171, 190; 2, 195–96. Mardi, 2, 270.* "The
Rose Farmer" in *Collected Poems*.

28. *Clarel, 1, 61; 2, 195.* Horsford, *Journal*, p. 139.

29. Lane, *Modern Egyptians* (2 vols. London, 1842), *1, 102, 106–7.*

30. *White Jacket*, chap. 31. *Pierre*, Bk. VII, p. v.

cance of Moslem titles like Mollah, Emir, Mufti, and Cadi, religious dissidents like the fanatical Wahabis, and, of course, institutions like the harem and the divan.[31] He is particularly entranced with the custom of Arab hospitality as practiced by the "wild Arab" and in the romantic setting of the Arabian tales.[32] Curiously enough, Melville's interest in the Bedouins does not focus on his favorite concept of Ishmael, the nomad. In the references to Bedouin life the greatest symbolic significance is attached to the perennial contrast between the desert and the oasis—the sea and the land in the topography of Melville's imagery. The Bedouin, like the sailor, is the noble warrior to whom the "pure desert air" and "doled diet pure" ensure "brave results."[33]

The model Bedouin of Arab tradition, the pre-Islamic poet and warrior Antar, is also referred to in *Clarel*.[34] His poetry, written in the last decade of the sixth century, was introduced to Western writers in the translation of Sir William Jones. The only complete poem of Antar that survives, "The Poem of Antara," ranked as one of the "Golden Verses"—"The Moallakat; or Seven Poems which were suspended on the Temple at Mecca," but was little known.[35] The romance of Antar, published in an English translation by Terrick Hamilton in 1819, achieved great popularity and must have attracted Melville's attention in Disraeli's *Tancred*.[36] The allusion to the poetry of Antar in *Clarel* was probably inspired by the "Fragments of the poems of Antar" quoted in Lamartine's *Pilgrimage to the*

31. The custom of indicating the tomb of a mufti by a surmounting stone-turban is referred to in *Clarel, 2, 54.*

32. *Typee,* chap. 27.

33. *Clarel, 1, 286.*

34. *Clarel, 1, 58.*

35. Jones, *Works, 10, 76* f.

36. *'Antar, a Bedoueen Romance,* trans. Terrick Hamilton, 4 vols. London, 1819. *Tancred,* Book IV, chap. 2.

Holy Land, which was published in an American edition in
1835 and upon which Melville drew for *Clarel.* That he did
so is clear not only from his explicit reference to Lamartine
but also from the way in which he follows the French poet
in linking his discussions of the Druze "secrets sacerdotal"
to the sojourn of Lady Hester Stanhope among this Arab
tribe.[37]

Melville's interest in the Druzes, a tribe of Syrian mountain villagers whose mysterious rituals aroused wide interest
in the nineteenth century, is embodied in the figure of the
Druze guide, Djalea. Melville himself had a Druze guide,
Abdallah, on his excursions from Jerusalem, and this guide,
no doubt, was the prototype of the character in *Clarel.*[38]
The name "Djalea," however, and the discussion of the
Druze religion—which is not mentioned in the *Journal*—
indicate that Melville's information on the Druzes was
based on his reading, most likely of Volney and Lamartine,
who had made a special study of the Druzes and, as we have
seen, are mentioned by name in *Clarel.*[39] Djalea

> was rumoured for an Emir's son,
> Or offspring of a lord undone
> In Ibrahim's time.[40]

The noble ancestry of the guide was probably inspired by
Volney's allusion to a Druze leader "Emir Yousef, who is
Djahel," who participated in a Syrian civil war at the end
of the eighteenth century.[41] Though this was long before
"Ibrahim's time," i.e. the time of Ibrahim Pasha (a governor), the name "Djalea" cannot be explained in any other
way except as a derivation from "Djahel," the epithet by

37. Lamartine, 2, 37, 49 f. *Clarel, 1,* 234; 2, 76–77.
38. Horsford, *Journal,* p. 127.
39. *Clarel, 1,* 234.
40. Ibid., p. 197.
41. Volney, 2, 60.

which most of the Druzes were designated on religious grounds. The word means "ignorant," in the French transliteration of the Arabic "Jāhil." Both Volney and Lamartine state that it is bestowed on most of the tribe with the exception of a small class of the initiated who are versed in the mysteries of the Druze religion and assume the name of "Akkal" ('āqil, intelligent). As Volney points out, these initiates wear a white turban as a symbol of their purity.[42] There is thus a discrepancy in Melville's characterization of his Druze guide. On the one hand he is depicted as wearing a white turban to show that he holds "the rank of Druze initiate." On the other hand, his name "Djalea" designates him as "Djahel" or ignorant, i.e. as a member of the profane majority which, as Volney shows in his allusion to the Emir Yousef, does not necessarily conflict with his secular rank. Melville obviously overlooked this discrepancy in naming his guide in Clarel, for the significance of the guide's spiritual rank in addition to his noble descent is of particular importance.

Melville's acquaintance with the history of Mohammed's successors is also attested in Clarel. The legend of Omar, the second Caliph, and his entry into Jerusalem in A.D. 637 which is related by Clarel, was known from Gibbon, the Universal History, and Washington Irving:

> An instance of the strict good faith of Omar is related as occurring on this visit to the Christian temples. While he was standing with the patriarch in the church of the Resurrection, one of the stated hours for Moslem worship arrived, and he demanded where he might pray. "Where you now are," replied the patriarch. Omar, however, refused, and went forth. The patriarch conducted him to the church of Constantine, and spread a mat for him to pray there; but again he

42. Ibid., p. 59; Lamartine, 2, 37.

refused. On going forth, he knelt, and prayed on the flight of steps leading down from the east gate of the church. This done, he turned to the patriarch, and gave him a generous reason for his conduct. "Had I prayed in either of the churches," said he, "the Moslems would have taken possession of it, and consecrated it as a mosque."[43]

Gibbon does not mention the coarse garb of Omar or the mat that the patriarch offered to spread for him. Both are an integral part of the traditional story and are incorporated in Clarel's account of Omar's magnanimity, which is contrasted with the later barbarism of the Crusaders. Another reference to the Caliphate in *Clarel* pertains to the mad al-Hakim, the sixth Fatimid Caliph (996–1021), whom Gibbon describes as "a frantic youth, who was delivered by his impiety and despotism from the fear either of God or man; and whose reign was a wild mixture of vice and folly."[44] Melville specifically alludes to Hakim's madness, the new religion which he founded, and his demolition of churches in Jerusalem.[45] The allusion to "the tribes not unrenowned" in Melville's account, which accepted the Mad Caliph's creed, refers to the Druzes, whose name is supposed to derive from a missionary, Ismail Al-Darazi, who preached the cult of al-Hakim. There is also a reference to the "Wahabees," the Moslem Puritans, who came into prominence in the nineteenth century by their conquest of Mecca in 1807 and were authoritatively described by Burckhardt, the famous "Sheik Ibrahim."[46]

On the whole, Melville's concern with the rise of Islam

43. *Mahomet and His Successors*, 2, chap. 18. Cf. *Clarel*, *1*, 123–24; Gibbon, *5*, chap. 51; *Universal History*, *1*, 294–95.
44. Gibbon, *5*, chap. 57.
45. *Clarel*, *1*, 139.
46. *Clarel*, *2*, 60.

and of Mohammed as a propagator of a new religion strikes one as comparatively slight. In his writings the Moslem prophet and his creed have metaphorical, not symbolic, significance. Unlike Zoroaster and Persian fire worship, they do not reach into the deepest levels of meaning but remain on the surface as decoration, rather than polysensua. There is one aspect in the later development of Islam, however, which was bound to stir Melville as profoundly as it did Emerson and the New England Transcendentalists. Like all mystical movements, Sufism concerned itself with "the open secret" which lay "under the rose" of the physical world.

The secret—the unattainable Yillah of the Melvillean quest—is "that divine mystery which lies everywhere in all Beings."[47] Its ardent devotees were Saadi, Hafiz, Jami— the school of Persian poetry which, in Melville's time, swept the Western literary world.

TAMERLANE AND THE TARTARS

In Chapter 65 of the *Decline and Fall* Gibbon's account of Tamerlane opens on a note of grandeur which resounds in Melville's Ahab: "The conquest and monarchy of the world was the first object of the ambition of Timour." The following portrayal is found in Malcolm's *History of Persia*, a standard work in the first half of the nineteenth century whose delineation of Timur's character is still highly regarded by modern scholars: "There was no feature more remarkable in the character of Timour than his extraordinary perseverance. No difficulties ever led him to recede from what he had once undertaken; and he often persisted in his efforts under circumstances which led all around him to despair."[1]

47. *On Heroes,* Lecture III.
1. Malcolm, *1,* 310.

Tamerlane became the legendary figure of an Oriental despot which kindled the imagination of European writers. Like Kublai Khan, the "Grand Khan of Tartary" lauded by Marco Polo, he symbolized the unknown splendor and might of the East. The romantic image of Tamerlane as an Oriental potentate was later joined by that of the Great Mogul, originally the Emperor of Hindustan, whose last vestige of power collapsed in Melville's time. In the works of Melville the figure of Tamerlane stands out among a host of allusions to Genghiz Khan, the Great Khan, the Grand Mogul and the tribes of Scythians, Huns, Tartars, and Calmucks. Most of these are found in *Mardi* and *Moby-Dick* and are used in an accumulation of images to convey opulence, despotism, and unbridled wildness.[2] The image of the Oriental despot is also latent in the ruthless might of the whale. For the shark "Tamerlane" in *Mardi* is a predecessor of "Timor Tom," the "famed leviathan" in *Moby-Dick* whose name denotes his origin from an island in the Malay archipelago but also suggests the name of the Tartar Khan.[3]

Ahab is a "Khan of the plank." There is a clear indication that the captain of the *Pequod* lording it over his faithful crew is the symbolic incarnation of the maimed Oriental conqueror: "Among whale-wise people it has often been argued whether, considering the paramount importance of his life to the success of the voyage, it is right for a whaling captain to jeopardize that life in the active perils of the chase. So Tamerlane's soldiers often argued with tears in their eyes, whether that invaluable life of his ought to be carried into the thickest of the fight."[4]

2. *Mardi, 1,* 135; *2,* 48, 54, 337. *White Jacket,* chap. 46. *Moby-Dick,* chaps. 39, 40, 43. See also "Fragment" in *Billy Budd and Other Prose Pieces,* p. 381.

3. *Mardi, 1,* 63. *Moby-Dick,* chap. 45.

4. *Moby-Dick,* chap. 50.

This particular reference has been connected with Zenocrate's plea to her husband in *Tamburlaine the Great*.[5] Melville bought Marlowe's plays in London in 1849, and the megalomania of Marlowe's Oriental hero doubtlessly contributed its share to the conception of Ahab. But apart from the imaginative insight, there is no authentic historical detail in Marlowe's play, whereas Melville's references to Tamerlane have identifiable historical origins.

The historical Timur did not emerge in Europe until the middle of the seventeenth century, when the main Eastern sources for his life began to be available in Latin, French, and English translations.[6] The most important of these was Petis de la Croix's *History of Timur-Bec, Known by the Name of Tamerlain the Great,* translated from the Persian, which was published in English in 1723.[7] Melville's reference to the pleas of Tamerlane's soldiers not to expose his life is actually traceable to a specific incident reported in this history. The incident is not mentioned by Gibbon or Samuel Purchas. Malcolm stresses the idolization of Timur by his soldiers, although there is nothing in his account to suggest Melville's description of the tearful plea to their lord. The story concerns the duel to which Yussuf Sufi, the ruler of Khwarizm, challenged Tamerlane on one of his campaigns. "The princes and Emirs of the

5. Explanatory Notes to *Moby-Dick*, ed. Luther S. Mansfield and Howard P. Vincent (New York, 1952), p. 737; cf. *Tamburlaine the Great*, Pt. II, 1.iv.9–11:

> Sweet Tamburlaine, when wilt thou leave these arms,
> And save thy sacred person free from scathe,
> And dangerous chances of the wrathful war?

6. Una Ellis-Fermor's introduction to *Tamburlaine the Great* (London, 1930), p. 17.

7. An English translation of Timur's "Institutes" by Major Davy appeared in Oxford in 1783. An English version of the "Memoirs" by Major Charles Stewart was published in 1830.

court cast themselves at his [Tamerlane's] feet," runs the chronicle in the English translation, "and told him it was not reasonable so great a monarch should fight a duel; but he had no regard to their speeches, and continued his way." One of the Emirs, Seifeddin, "full of affection to him, which transported him beyond all bounds, took hold of the horse's bridle, to strive to conquer the stubbornness of the emperor; he cast himself at his knees, and told him he ought not to be guilty of exposing his royal person. . . . Timur was wroth, reprimanded Seifeddin, and drew his sword to strike him."[8] This passage, besides explaining Melville's reference to the loyalty of Tamerlane's soldiers, offers a striking parallel to the attempt of Starbuck, "the first Emir," to restrain Ahab's foolhardiness, and Starbuck's retreat in the face of the captain's loaded musket.[9]

A reference in *Mardi* is also sufficiently specific to show that Melville must have read some historical account of Tamerlane. Melville speaks of "the gaunt tribes of Tamerlane" which "o'erspread the tented pastures of the Khan."[10] This image, too, is historically authentic and refers to Timur's campaign against Toktamish Khan, the ruler of the Kapchak, a nomadic tribe of Tartars which was part of the raiders known as the Golden Horde. In this campaign Timur's troops were dispersed across the steppes of Asia and suffered great hardships for want of provisions, which may have suggested Melville's use of the adjective "gaunt."[11]

Melville's preoccupation with Tartar images is not extraordinary: Tartar and Tartary, introduced into European literature by Marco Polo, were part of the common romantic vocabulary. In *Mardi* "the sacred bay steed of the Great

8. *History of Timur-Bec, 1,* 195.
9. *Moby-Dick,* chap. 109.
10. *Mardi, 1,* 225.
11. Malcolm, *History of Persia, 1,* 310.

Khan of Tartary" has the flavor of the romantic guides, Marco Polo and Samuel Purchas. The recurring reference to the Tartar termagant—Samoa's wife is "a regular Calmuck"—also stems from the popular conception of Tartar life. But in *Moby-Dick* the helmsman in a storm "felt like a Tartar, when he holds back his fiery steed by clutching its jaw"—an image which gives one a sense of actual physical experience.[12] An interesting account of the Calmuc Tartars by Jonas Hanway, an eighteenth-century merchant who traveled in Russia and Persia, also describes the Tartar worship of idols consisting of "a small bit of wood" on which marks are carved to resemble human features, like Queequeg's Yojo, the black wooden idol in *Moby-Dick*.[13] In the nineteenth century there were fascinating accounts of Tartar life by contemporary travelers like Edmund Spencer and Clarke. Of American travelers whom Melville knew, John Ledyard—with whom Melville's uncle, Captain John D'Wolf was associated—visited the Tartars. Ledyard's travels to Siberia and Tartary by sledge, rather than the account of Marco Polo, were in Melville's mind in the chapter "Dreams" in *Mardi:* "But far to the south, past my Sicily suns and my vineyards, stretches the Antarctic barrier of ice: a China wall, built up from the sea, and nodding its frosted towers in the dun, clouded sky. Do Tartary and Siberia lie beyond? Deathful, desolate dominions those." Inevitably, in the Melvillean vision the romantic land of Xanadu was peopled with "frozen cemeteries of skeletons and bones."

12. *Mardi, 1,* 86, 100, 102, 128, 298; *2,* 141, 187. *Moby-Dick,* chaps. 16, 54.

13. Jonas Hanway, *Journal of Travels* (4 vols. London, 1753), *1,* 101; cf. *Moby-Dick* (Hendricks House), Explanatory Notes, p. 629, where "Yojo" is connected with Yajooj and Majooj, the Moslem equivalent of Gog and Magog.

SULEIMAN THE MAGNIFICENT
AND THE TURKS

The landmark in Melville's reading about Turkey is his purchase of Thomas Hope's *Anastasius* on his trip to London and the Continent in 1849–50. But allusions to Turkish history and Turkish manners were part and parcel of the Near Eastern imagery in his first two books. In *Typee* there is a reference to "Sultan Solyman"—like Tamerlane, one of Melville's favorite Eastern potentates. In *Omoo* Melville shows his familiarity with the indications of Ottoman military rank—Omoo is a "Bashaw with Two Tails."

The source of Melville's information about Suleiman the Magnificent (1494–1566) is difficult to determine among the multitude of books on Turkey from which nineteenth-century writers drew their information. Byron, among his reading, mentions Knolles, Cantemir, Baron de Tott, Lady Mary Wortley Montagu, and Hawkins' translation of Mignot's *History of the Turkish Empire*.[1] We do not know if Melville read any of these books, though they were standard works and easily available. What does appear, however, is that there was considerable confusion in Melville's mind about Suleiman's historical role and other details of Turkish history—for example, the various sieges of Constantinople—which he probably picked up at random. "Having heard only four reports from the musket," says the narrator in *Typee,* when watching a skirmish between the Typees and Happars "I was led to believe that they were worked by the islanders in the same manner as the Sultan Solyman's

1. Moore, *Life of Byron* (London, 1851), p. 119, n. 2. The following works were available at the New York Society Library when Melville was a member: R. Knolles, *Turkish History*, London, 1687; D. Cantemir, *History of the Growth and Decay of the Othman Empire,* trans. N. Tindal, London, 1756; Baron de Tott, *Memoirs,* 3 vols. London, 1785; Lady Mary W. Montagu, *Letters,* London, 1783; V. Mignot, *History of the Turkish Empire,* trans. A. Hawkins, 4 vols. Exeter, 1787. See *Analytical Catalogue* (1850), pp. 75, 243, 297, 304, 443.

ponderous artillery at the siege of Byzantium, one of them taking an hour or two to load and train."[2] Evidently, the allusion is to the siege of Constantinople marking the end of the Roman Empire, which is brilliantly described by Gibbon. But this siege was not conducted by Suleiman, and Gibbon was not necessarily the source of Melville's idea that it took an hour or two to load one of the muskets, though we find there that "under a master who counted the moments the great cannon could be loaded and fired no more than seven times a day."[3] In his imagination Melville confused the siege of Byzantium of 1453, when cannons were used by the Turks, with the earlier eighth-century siege of Constantinople by the Arabs which was also described by Gibbon and was led by one Solyman, brother of the Caliph Walid.[4] The "ponderous artillery" which ensured the capture of the city by the Turks in 1453 had nothing to do with "Sultan Solyman," for the siege was undertaken by Mohammed II (1431–81), about whom Melville had probably also read in the *Penny Magazine*.[5] It is the name of this sultan that is associated with the use of the famous great cannon. Melville's description of the Turkish musket which took "an hour or two to load" is, curiously enough, reminiscent of the most authoritative nineteenth-century account of Turkey, Hammer-Purgstall's German history of the Ottoman Empire, available both in a French translation and an English abridgment, and continuously referred to by all writers on the Ottomans in Melville's time.[6] It is Hammer who states that the great Turkish

2. *Typee,* chap. 17.
3. Gibbon, chap. 68.
4. Ibid., chap. 52.
5. *Penny Magazine* (April 12, 1834), pp. 140–42.
6. *Campaigns of Osman Sultans, Chiefly in Western Asia. From the German of Joseph von Hammer,* trans. Thomas Aquila Dale, London, 1835.

cannon planted at the gate of St. Romanus at the siege of
Constantinople required "two hours for loading."[7] Hammer, it will be seen, also provides a clue to Melville's choice
of the name Mohi for the chronicler and historian in *Mardi;*
it looks therefore as if Melville had some casual acquaintance with Hammer's work. That he had read Gibbon on
the various sieges is clear from an allusion in *Mardi* which
shows that Melville combined the first siege of Constantinople by the French and Venetian crusaders in 1203 and
the later fight against the Turks into one image. The reference is to Dandolo, the old doge of Venice, who was one of
the leaders of the Latin attack against the Greeks at Constantinople undertaken in order that the Eastern church
be subjected to the Pope. Melville mentions "the blind old
Doge" in a characteristic accumulation of boat and barge
images heaped around the archetypal concept of "King
Bello's State Canoe," i.e. Great Britain's navy. "But from
another sort of prow leaped Dandolo," says Melville, "when
at Constantinople, he foremost sprang ashore, and with a
right arm ninety years old, planted the standard of St. Mark
full among the long chin-pennons of the long-bearded
Turks."[8] The incident is related in Gibbon: "In the midst
of the conflict the doge, a venerable and conspicuous form,
stood aloft in complete armour on the prow of his galley.
The great standard of St. Mark was displayed before him;
his threats, promises, and exhortations, urged the diligence
of the rowers; his vessel was the first that struck; Dandolo
was the first warrior on the shore. The nations admired the
magnanimity of the blind old man, without reflecting that
his age and infirmities diminished the price of life, and enhanced the value of immortal glory." Gibbon also points

7. Cf. *Geschichte des Osmanischen Reiches* (10 vols. Pest, 1827–35),
1, 526.
8. *Mardi, 2,* 186.

out that Dandolo died at Constantinople and was ninety-seven at his death.[9]

Another allusion in *Mardi* which stems from Melville's reading about Suleiman the Magnificent refers to "The Grand Turk and his Vizier Mustapha sitting down before Vienna" in a comparison of the way in which the narrator and his companion Jarl besieged the "bread-barge" of the *Parki*.[10] The unsuccessful siege of Vienna by the Turks under Suleiman took place in 1529 and was abandoned after three weeks. Suleiman's vizier on that occasion was Ibrahim, while Mustapha was Suleiman's eldest son who accompanied him but whom he subsequently murdered.[11] Finally, "the proud paternal glance of the Grand Turk Solyman, looking round upon a hundred sons, all bone of his bone, and squinting with his squint," is Melville's own artistic contribution to the history of the great Ottoman sultan.[12]

There is only one other Turkish ruler whom Melville is fond of mentioning by name. Bajazet in *Mardi* refers to Bayezid I (1347–1403), whose history is connected with that of Tamerlane by whom he was defeated and made captive.[13] In *Clarel* the allusion to "Ibrahim's rule, the Turk" deals with contemporary nineteenth-century history referring to Ibrahim Pasha (1789–1848), son of the famous Mohammed Ali, ruler of Egypt. It was Mohammed Ali who perpetrated the infamous murder of the Mamelukes in the Cairo Citadel in 1811 which Melville mentions in *Clarel*.[14] In *Mardi* storms are compared to Mamelukes: "they charge, and away."[15]

9. Gibbon, chap. 60.

10. *Mardi, 1,* 73.

11. Purchas, 5, 285; cf. R. B. Merriman, *Suleiman the Magnificent* (Cambridge, Mass., 1944), pp. 16, 184, 186.

12. *Mardi, 1,* 284.

13. Ibid., *2,* 54.

14. *Clarel, 1,* 89.

15. *Mardi, 1,* 135.

Melville's spelling of Turkish designations may at times be a guide to his reading. His vagaries of spelling, like his almost illegible handwriting, are a matter of common knowledge; his general arbitrariness affected foreign and unusual words, e.g. *bazaar,* which he spells in four different ways in seven lines.[16] This consideration, however, does not necessarily apply if Melville's variants are found in other authors. Thus in *Clarel* the appearance of the Arabic name for Jerusalem in the transliteration "El Cods" clearly indicates a French source. Similarly, the Turkish title of "Janizary," spelled with a capital in *Mardi,* and the consistent use of "Bashaw" for Pasha obviously represent Melville's own preference for the more picturesque older forms. There was no established rule for the correct rendering of Oriental words into European languages, and every writer did as he pleased, following his source, if he had one, or the usage prevalent in his language at a particular time.[17]

Melville's spelling of "janissary" commonly follows that of seventeenth- or eighteenth-century travel books, like Thevenot's *Travels* mentioned in *Mardi.* He spells it "Janizary" or "janizary" while most nineteenth-century writers used "janissary," although the latter form appears in Melville's later Near Eastern *Journal.*[18] In one of his "catalogues," also in *Mardi,* he uses both "Sultans" and the earlier "Soldans," listing the two spellings as given in

16. Horsford, *Journal,* intro. p. 46; B 35, p. 91.

17. The name of the Persian poet Jami, for example, was spelled "Dschami" by Emerson, according to the German transliteration of Hammer-Purgstall (*Works, 8,* 191; Hammer-Purgstall, *Geschichte der schoenen Redekuenste Persiens,* p. 273). Other spellings were "Djami" on the pattern of French (cf. Hammer-Purgstall, *Mines d'Orient, 1,* 456, 468) and the common English form "Jami," introduced by Sir William Jones.

18. See *Mardi, 2,* 394–449; and Horsford, *Journal,* p. 92. Cf. E. Warburton, *The Crescent and the Cross* (New York, 1845), p. 142.

Ephraim Chambers' *Cyclopaedia,* which he owned, in a decorative cumulative effect as two distinct titles.[19]

The main difficulty in regarding Melville's various spelling of Oriental words as an indication of his reading is the absence of almost all his manuscripts and the likelihood that in his books his spelling was normalized in accordance with prevalent American usage. (In Bayard Taylor's *Cyclopaedia of Modern Travel,* for example, the spelling of "Wahabys" is changed in quotation to "Wahabees.")[20]

But the printed works may be relied on to reproduce Melville's original spelling of names. A case in point is "Bobadil" in *White Jacket,* where the reference is evidently to Boabdil, King of Granada, the hero of Washington Irving's *Alhambra.*[21] Also in *White Jacket,* "Koriesh" is spelled for the tribe of Mohammed "Koreish," and "Mohammed" is spelled as in *Pierre,* while the *Confidence-Man* has "Mahomet," in the spelling of Bayle, Beckford, Goethe, Carlyle, and Washington Irving.[22] On the other hand, the printed works do not necessarily convey the manuscript spelling of *common* Oriental words like "harem," "sheik," or "Ramadan." The spelling of these words in Melville's text should not be taken for granted, for contemporary writers, like Warburton, spelled "hareem"; Curtis, in *Nile Notes of a Howadji,* spells "shekk"; and Thackeray spells "Ramazan," in the Turkish and Persian manner, which

19. *Mardi,* 2, 337; Chambers' *Cyclopaedia: or, An Universal Dictionary of Arts and Sciences* (2 vols. London, 1728), 2, 150. The book was given to Melville by his uncle, Herman Gansevoort, in 1846 (Leyda, *Log,* p. 231). Mr. Leyda has been good enough to draw my attention to the importance of the *Cyclopaedia* in Melville's reading.

20. See article on "Burckhardt's Travels in Syria, Africa, and Arabia."

21. *White Jacket,* chap. 52.

22. *White Jacket,* chap. 65. *Pierre,* Bk. XXI, sec. iii. *Confidence-Man,* chap. 24.

also appears in *Purchas His Pilgrims,* Harris' *Collection,*
and the Notes in Hope's *Anastasius.*[23]

With regard to "Ramadan," which forms a chapter head-
ing in *Moby-Dick,* we have, in fact, definite evidence that
Melville also used a variant. In the poem "The Rose
Farmer," one of the few manuscripts extant, Melville spells
"Rhamadan," using a less common eighteenth-century form
which, for example, appears in Hume's "Natural History of
Religion" which he recalled while writing the *Confidence-
Man.*[24] The variation in spelling is particularly striking, as
the word occurs in a context which evokes Queequeg's
"Ramadan" in *Moby-Dick:* "When I against his Rhamadan
/ Prepared a *chowder* for his feast."[25] The identification of
the Ramadan with Lent, which Melville makes in *Moby-
Dick* and *Clarel,* was, on the other hand, a commonplace in
his time. The Moslem fast was explained as "a kind of Lent"
in sixteenth- and seventeenth-century travel books, by Lady
Mary Wortley Montagu, by Denon, and, among writers that
Melville is definitely known to have read, by De Quincey,
in Harris' *Collection,* and in Hope's *Anastasius.*[26]

The Islamic terms in Melville's writings do not necessarily derive from romantic novels like *Vathek* or *Anastasius,*
as has been suggested.[27] Melville's spelling of words like

23. See *Mardi, 1,* 280; *Clarel, 1,* 233; *Moby-Dick,* chap. 17. Cf. *The
Crescent and the Cross,* p. 81; *Nile Notes of a Howadji,* p. 127;
Thackeray, *Journey from Cornhill to Cairo* (London, 1846), p. 345;
Purchas, 2, 1602; Harris, 2, index; *Anastasius, 1,* 419.

24. David Hume, "The Natural History of Religion" in *Essays and
Treatises, 4,* 320. On Melville's reading of Hume see the *Confidence-
Man,* chap. 24; Foster, Explanatory Notes in Hendricks House edition
(New York, 1954), p. 329.

25. *Collected Poems,* p. 304.

26. *Moby-Dick,* chap. 16. *Clarel, 2,* 78. Cf. Lady Mary Wortley Montagu, *Letters and Works* (3 vols. London, 1837), *2,* 94; Denon, *2,* 150;
Chateaubriand, p. 351; De Quincey, *Opium-Eater* (Boston, 1841), p.
116; Harris' *Collection, 1,* index; *Anastasius, 1,* 136.

27. By Bezanson, "Herman Melville's *Clarel.*"

"Bedouin," "Mameluke," "Osmanli," and "Wahabee" shows the influence of authentic nineteenth-century travel books and histories of the Near East, which, of course, he is known to have read. The spelling in *Anastasius,* for example, is so arbitrary that a direct influence in this respect could only be assumed if Melville had written Osmanlee, Stambool, Mamluke, Bedawee, Arnaoot, Spahee.

That most of Melville's information on Turkey derived from travel books rather than from romances may also be gathered from the aspects of Turkish life he used for his images. The term "seraglio" (Italian for Turkish "serai"), denoting the women's apartment, for instance, is associated with seventeenth-century accounts of Turkish life—Purchas, Thevenot, Tavernier, Sandys—rather than with nineteenth-century books like *Anastasius,* which used the Arabic term "harem" to describe the apartment in Turkey as well as in Egypt. In *Moby-Dick* the "Ottoman" whale has a "harem."[28]

In *Mardi* Donjalolo's "seraglio" reflects Thevenot's description of the Grand Signior's private apartments.[29] In reporting the Grand Signior's jealousy concerning his seraglio, Thevenot points out that no boats are suffered to come nearer than four hundred paces of the palace garden when the sultanas are there. Accounts such as this, rather than the *Arabian Nights,* seem to have prompted Melville to compare the difficulties which the narrator and Jarl encountered in securing a boat for their escape from their ship to the attempt of "any dashing young Janizary to run off with a sultana from the Grand Turk's seraglio."[30]

Similarly, in *Omoo,* the description of the narrator's Eastern turban is accurate enough to recall the accounts of Turkish headgear in Thevenot: "It was then that I mounted

28. *Moby-Dick,* chap. 88.
29. *Mardi, 1,* chap. 80. Thevenot, *Travels,* chap. 18, in Harris' *Collection, 2,* 398.
30. *Mardi, 1,* 24.

the turban," says the hero in *Omoo*. "Taking a new Regatta frock of the doctor's, which was of a gay calico, and winding it round my head in folds, I allowed the sleeves to drop behind. . . . The pendent sleeves adding much to the effect, the doctor always called me the Bashaw with Two Tails."[31] The following description is given by Thevenot: "The Habit of the Janizaries differs not from that of other Turks, but they have another kind of Head-attire; for on their head they wear a Cap hanging down behind, and shaped like the sleeve of a Casque; in one end of which they put their head, and the other hangs down their back, like a large Livery-hood."[32]

The "Eastern title" of "Bashaw with Two Tails" which the narrator receives from Doctor Long Ghost as the result of his headgear indicates the Ottoman custom of differentiating between the ranks of pashas by the number of horse-tails borne on the standard of each—a custom referred to by Byron in the *Siege of Corinth*.[33] There were pashas of one, two, or three tails, that of three tails being the highest in rank. The earlier spelling of "Bashaw" rather than the modern "Pasha," which Byron uses, consistently appears in Melville's writings as it does in seventeenth- and eighteenth-century travel books.

As displayed in Donjalolo and Media in *Mardi*, among the whales in *Moby-Dick*, and by the Creole Dog-King in the "Encantadas," the Grand Turk among his Bashaws, in his seraglio, surrounded by janizaries, is Melville's favorite image for the opulent willfulness of absolute power. The Great Khan Tamerlane, resurrected in austere Ahab, embodies heroism and tragedy.

31. *Omoo*, chaps. 61, 74.
32. Thevenot, *Travels*, p. 70.
33. *Siege of Corinth*, Stanza XXII, n. 8, in *Works, 3,* 223. Cf. *Eothen* (New York, 1846), p. 5.

6. Islamic Characters and Symbols

The role of the *Arabian Nights* in Melville's concept of "romance" is apparent in his first compositions, "Fragments from a Writing Desk." A decade later the articles on the *Arabian Nights* which appeared in the *Literary World* from February 12, 1848, to May 13, 1848, seem relevant to the material which shaped Melville's ideas in the early months of 1848. In these articles the Persian origin of the *Arabian Nights* was discussed at length. Thus what we may call "the matter of Persia" was brought to the attention of every reader of the *Literary World* at the very time Melville was contemplating his own Oriental romance. The Arabian overtones of *Mardi* are visible at first sight in the Arabian names of the main characters, Taji, Yillah, Yoomy, Mohi, Babbalanja, not to speak of Donjalolo and his harem of thirty wives. The specifically Persian element is evident from numerous allusions in the text and directly relates to its "meaning."

"My romance I assure you is no dish water nor its model borrowed from the Circulating Library," wrote Melville to John Murray, his publisher, on March 25, 1848. "It opens like a true narrative— . . . & the romance & poetry of the thing thence grow continu[al]ly, till it becomes a story old enough I assure you & with a meaning too."[1] The marriage of romance and mysticism which Melville strove to achieve

1. *Letters,* pp. 70–71.

in "the thing" has, in fact, the same "Persian air" as Yoomy, the poet, for it is the distinguishing mark of the movement of Moslem mysticism known by the name of Sufism, which flourished in Persia in the Middle Ages and aroused intense interest in the West through its manifestation in the Persian poets, many of whom were practicing mystics and dervishes.

The *Literary World* referred its readers to the writings of Sir John Malcolm, the most popular nineteenth-century historian of Persia, and an article "Ancient Persian Poetry" in the *Foreign Quarterly Review* of October 1836.[2] The mystical movement of Sufism is discussed at length in Malcolm's *History of Persia,* where it is stressed that traces of the Sufi doctrine are found in every religion of the world. "The Soofees represent themselves as devoted to the search of truth, and incessantly occupied in adoring the Almighty, an union with whom they desire with all the fervour of divine love. The Creator, according to their belief, is diffused over all his creation. He exists everywhere, and in everything. . . . It is for this reabsorption into the divine essence, to which their immortal part belongs, that they continually sigh." The doctrine of the Sufis is termed by Malcolm "the belief of the imagination" which insists on striving "through fervent piety and enthusiastic devotion, of attaining for the soul, even when the body inhabits the earth, a state of celestial beatitude."[3] Sufi fraternities, which became widespread in the tenth and eleventh centuries, like the famous Assassins of the Ismailiya, gave rise to the orders of dervishes and other related mystical sects which indulged in the practice of exciting religious ecstasy by music, dancing, intoxication, and various kinds of hypnotic suggestion.

The tenets of Sufism underlay the poetry of practically all medieval Persian poets, whose imagery formed an elaborate system of Sufi symbolism. This symbolism centered on the

2. *Literary World, 3* (1848), 27.
3. *History of Persia, 2,* 269–71.

imagery of wine and love, in which wine stood for esoteric
knowledge and love for the relationship between the mystic
and the divine. The special position accorded to wine and
other intoxicants, venerated as vehicles of religious ecstasy
by the Sufis but forbidden by orthodox Islam, indicates that
some of the sources of Sufism were outside the Islamic tradition. They are connected with the influence of various types
of religious thought which left its impact on Persia in the
period immediately preceding the Moslem conquest in the
seventh century, i.e. Zoroastrian or Magian worship, Nestorian Christianity and Gnosticism, Greek Neo-Platonism,
and Indian Buddhism.⁴ All these religious and mystical
movements were the subject of intense study by Melville's
contemporaries and, as we know, by Melville himself. In the
face of this general preoccupation with Oriental religious
thought it can hardly be doubted that Melville was as familiar with Sufism as Thoreau, Emerson, *The Dial,* the *Atlantic
Monthly,* and the *Literary World.*⁵ What remains to be
examined is the extent to which this general interest is reflected in the characters and symbols of *Mardi, Moby-Dick,*
and his other works, all of which bear unmistakable traces
of what may be called the nineteenth-century "Gesta
Arabum et Persarum."

TAJI, YILLAH, AND THEIR COMPANIONS

Mardi: And a Voyage Thither was proclaimed by Melville as "a *real* romance" in a letter to his publisher.⁶ It was
not to be, as he had planned at first, a narrative of Polynesian adventure like *Omoo,* but a "Romance of Polynesian
Adventure." True enough, the narrator and hero of *Mardi,*

4. See A. J. Arberry, *Sufism,* New York, 1950.
5. On the Transcendentalist interest in Sufism see A. Christy, *The
Orient in American Transcendentalism* (New York, 1932), pp. 34, 138.
6. *Letters,* p. 70.

like the narrators of *Typee* and *Omoo* before him, jumps
ship in the South Seas and heads "Westward" in an open
boat. But he soon finds himself, in the guise of "Taji," in
the archipelago of "Mardi," a "world" of islands which is
the setting for the main action and theme of the book—the
quest for "Yillah." "The narrator's journey to the Mardian
archipelago is a voyage away from verisimilitude," writes
Feidelson. The action of the book is a part symbolic, part
allegorical, part fanciful journey "in quest of some object,
mysteriously hinted." At the end, after a chartless voyage,
with Yillah unattained, the narrator darts on toward a realm
of shades, over an endless sea.[7]

What Melville accomplished in *Mardi* was an extraordinary and complex departure from what his contemporaries
regarded as "romance." In *Mardi* Melville plunged into his
true element of openly symbolic writing. But considering
his public, he was bound to use the familiar trappings of
romantic machinery, which, almost inevitably in the first
half of the nineteenth century, led to the setting and
atmosphere of Persian poetry and the *Arabian Nights*.

A. *Taji*

At the very beginning of *Mardi* as a "Romance," in
Chapter 39 at the point of transition when the book changes
its character from a narrative of sea adventure through the
first encounter with Yillah, the following description is
given by the Narrator, soon to be turned into Taji: "Here
it must be mentioned, that from the various gay cloths and
other things provided for barter by the captain of the *Parki,*
I had very strikingly improved my costume; making it free,
flowing, and Eastern. I looked like an Emir!"[8] Taji thus
makes his entrance as an Arabian prince, like Taj el-
Mulook, a figure of Arabian romance.

7. Feidelson, pp. 166 f.
8. *Mardi, 1,* 146–47.

"Taji" in Arabic means "my crown." That Melville knew the Arabic meaning of the word seems to be attested by the frequency with which the words "crest" and "crown" are associated with Taji in *Mardi*. At the very beginning of Taji's romantic adventure, on first meeting the dignitaries of Mardi as "a gentleman from the sun," the Narrator says: "Taji seemed oozing from my fingers' ends. But courage! and erecting *my crest*, I strove to look every inch the character I had determined to assume."[9] Next, when the Narrator discovers the unconcern with which the Mardians regard his assumed godship, he makes the following remark: "Look to thy ways, then, Taji, thought I, and carry not *thy crest* too high."[10] At the end of the quest, when Taji tries to penetrate the mystery of Hautia and Yillah, he describes Yillah as *"my crown* of felicity."[11] Finally, when Taji comes to Hautia's abode, he is greeted by Hautia's order to the damsels: *"Crown* him with your flowers!"[12]

Melville implies that Hautia loved the name of Taji because of its sound: "Taji! Taji!—as a berry, that name is juicy in my mouth!—"[13] But the numerous allusions to "crest" and "crown" in connection with Taji seem to show that Melville was attracted also because of its Arabic signification. To follow Cassirer, "the notion that the name and essence bear a necessary and internal relation to each other, that the name does not merely denote but actually *is* the essence of the object, that the potency of the real thing is contained in the name—that is one of the fundamental assumptions of the mythmaking consciousness itself."[14]

9. Ibid., p. 193. Italics mine.
10. Ibid., p. 205.
11. Ibid., 2, 386.
12. Ibid., p. 390.
13. Ibid., p. 395.
14. Ernst Cassirer, *Language and Myth* (New York, 1946), p. 3.

The meaning of the word "Taj," i.e. "crown," is explained by Lane in his annotation of the *Arabian Nights* in connection with "The Story of Prince Taj-el-Mulook and the Lady Dunya" (The Crown of the Kings and the Lady World).[15] In the tale, Prince Taj el-Mulook journeys in quest of his beloved Lady Dunya in the company of his father's vizier and a poetically inclined youth. When the prince finally arrives in the land of his quest, the country of Lady Dunya, his handsome person creates the impression that he is no mortal. He is considered to be an angel by Lady Dunya's nurse.[16] The tale thus presents the basic theme of the quest for the beloved which we find in *Mardi* as well as the assumed supernatural character of the hero. There can be no question that Taji was modeled on the heroes of Arabian romance, and considering this, the emir Taj el-Mulook of the *Arabian Nights* would provide a plausible explanation of Taji's name.

Another key to the romantic aspect of the character is found in the essay on "Ancient Persian Poetry" referred to in the article on the *Arabian Nights* in the *Literary World* of February 12, 1848.[17] The subject of this essay was "the most ancient Persian Romantic Poem," in the German translation of the Orientalist Joseph von Hammer, whose plot in many ways typifies the theme on which Melville modeled the love story of Taji and Yillah in *Mardi*. The romance describes the mystic love of Wamik and Asra and their separation after experiencing great happiness in each other's company. Their reunion on earth becomes hopeless, and they are finally turned into mythological figures in the skies, "where she appears as the Virgin and he is Arc-

15. *Arabian Nights* (London, 1841), *1*, 607, n. 11.
16. Ibid., chap. 8.
17. *Literary World*, *3*, 27. *Foreign Quarterly Review*, *18* (1836), 119–58.

turus."[18] Melville need not, of course, have drawn on this particular story in delineating the association between Taji and Yillah. But the story shows that the mystical nature and ending of the relationship was a typical Arabian theme which includes mythological elements and may even be linked to the symbolism of the Narrator's ship "Arcturion" and Taji's imaginary progress through the Milky Way.[19]

Another variation on the theme of a lover's desperate quest for his beloved is the famous Arabian romance of "Mejnoun and Leila," one of the favorite subjects of Eastern poetry, which Isaac D'Israeli, whose books Melville later acquired,[20] popularized in the literature of England and

18. A variation on the theme is also found in "Weddah and Om-El-Bonain," a poem by James Thomson which, in 1884, gave Melville "more pleasure than anything of modern poetry that I have seen in a long while" (*Letters of Herman Melville*, p. 276). Thomson "found this Story . . . in the *De l'Amour* of De Stendhal . . . among 'Fragments Extracted and Translated from an Arabic Collection, entitled *The Divan of Love*, compiled by Ebn-Abi-Hadglat' ": "Note" in "Vane's Story," *Weddah and Om-El-Bonain, and Other Poems* (London, 1881), p. 58.

19. The term "taj" is used in Arabic in astronomy, e.g. Taj-i-Sa'dān—"the crown of the two planets"—Saturn (*Encyclopaedia of Islam, 4, 597*). Melville, too, linked the sparkling *crowns* of the kings of Mardi to the constellation Corona Borealis (*Mardi, 1, 293*). But the suggestion of Merrell Davis (Melville's *Mardi*, p. 69) which connects Melville's Taji with a comet "Taije" purported to be mentioned in a letter of the Boston Professor Edward Everett to the French Astronomer Le Verrier is based on a typographical error. According to the reprint of Mr. Davis, Everett's letter of October 1, 1847, refers to Leverrier's "noble memoire sur les cometes de *Taije* et de Vico." It is obvious from Leverrier's "memoires" in the "Comptes Rendus de l'Academie des Sciences" that the reference is to "les cometes de *Faye* et de Vico," i.e. the two comets discovered by Faye and Vico respectively, in 1843 and 1844, which bear their names (cf. *Comptes Rendus des Séances de l'Academie des Sciences* (Paris, Bachelier, 1845), 20, 1072, 1309). Italics mine.

20. Sealts, Nos. 184–87.

America. D'Israeli explained that the story of the two lovers "told by various poets is as popular in the East, as the loves of Abelard and Eloisa, or those of Petrarch and Laura, are in the West."[21] That D'Israeli's version of the romance was well known in America is attested by a reference to it in the second article on the *Arabian Nights* which appeared in the *Literary World* of March 18, 1848.[22] The story describes the unfortunate love of a gifted Bedouin poet for the beautiful Leila, daughter of a haughty emir. The lovers had known each other from childhood and had pledged their troth, but Leila's father refused to permit his daughter to marry the son of a Bedouin sheikh who was beneath her in rank. The poet's sanity succumbed under this blow. He spent the rest of his life in the wilderness as a madman (Mejnoun), while Leila was married to another man who, however, respected her love for Mejnoun. Death finally united the lovers.

There are several features in this tale which are of interest in relation to Taji and Yillah. Like most lovers in Arabian romance, Mejnoun and Leila had known each other from infancy, a fact which recalls the Narrator's successful attempt in *Mardi* to convince Yillah that they had known each other as children. Like all lovers in Arabian tales, Mejnoun raves, and so does Taji. Taji, on losing Yillah, falls into a mood of distraction and delirious despair: "For a time I raved. Then, falling into outer repose, lived for a space in moods and reveries, with eyes that knew no closing, one glance forever fixed.

"They strove to rouse me. Girls danced and sang; and tales of fairy times were told. . . . Yet still I moved not, hearing all, yet noting naught."[23] The situation closely resembles that of Mejnoun whom his family attempts to cure

21. I. D'Israeli, *Romances* (London, 1799), "Advertisement."
22. *Literary World, 3* (1848), 124.
23. *Mardi, 1,* 227.

of his despair at the loss of his beloved by continued festivals and the performance of beautiful dancing girls.[24] But more important than these details is the mystical significance of the tale. For Mejnoun and Leila came to occupy the same place in Moslem mysticism as the lovers of the Song of Songs in the interpretations of Jewish and Christian mystics. Their history was allegorized; their love, like Taji's for Yillah, was interpreted as a symbolical representation of the human soul groping for divine love. "Megnoun," says an eighteenth-century dictionary of the religious ceremonies of Eastern nations, "which properly signifies in Arabic, a Fool, and a Madman, means also, in particular, a man who is transported by love, either divine or profane."[25] A note to *Vathek* points out that the Moslems regard the love of Mejnoun and Leila "in the same light as the Bridegroom and Spouse, and the Song of Songs are regarded by the Jews."[26] Similarly, Taji's longing for Yillah is cast in the language of the Song of Songs: "Was not Yillah my shore and my grove? my meadow, my mead, my soft shady vine, and my arbour?"[27]

Like all of Melville's characters, Taji is a composite figure whose derivation and meaning encompass romantic, mythological, and mystical elements in a series of linked analogies. He is the hero of romance, but also a demigod. At the most significant level of his characterization he is the ecstatic mystic striving for union with the divine. All these aspects of Taji may be related to a variety of sources within "the matter of Persia" of Melville's time. One of the most striking analogies, however, leads to an association of Taji's name with the terminology and practice of the dervish

24. D'Israeli, p. 116.
25. *A Dictionary of the Religious Ceremonies of the Eastern Nations* (Calcutta, 1787), article on "Megnoun."
26. *Vathek* (Bentley), p. 101.
27. *Mardi, 1,* 168.

orders, the religious fraternities of Sufi mystics who strove for an intimate union with God through the inducement of ecstatic states.

Melville's interest in the "dancing religion" of Shakers and dervishes is well attested.[28] On July 21, 1850, Melville visited the Shaker settlement at Hancock, Massachusetts, and acquired a work on the "United Society of Believers, Commonly Called Shakers" which he thoroughly studied and marked.[29] In the course of the same summer he was interested enough to return to the Hancock settlement and to visit the nearby Shaker settlement at Lebanon in the company of Hawthorne, Evert Duyckinck, and a party of other friends who had visited him at Pittsfield. The visit to the Lebanon settlement was repeated on August 15, and, again, in the following year.[30] Finally, during his visit to Constantinople in 1856, he recorded the resemblance of the Moslem Dancing Dervishes to the Shakers.[31] Merton Sealts, who has made a special study of Melville's interest in the Shakers, has expressed the view that "what seemingly attracted him most was the prophetic strain in the Shaker religion, with its association of exalted bodily and mental states." The sympathetic chord was struck by "the themes of inspiration and prophetic utterance" in the Shaker tradition which manifested themselves not only in *Moby-Dick* but as early as *Mardi* (1849).[32]

28. See Merton Sealts, "Melville and the Shakers," *Studies in Bibliography*, Papers of the Bibliographical Society of the University of Virginia, 2 (1949–50), 105–14, esp. p. 107, where attention is drawn to a note by Melville on Shaker dancing.

29. *A Summary View of the Millenial Church, or United Society of Believers, Commonly Called Shakers* (Albany, 1848). Melville's copy is in the Stone Collection in the Alderman Library, the University of Virginia (Sealts, p. 105).

30. Leyda, *Log, 1*, 381, 385, 388, 422.

31. Horsford, *Journal*, p. 89.

32. Sealts, pp. 107, 114.

Whatever other elements of the tradition may be traced in *Mardi*, the exaltation of Taji's mental and bodily state in his pursuit of Yillah suggests the experience of a religious mystic that is closely related to the practice of the "zikr" by Moslem dervishes. Melville's acquaintance with some aspect of this phenomenon as early as *Mardi* need not be doubted in view of his reading of the *Arabian Nights*. There is an elaborate note "On Muslim Saints, or Devotees" in Lane's *Arabian Nights* which explains the practice of the dervishes in repeating the zikr, i.e. the chantlike invocation of the formula "la ilaha illa-llah" "There is no God but God," until they reach a state of mental and bodily exaltation.[33] In the same note, Lane also explains the Moslem view of insanity "as a quality that entitles the subject of it to be esteemed as a saint; being supposed to be the abstraction of the mind from worldly affairs and its total devotion to God."[34] We know from *Clarel* that Melville was greatly interested in this aspect of the Moslem "santon."[35] "So man's insanity is heaven's sense," he says in *Moby-Dick* of the idiot, Pip.[36]

In *Mardi* there is a facetious emphasis on "cracked crowns" in the conversation of Babbalanja, the philosopher: "Cracked are our crowns by nature, and henceforth forever cracked shall they be by hard raps." Babbalanja quotes "old Bardianna" in asserting "that to those identical cracks was he indebted for what little light he had in his brain."[37] There is a relationship between the image of "cracked crowns" and the idea of spiritual abstraction from worldly affairs in a mystical quest for light. The relationship be-

---

33. *Arabian Nights*, notes to chap. 3 ("The Story of the Three Royal Mendicants"), pp. 232, 237.

34. Ibid., p. 237.

35. *Clarel*, *1*, 36, 205; *2*, 131. Horsford, *Journal*, pp. 169–70.

36. *Moby-Dick*, chap. 94.

37. *Mardi*, 2, 141–42.

comes particularly intriguing when viewed in connection
with a feature pertaining to the "crowns" of the Howling
Dervishes, i.e. the importance attached to the headgear
known as "crown" or "taj." "The darweeshes I found to be
of different nations, as well as of different orders," writes
Lane in his *Modern Egyptians* to which frequent reference
is made in his notes to the *Arabian Nights*. "Some of them
wore the ordinary turban and dress of Egypt: Others wore
the Turkish . . . padded cap; and others again, wore high
caps . . . mostly of the sugar-loaf shape. One of them had a
white cap of the form last mentioned, upon which were
worked in black letters, invocations to the first four Khaleef-
ehs."[38] The headgear of the dervishes had special religious
significance. The assumption of the taj was an essential part
of the initiation ceremony of the mystic, signifying his
abandonment of carnal sins and his complete devotion to
Allah. Lane does not mention the term in his description of
the various types of headgear, but there were interesting
illustrations of the orders and their headgears in D'Ohsson's
Tableau général de l'Empire Othoman (1790), where the
significance of the taj is pointed out.[39]

The details of dervish appearance and practice were well
known to the American public in the second half of the
nineteenth century. There was a scholarly article on the
subject in the *Knickerbocker Magazine* of 1856, and its
author, John Brown of the American Legation of Constantinople, subsequently published an authoritative work, *The
Dervishes*, which appeared in Philadelphia in 1868.[40] But

38. *Modern Egyptians* (London, 1842), p. 190. The first edition of
this work was published in the "Library of Entertaining Knowledge,"
London, 1836–37.

39. M. D'Ohsson, *Tableau général de l'Empire Othoman* (Paris,
1790), 2, 298.

40. *Knickerbocker*, *48* (1856), 386, 389. John P. Brown, *The Dervishes; or Oriental Spiritualism*, Philadelphia, 1868.

there was enough information before that, for example, in the writings of D'Ohsson, Malcolm, Lane, the famous Orientalists Hammer-Purgstall and de Sacy, and the popular *Travels* of J. S. Buckingham, who lectured extensively in the United States.[41] Melville's interest in the meaning of the dervish headgear is clear from his markings in his copy of *Anastasius,* where he scored a reference to a Turkish town looking "like a sugar-loaf, built on the model of a derwish's cap; with the church at the top, by way of a tuft!"[42] In his own works we need only consider the symbolical importance of headgears in *Moby-Dick* and *Clarel* to realize the significance of Taji's invocation of Yillah as his *"crown* of felicity."[43]

In *Moby-Dick* the chapter "The Hat" is linked to the "mystic watch" of Fedallah, the mysterious Parsi with the Mohammedan name who is joined to Ahab in the "potent spell" of a mystic fraternity.[44] As Ahab, perched aloft, gazes upon the dim and distant horizon, a black red-billed sky-hawk removes his hat and with a scream darts away with his prize. "An eagle flew thrice round Tarquin's head, removing his cap to replace it, and thereupon Tanaquil, his wife, declared that Tarquin would be king of Rome. But only by the replacing of the cap was that omen accounted good. Ahab's hat was never restored."[45]

In the image of Tarquin the symbolical identification of cap and crown is self-evident. As applied to Ahab, the removal of his "crown" was final and therefore disastrous. It

41. Malcolm, *History of Persia,* 2, 327, 503. Hammer-Purgstall, *The History of the Assassins,* London, 1835. Silvestre de Sacy, *Exposé de la religion des Druzes,* Paris, 1838. J. S. Buckingham, *Travels in Assyria, Media, and Persia* (London, 1830), *1,* 275.

42. Melville's copy of *Anastasius, 1,* 201.

43. *Mardi,* 2, 386. Italics mine.

44. *Moby-Dick,* chap. 130.

45. Ibid.

acquires the symbolical significance associated with the
crown of a dervish. For a dervish to lose his cap is identical
with losing divine grace, since the headgear is held to be of
divine origin, an emblem of "the vase of light" which contains the immortal soul of Mohammed.[46] The significance
of the hat or cap as an emblem of man's soul, i.e. the divine
spirit in man, is stressed again in *Clarel* in the canto "Man
and Bird."[47] The story of the man and the bird is essentially
the same as Ahab's, but in *Clarel* there is an explicit identification of the cap with the soul and of the black red-billed
bird, which carries it away, with the devil. Most significantly, the lost cap is described as a "wool" cap—an image
of the greatest importance if we consider that the Sufi mystics derived their name from the Arabic word for "wool,"
i.e. "suf," because of their ascetic predilection for woolen
garments. This association of Sufi with wool was well
known to Melville's contemporaries, and was even discussed
in Chambers' *Cyclopaedia* of 1728 which Melville, in 1846,
received from his uncle.[48]

The mystical significance of Ahab's hat which is associated with the influence of Fedallah and the pursuit of the
White Whale is obvious. The reiteration of the theme in
Clarel clearly suggests Sufi elements. In view of this, it is
hardly surprising that the Islamic connotations of the Arabian names "Taji" and "Yillah" should accurately reflect
the ecstatic aspiration of the Moslem mystic for the divine.

46. Brown, *The Dervishes,* pp. 99, 124.

47. *Clarel, 2,* 129–30.

48. Chambers, *2,* 97. An additional sign of Sufi influence in *Clarel*
is the woolen shirt of the mariner who lost his "old wool cap" to the
bird. The "quilted patches" of the mariner's shirt are given special
significance by Melville. An interesting analogy is found in the sections, or patches, which make up the caps of the dervishes, each section standing for the abandonment of a sin (see Brown, *The Dervishes,*
p. 99). Cf. the symbolic significance of Mortmain's "Skull-Cap" (*Clarel,
1,* 179–80) and of the "Phrygian cap" of the Cypriote (ibid., *2,* 16).

B. *Yillah*

The appearance of Yillah in *Mardi* marks the transition from the realistic narrative of sea adventure to the romantic pursuit of a mystical phantom. In the figure of Yillah Melville fused the anthropological and mythological elements of his tale into a symbolism of the divine absolute which is incessantly pursued by man. The human Yillah, whom the Narrator, Jarl, and Samoa encounter, is a white maiden who has been dedicated for sacrifice to the gods by Aleema, the priest. Yillah, the phantom, the object of Taji's quest, is an apparition whose complex meanings suggest a combination of origins.

There are two features relating to the human Yillah that appear in Oriental romances by English writers which achieved great popularity in the nineteenth century and preceded Melville's *Mardi*. The account of Yillah's European origin, which the Narrator suspects from her appearance and which forms the rationale of the myth, is paralleled in the hidden European origin of the white maiden Ayesha whom Lord Osmond, the hero of Morier's tale *Ayesha, the Maid of Kars,* encounters in his travels in Turkey.[49] Yillah's rescue by the Narrator recalls a similar episode in which a maiden who was to be thrown into the sea in accordance with native practice was saved by the hero in Byron's Oriental romance, *The Giaour.*[50]

The Narrator's account of Yillah's origin as the child of European parents who were massacred by the natives resolves in the description of Yillah's dreamlike existence in Ardair, and finally her phantom-like disappearance. This mythological Yillah is the riddle in Melville's romance, and her name seems to indicate an Islamic origin.

49. J. Morier, *Ayesha, The Maid of Kars* (Paris, 1834), p. 35.
50. Byron, *Works,* 2, "Advertisement."

It is evident that in its Arabic connotation Yillah suggests the Mohammedan name of God, Allah, and in particular the invocation of faith "La ilaha illa-llah." A description of this formula chanted at a wake, as found in Lane's notes to the *Arabian Nights*,[51] acquires added significance when one remembers that Taji and his companions "leave their wake around the world" for Yillah,[52] and Yillah is both a maiden destined for death and the symbol of the divine absolute. According to Lane, the words "La ilaha illa-llah" (There is no God but God) were chanted "in a very deep and hoarse tone; laying the principal emphasis upon the word 'La' and the first syllable of the last word 'Allah'; and uttering i, apparently, with a considerable effort."[53] The first two elements emphasized by Lane recall the name Lallah, reminiscent of Thomas Moore's *Lalla Rookh,* while "illa" uttered "with considerable effort" would produce "Yillah." D'Ohsson transliterated the chant as "La ilahy ill' allah."[54]

This connotative significance of the name does not exclude the probability, pointed out by Merrell Davis, that Yillah is also an anagram of "lily," the symbol for innocence, purity, and the return of happiness, with which Yillah is identified throughout *Mardi*. It is also an anagram of Laylah (night), the popular name of Arabian maidens in Oriental romance and the name of the heroine in "Mejnoun and Leila." But we know from Melville's later works that he was thoroughly familiar with the "Islam wail."[55] A reference to the "wailful cries of 'La Ilah illa Alla!' . . . commonly uttered under some violent emotion of mind" is also found in Beckford's *Vathek*.[56] It is only to be expected that, like

51. *Arabian Nights, 1,* 612, n. 37, "On the Ceremony called Zikr."
52. *Mardi,* 2, 270.
53. *Arabian Nights, 1,* 613–14.
54. D'Ohsson, 2, 299.
55. *Clarel, 1,* 84, 99, 156.
56. *Vathek,* "Notes."

other examples of name coinage in Melville, the name of
Yillah should reflect the complex accumulative symbolism
of the figure. The correlation in the meaning and pronunciation which exists between the name and the Mohammedan profession of faith is therefore of great interest, particularly as it appears in a context which would also explain
the name of Taji.

Yillah's home in *Mardi* is "the valley of Ardair," a name
the interpretation of which has so far not been attempted.
The following passage is found in Lane's Notes to the Story
of Taj el-Mulook: "The scenes of the events narrated in the
story of Taj el-Mulook are in Persia and, probably, in India; but imaginary names appear to be given to the several
kingdoms mentioned in it: the kingdom of El-Ard El-
Khadra (the Green Country) and . . . that of El-Ard El-
Beyda (The White Country) . . . and as to the Islands of
Camphor, I fancy we must be content to consider them
vaguely as appertaining to India."[57] Apart from the possible significance of "the Islands of Camphor" for the idea
of "the Isles of Myrrh" in *Mardi*,[58] this note offers a plausible explanation of the meaning of Yillah's abode "Ardair,"
i.e. "The Country of Air." The Arabic meaning of the word
"Ard" is "country, earth, and world," equivalent to the
Latin "terra." In fact, if we accept the suggestion that Melville knew the meaning of the Arabic word "ard" from his
reading of Lane, we are faced with a surprising conclusion
about the word "Mardi."

The symbolical identity between Mardi and the world
or earth is obvious. Mardi is constantly referred to as "the
world" and in several instances simply translated by Melville, e.g. when he speaks of "round Mardi," or of Vivenza
(North America) as "that New Mardi."[59] The following

57. *Arabian Nights*, *1*, 607, n. 11.
58. *Mardi*, 2, 268.
59. *Mardi*, *1*, 171, 205, 210, 222, 277, 315; 2, 109.

question therefore presents itself: Could Melville have
coined the word "Mardi" or taken it from Anthon's Classical Dictionary, as has been suggested,[60] in the knowledge
of the Arabic word "ard" which he used in "Ardair"?
"Mardi" would then simply mean "my earth, my world"
on the model of the Lady World (Arabic "dunya") which
Prince Taj pursues in the *Arabian Nights*.[61]

Be that as it may, the picture of Yillah in Ardair is a
stock tableau of Arabian romance and the Oriental tales of
European writers. Its stage props include the enraptured
youth, gazing on his beloved from a secret recess in the inaccessible garden to which his heroine is confined, and the
allegorical bird which is the maiden's companion. The bird
is a variation of the "bulbul" of Persian romance, which is
generally translated as a nightingale by Western writers and
celebrated in Persian literature as "the almost inseparable
companion of the rose, and the beautiful Persian Peries."[62]

The chapter entitled "Yillah in Ardair" stresses the airy
substance of the mythological Yillah. This verdant glen, in
which Yillah abode, looked "like a lake of cool, balmy air.
. . . Aerial trees shot up from its surface."[63] The element
air is contained in its name. The "unearthly" story which
the Narrator hears from Yillah's lips fuses the elements of
air and water in her "more than terrestrial origin." The
literary parallelism between Yillah and the water nymph
of La Motte-Fouqué's German romance *Undine*, which
Melville probably read in Tracy's translation, has been discussed by Merrell Davis.[64] Like a mermaid, Yillah dreams
of the whirlpool and sweet mosses and finally disappears
like Undine. Yet Yillah is more than an undine. Ultimately

60. Davis, *Melville's "Mardi,"* p. 77, n. 2.
61. *Arabian Nights, 1,* 607, n. 11.
62. Ouseley, *Persian Miscellanies,* p. xxx.
63. *Mardi, 1,* 179.
64. Davis, p. 59.

she is the intangible symbol of divine love. But even as a mythological figure she is more than a water nymph. Like Shakespeare's Ariel, she is also of aerial extraction. Then, there is the flower symbolism which connects her with fairy mythology. Yillah

> declared herself more than mortal, a maiden from Oroolia, the *Island of Delights*. . . . To this while yet an infant, by some mystical power, she had been spirited from Amma, the place of her nativity. . . . And hardly had the waters of Oroolia washed white her olive skin, and tinged her hair with gold, when one day strolling in the woodlands, she was snared in the tendrils of a vine. Drawing her into its bowers, it gently transformed her into one of its blossoms, leaving her conscious soul folded up in the transparent petals. Here hung Yillah in a trance, the without all tinged with the rosy hue of her prison. At length, when her spirit was about to burst forth in the opening flower, the blossom was snapped from its stem, and borne by a soft wind to the sea; where it fell into the opening valve of a shell; which in good time was cast upon the beach of the island of Amma.
>
> In a dream, these events were revealed to Aleema the priest; who by a spell unlocking its pearly casket, took forth the bud, which now showed signs of opening in the reviving air, and bore faint shadowy revealings, as of the dawn behind crimson clouds. Suddenly expanding, the blossom exhaled away in perfumes; floating a rosy mist in the air. Condensing at last, there emerged from this mist the same radiant young Yillah as before; her locks all moist, and a rose-coloured pearl on her bosom.[65]

65. *Mardi, 1,* 159–60.

The account of Yillah's mythological origin contains several features which suggest various mythologies, both Western and Eastern. Emergence from the sea shell recalls the
birth of Venus. But condensation from a mist in the air
was generally familiar from the *Arabian Nights* as the manner in which the Arabian spirits called genii (jinn) assumed
corporeal shape. Of these spirits, some were celebrated for
their purity, beauty, and goodness, and were called by the
Persian name of peris.

The peris had been popularized in nineteenth-century
English literature by translations of Persian tales, particularly Jonathan Scott's translation of the *Bahar Danush,* a
collection of romances on which Moore drew for his *Lalla
Rookh.*[66] Moore's Oriental frame-tale was published in
1817 and was acclaimed for its genuinely Oriental flavor.
Its Oriental machinery, elaborately explained in the notes,
aroused general interest and became common knowledge.
Lalla Rookh, which contains four stories in verse connected
by a prose narrative, was especially praised by contemporary
critics for the story called "Paradise and the Peri."[67] Its
particular significance is that it "added a new and very at-
tractive figure to the gallery of fairy mythology."[68] In 1813
a poem about the love of a peri and a mortal had also been
planned by Byron. He dropped this idea, however, on
learning that Moore had already made the daughter of a
peri the heroine of one of his tales.[69] This tale, which was
left unfinished but inspired "Paradise and the Peri," is

66. Jonathan Scott, *Bahar-Danush; or Garden of Knowledge,* translated from the Persic of Einaiut Oollah (Inayat Allah), 3 vols. Shrewsbury, 1799. The story of Lalla Rookh is given in the Appendix to
Vol. 3, pp. 298–304. See also "Story of the Merchant's Son and the
Peries," 2, 213–24.

67. *Blackwood's Magazine, 1* (June 1817), 285.

68. R. Garnett, *Essays of an Ex-Librarian* (New York, 1901), p. 216.

69. Moore, *Life of Byron,* pp. 193, 194.

mentioned by Moore in his preface to the twentieth edition of *Lalla Rookh,* reprinted in America in 1845: "The Peri's Daughter was meant to relate the loves of a nymph of this aerial extraction with a youth of mortal race, the rightful prince of Ormuz, who had been, from his infancy, brought up, in seclusion, on the banks of the river Amou, by an aged guardian named Mohassan. The story opens with the first meeting of these destined lovers, then in their childhood; the Peri having wafted her daughter to this holy retreat, in a bright, enchanted boat. . . ."[70] Melville's copy of the *Poetical Works of Thomas Moore,* where the preface to *Lalla Rookh* is marked, was acquired only in 1862.[71] But he was thoroughly familiar with the machinery of Oriental romance as popularized by Byron and Moore when he was writing *Mardi,* and peris are mentioned in *Redburn.*[72]

There is an evident correspondence between the story of the nymph of aerial extraction who loved a youth "brought up in seclusion, on the banks of the river Amou, by an aged guardian" and the account of Yillah, guarded by an old priest "in the silent interior of Amma." Lalla Rookh, the heroine, is characterized by a "rose-coloured veil"; Yillah by a "rose-coloured pearl." There is a resemblance in the appearance and dress of the youthful poet who accompanies Lalla Rookh and Taji's companion, Yoomy. Lalla Rookh's poet is subjected to the same type of harangue on the part of the counsellor Fadladeen as Yoomy is by

---

70. *Lalla Rookh* (Philadelphia, 1845), p. xvii.

71. See Melville's copy of Moore's *Poetical Works* (Boston, 1861), *6,* 4 f. (Houghton Library, Harvard University).

72. *Redburn,* chap. 43. Moore's *Loves of the Angels* is mentioned in *White Jacket,* chap. 41. There is also a reference to peris in an extract from Moore in *The London Carcanet* (New York, 1831), p. 209, an anthology which Melville received as an award from the Albany Academy in 1831. The book is in the Yale Collection of American Literature, Yale University.

Babbalanja. Also, there is a parallelism of the political allegory of *Lalla Rookh,* with its references to the woes of Ireland, and the political satire in *Mardi.*[73]

In all this machinery the peris were creatures of importance. Their nature was discussed in the second article on the *Arabian Nights* that appeared in the *Literary World* on March 18, 1848:

> The human race is considered, by the Mohammedans, to have been secretly surrounded by an invisible creation of two distinct species; the Peris or fairies, beautiful and benevolent, but imperfect and offending, who were friendly to man, and the Dives, hideous in form and appearance, of an indignant disposition, and constantly exercising their ingenuity in involving humanity in every disquietude of error and of guilt. . . .
>
> In a note to the late Mr. D'Israeli's "Mejnoun and Leila" . . . we find "The Dives are all males, and the Peris all females. Such is the envenomed character of the Dives that they can endure nothing fragrant; the contrast is strongly marked when it is remembered that the perfume of flowers was the only sustenance of the Peris."[74]

The article explains that the peris lived in a "fairy-land which was supposed by some to have been . . . in the land of Eden, the Garden of Paradise." One of the provinces of this "happy land" was called "the Country of Delight." To this a parallelism may be easily found in *Mardi.* Corresponding to the "Country of Delights," Yillah's abode is called the "Island of Delights." Yillah, to Taji, seems a "spirit." The question he asks himself in relation to her remains unsolved throughout the book: "Did I commune

73. *Lalla Rookh,* pp. xvii, 16, 22. *Mardi, 1,* 158, 159, 230.
74. *Literary World, 3* (1848), 124.

with a spirit? Often I thought that Paradise had overtaken me on earth, and that Yillah was verily an angel and hence the mysteries that hallowed her."[75]

There was much literature on the peris, besides D'Israeli's note, which could have supplied information for the article in the *Literary World*. One of the sources to which most frequent reference was made by English writers of Oriental romance, including D'Israeli, was Sir William Ouseley's *Persian Miscellanies* (1795). There the nature of the peris is extensively described. Ouseley speaks of "the extraordinary degree of beauty which the Persians assign to the imaginary being called Peri." He describes them as "the fairest creatures of poetical imagination" whose beauty and goodness are proverbial. He translates the word as angel "for want of a better term," for "however they may correspond in beauty with our idea of angels . . . the Persian Peris seem to be a distinct species of imaginary beings, and I know not any class of airy creatures, in which they can, with exact propriety be ranked." Like angels and "other creatures endued with uncommon purity of nature," the peris were believed to be formed of fragrant substances and to exist on the perfume of flowers. They are not immortal, and "when . . . in danger of being overpowered by their foes, they always solicit the assistance of some mortal hero; which furnishes a wonderful fund of fanciful machinery for Eastern Poetry and Romance."[76] Beckford, in *Vathek,* defines "Peri" as signifying "that beautiful race of creatures which constitutes the link between angels and men."[77] Other writers simply identify the peris with the fairies of Western mythology to the point of establishing an etymological relationship between the words "fairy" and "peri."[78]

75. *Mardi, 1,* 226.
76. *Persian Miscellanies,* p. 136.
77. *Vathek,* "Notes."
78. *Oriental Collections, 1,* 361.

But all agree that the peris were "uniformly described as beneficent, beautiful, and mild" and that they represented the ideal of beauty and goodness to the Persian poets. "Perfection of beauty, Peri of my soul!" says Mejnoun to Leila in D'Israeli's version, "when we again meet, I shall open for thee the silver gate of Paradise!"[79] In the context of the popular Oriental romance of Melville's day, Yillah was the peri of Taji's soul.

c. *Hautia*

The figure of Hautia stands behind Yillah as the symbol of sensuous woman, the temptress, "the vortex that draws all in." Though seductive queens like Hautia, who dwell in palaces of pleasure, commonly appear in romantic tradition—Nathalia Wright has pointed to Hautia's connection with the sorceress Acrasia in Spenser's *Faerie Queene*[80]—there are specific traits relating to Taji's temptress which also evoke the houris, the sensuous creatures of the Moslem paradise as described in the Koran. In Oriental romance there is a connection between the peris and the houris. This is reflected in Melville's use of both terms for "charmers" in *Redburn*.[81] In Arabian legend both peris and houris were symbols of beauty and were celebrated for their power of charming and enchanting. Both were considered "superior spirits." But while the peris are idealized as incarnations of love at its highest and purest, the houris are symbols of sexual love and sensuous delight.

Melville emphasizes the dark carnal nature of Hautia by making her the queen of "black-eyed damsels," to contrast

79. *Romances,* p. 141.
80. Nathalia Wright, "A Note on Melville's Use of Spenser: Hautia and the Bower of Bliss," *American Literature, 24* (1953), 83–84.
81. *Redburn,* chap. 43.

with the blue-eyed ideal of Yillah's innocence.[82] In nineteenth-century romantic tradition the houris are the black-eyed damsels par excellence. Their name was derived from the epithet "black-eyed." They were described as dwelling in luxury in splendid palaces of pleasure surrounded by female attendants. Like Hautia's damsels who beckon Taji by waving "verdant scarfs of vine," the houris were pictured as waving "green" kerchiefs to beckon their lovers to their abode—a frequent image which is used in the Oriental romances of both Byron and Moore.[83] Wine and the fragrance of flowers, the chief ingredients of the Moslem paradise, are offered Taji as the delights of Hautia's bower. Like houris, her damsels dance, make music and proffer Taji "clustering grapes."[84]

Hautia herself, however, is "scentless."[85] This significant characteristic acquires special interest in an Islamic context when we remember that the fragrance of the Arabian fairies was connected with the purity of their nature. "Of musk, camphor, ambergris and similar fragrant substances, the Persians believe angels to be formed, and other creatures endued with uncommon purity of nature," says Ouseley in the *Persian Miscellanies*.[86] The connection between the purity of the peris and the fragrant substances out of which they are created is also pointed out by D'Israeli in a note to *Mejnoun and Leila*.[87] This image is echoed in Southey's *Thalaba*.[88] Its meaning is reflected in *Moby-Dick*, where Melville speaks of the young women of Salem who "breathe

82. *Mardi*, 2, 392.
83. Ibid., p. 150; Byron, *The Giaour (Works)*, 2, 245, 280.
84. *Mardi*, 2, 150.
85. Ibid., pp. 389–90.
86. *Persian Miscellanies*, p. 62.
87. *Romances*, p. 14.
88. *Thalaba, the Destroyer* (London, 1814), 2, 17, 33.

such musk, their sailor sweethearts smell them miles off
shore, as though they were drawing nigh the odorous Mo-
luccas instead of the Puritanic sands."[89]

Hautia is scentless because she is impure, though her
abode, like the enticing Moslem paradise of the houris, is
suffused with perfumes. Hautia is "a dahlia on its stalk," a
dahlia being the symbol for "heartless beauty."[90] In the
story of Prince Taj el-Mulook in the *Arabian Nights* she
has her parallel in the "daughter of the enchantress Delee-
leh" whose name, says Lane, is used as an epithet indicating
artifice, machination, and fraud.[91] There is also a similarity
in the situation. The temptress in the Arabian story lures
the hero away from his true love, but, like Hautia, cannot
destroy him because of the protection given him by the
spirit of the pure maiden who is his ideal.

There is another suggestion of Hautia in an illustration
to the *Arabian Nights*. The figure appears in an illustrated
article in the *Literary World* of October 14, 1848, which
gives excerpts from Harper's edition of Lane's translation
and shows a female figure, like Hautia's "incognito," en-
veloped in a robe so as to expose one solitary eye.[92] The appearance of Arab women in the streets of Cairo "with one
eye gleaming above the veil which is drawn *across* the face"
was described by Warburton in *The Crescent and the Cross*
(1845).[93] In *Mardi* and later, in "Benito Cereno," Melville
associated this costume with the appearance of women at
Lima, but he could hardly have been unaware of its fre-

89. *Moby-Dick*, chap. 6.
90. *Mardi*, 2, 389. M. Davis, "The Flower Symbolism in *Mardi*,"
Modern Language Quarterly, 2 (1941), 637.
91. *Arabian Nights*, 1, 562, 614.
92. *Literary World*, 3, 724.
93. *The Crescent and the Cross*, p. 69.

quency in Islamic countries, if only from a perusal of the *Arabian Nights*.[94]

Hautia's flower messages to Taji represent an Oriental custom which was the subject of lively interest in the West. The first information concerning the use of fruits and flowers to communicate messages was transmitted to Europe as early as 1688 by the French Orientalist Du Vigneau, who, on his return from a diplomatic mission to Turkey, published a work on "the language of flowers."[95] But European interest in this Oriental habit was not generally aroused until the first half of the eighteenth century, when Lady Mary Wortley Montagu, who accompanied her husband on his Turkish mission, described in one of her letters from the East the way in which Turkish ladies communicated with their lovers from the seclusion of their harems by using the names of fruits and flowers as a code, e.g. jonquil— "Have pity on my passion."[96] This secret flower language was discussed by Goethe in his notes to the *West-East Divan*,[97] and by Lane, in a note on "conversing and corresponding by means of signs, emblems, metaphors, etc." appended to the Story of Taj el-Mulook:

> Many persons of the instructed classes, and some others, among the Arabs, often take delight, and show

94. *Mardi, 1,* 217. "Benito Cereno," in Leyda, *Complete Stories,* p. 256. Cf. *Pierre,* Bk. VIII, sec. ii. Foster, Explanatory Notes (Hendricks House), p. 466. The "incognito" is *not* to be attributed to the priest, Aleema (see Richard Chase, *Herman Melville,* New York, 1949, p. 18).

95. Du Vigneau, *Le Secrétaire Turc contenant l'art d'exprimer ses pensées sans se voir, sans se parler & sans s'écrire* (Paris, 1688), "Dictionnaire," pp. 198–211.

96. *Letters and Works* (3 vols. London, 1837), 2, 56.

97. Goethe, *West-Oestlicher Divan, Noten und Abhandlungen,* ed. Ernst Grumach (Berlin, 1952), pp. 98–101. On Goethe and the Near East see H. H. Schaeder, *Goethes Erlebnis des Ostens,* Leipzig, 1938.

much ingenuity and quickness of apprehension, in
conversing and corresponding by means of signs, emblems, &c., or in a conventional, metaphorical language, not understood by the vulgar in general. . . .
Many of the women are said to be adepts in this art,
or science, and to convey messages, declarations of love,
&c., by means of fruits, flowers, and other emblems. . . .
The language of flowers employed by the Turks . . .
consists of a collection of words and phrases or sen-
tences which rhyme with the names of the objects used
as the signs.

Lane illustrates the "remarkable faculty" displayed "in
catching the meaning of secret signs" by the story of a poet
who was "a wonderful guesser." In this note he refers to
Lady Mary Wortley Montagu's letter, a paper on the language of flowers by Hammer-Purgstall, a note on the subject in a French collection of Arabian tales, and the work
of Du Vigneau.[98]
There are several features in Lane's note that may be
related to Melville's idea of having Hautia send Taji flower
messages that are interpreted by "Hautia's dragoman,"
Yoomy, the poet. The note was a commentary on the story
of Taj el-Mulook which, as has been seen, may bear on
Melville's use of the names Taji and Yillah. It describes at
some length the custom of using the language of flowers for
messages and even mentions a poet as the interpreter of
such messages.
A key to the emblematical use of flowers is provided in
Lane's reference to Hammer-Purgstall's and Du Vigneau's
papers on "le langage des fleurs." Du Vigneau's list of flowers and their meanings, as used in such messages, includes

98. *Arabian Nights, 1,* 608.

179 items and Hammer-Purgstall's 120.[99] Most of "ces hieroglyphes turcs d'amour" cited by Hammer-Purgstall are identical with Du Vigneau's. It is also of interest to find that this correspondence was known by the name of "Salaam" or "Greeting." On their first appearance Hautia's messengers were ushered into Taji's presence "with many salaams" and, when he failed to understand their flower messages, exclaimed: "he mocks our mistress," being unable to imagine that their mistress' lover was ignorant of the flower language.[100] In view of the Oriental character of *Mardi,* it can hardly be doubted that Melville's flower symbolism was inspired by descriptions of the Oriental flower language and, possibly in particular, by Lane. But he turned to an English or American flower book in order to adapt his flower symbolism to Western usage, and to enable the reader to identify the flowers and their meaning according to the sentiments attached to them in popular flower books.[101]

D. *Mohi*

The link between Yillah and Hautia is established by Mohi, the historian, who tells Taji that "the maidens of Hautia are all Yillahs, held captive, unknown to themselves."[102] The name and character of this historian also suggest an Islamic source. Old Mohi "was a venerable teller of stories and legends, one of the Keepers of the Chronicles of the Kings of Mardi."[103] There was, in fact, a Turkish

99. See J. J. Marcel, *Contes du Cheykh El-Mohdy* (Paris, 1833), *3,* 328; *Mines de l'Orient, 1,* "Dictionnaire du langage des fleurs," pp. 36–42.

100. *Mardi, 1,* 218.

101. See Merrell Davis, "A 'Flower Dictionary' for *Mardi"* (from the *Poetry of Flowers and Flowers of Poetry* by Frances S. Osgood, New York, 1840), *Modern Language Quarterly,* 2 (1941), 636–38.

102. *Mardi, 2,* 392.

103. Ibid., *1,* 229.

chronicler and historian named "Muhyi" (Muhyi ed-Dīn
ibn 'Ali ed-Dīn al-Jamāli) who lived in the sixteenth century and is mentioned by Hammer-Purgstall in his history
of the Ottoman Empire, which appeared in 1827–35 and
was partly rendered into English.[104] A complete French
translation of the work was in the possession of the New
York Society Library.[105] In the introduction Hammer-
Purgstall gives the name of the Turkish historian as Muhijeddin Dschemali, who described the history of the Ottomans from its inception to the year 957 (1550).[106] He also
mentions another Muhyi who was considered the greatest
of all mystic sheikhs of Islam, Mohijeddin Al-Arabi. The
grave of this "Mohi" was on the outskirts of Damascus and
was a holy site for Moslem pilgrims.[107] Hammer-Purgstall
varies the transliteration of the name, spelling the historian
"Muhijeddin" and the name of the mystic both "Muhijeddin" and "Mohijeddin."[108]

E. *Yoomy*

Yoomy, the poet in *Mardi,* is described as "a youthful,
long-haired, blue-eyed minstrel; all fits and starts; at times,
absent of mind, and wan of cheek; but always very neat and
pretty in his apparel; wearing the most becoming of tur-
bans, a bird-of-paradise feather in its plume, and sporting
the gayest of sashes."[109] His appearance, like Taji's in his

104. T. A. Dale, *Campaigns of Osman Sultans,* from the German
of Joseph von Hammer, London, 1835.

105. Joseph von Hammer, *Histoire de l'Empire Ottoman,* 2 vols.
Paris, 1844. *Alphabetical and Analytical Catalogue of the New York
Society Library* (New York, 1850), p. 194.

106. *Geschichte des Osmanischen Reiches, 1,* xxxvi.

107. Ibid., *2,* 489; *10,* 529.

108. In the index the name appears in both transliterations: ibid.,
10, 529.

109. *Mardi, 1,* 230.

flowing robes, immediately evokes the land of Arabian romance. He is reminiscent of the graceful and elegant young poet in *Lalla Rookh* who suffers from the unfeeling harangue of Lalla Rookh's chamberlain, Fadladeen, as Yoomy suffers from Babbalanja. Even more suggestive of an Islamic prototype is Yoomy's name. Its spelling suggests a play on the name of Jami, the last great classical poet of Persia and a pronounced Sufi, who, together with Saadi and Hafiz, was well known in the translations of Sir William Jones and Joseph von Hammer-Purgstall.[110]

Jami was particularly celebrated for his poetic rendering of famous Arabian romances, one of which was the story of Mejnoun and Leila. In the first decade of the nineteenth century Jami's version of the tale was translated into French and German. D'Israeli, in his notes to "Mejnoun and Leila," describes Jami as "a tender elegiac persian poet."[111]

In America, Emerson mentions Jami in his poem "Saadi," which appeared in the *Dial* in October 1842. There the name of the poet is spelled "Dschami," for "Mr. Emerson had, of course, when he wrote of the Persians, only Von Hammer's translations to work on. The Germans had no way of rendering the sound *J* but by the clumsy *dsch*, so he usually spelled Jami, as in the poem 'Saadi', Dschami."[112] Four lines from Jami are among the sixty-four Persian poems which Emerson translated from Hammer-Purgstall's German version.[113] Hammer's *Geschichte der schoenen Redekuenste Persiens*, which Emerson, like Goethe, used for his adaptations from Persian poetry, compares

110. *Literary History of Persia, 3*, 427. *Asiatic Miscellany*, p. 98. Hammer, *Geschichte der schoenen Redekuenste Persiens*, pp. 312–48.

111. *Romances*, p. 180.

112. E. W. Emerson in notes to essay "Persian Poetry," *Works, 8*, 421.

113. See Yohannan, "Emerson's Translations of Persian Poetry from German Sources," *American Literature, 14* (1943), 418, No. 23.

Jami's work to Saadi's and discusses it as reflecting the characteristics of Persian literature: the interweaving of prose and verse, the mixture of philosophical observations with narrative, and the skillful use of punning[114]—all of which are common characteristics of Oriental tales adopted in the stylistic peculiarities of *Mardi*.

It stands to reason that Melville's interest in the Persian poets, which is attested by his allusions to Hafiz in *Mardi* and his later preoccupation with Saadi, also brought Jami to his attention. That Yoomy is modeled on a Persian poet is made explicitly clear: " 'Oh, morning life!' cried Yoomy, with a Persian air; 'would that all time were a sunrise, and all life a youth!' "[115] Besides, a minstrel by the name of "Jarmi" is mentioned by Yoomy in *Mardi:* " 'At the sacred games of Luzella,' said Yoomy, 'slyly crowned from behind with a laurel fillet, for many hours, the minstrel Jarmi wandered about ignorant of the honours he bore.' "[116] The name of the minstrel is identical with Jami in pronunciation if not in spelling. "Jarmi" and "Yoomy" are probably variations on the same name, like Pierre and Glendinning Stanly in *Pierre*.

Yoomy is the most conspicuously Persian character in *Mardi*. His role as a Persian poet is not limited to his name and appearance. As the interpreter of Hautia's flower messages he is the classic Western image of a Persian poet, for the flower imagery of love was generally associated with "the Rose Garden of Persia"—as the most popular contemporary anthology of Persian poetry was called.[117] Yoomy also represents the image of the Persian poet as a mystic,

114. *Geschichte der schoenen Redekuenste Persiens,* p. 313.
115. *Mardi,* 2, 188.
116. Ibid., p. 88.
117. Louisa Stuart Costello, *The Rose Garden of Persia,* London, 1845.

for several of his poems describe the character of the lost maiden Yillah and the nature of her disappearance. They express the mystic apprehension of the divine absolute in the poetic terms of beauty, nature, and love. The mysticism of Yoomy's poetic invocation of Yillah is satirized by Babbalanja, the philosopher, in a way that evokes the comments of contemporary writers on the mystical interpretation of Persian poetry: "it must be confessed, that the following ode of Hafiz requires to be studied with more than ordinary attention, in order that the full meaning of its *devotional* fervour may be comprehended; otherwise, it might appear to the *unguarded* reader a mere Bacchanalian effusion, not unworthy of Anacreon!"[118] Melville's statement that Yoomy "was miraculously gifted with three voices" serves to emphasize the "Persian air" of Yoomy's songs, for a Persian poem was considered on three levels, the perfection of its composition, the lyrical content of the poem and, finally, its mystical significance.

F. *Aleema, Alma, and Other Names*

In their Arabic connotation the names of Aleema and Alma in *Mardi* suggest a common root "'ālim," which Lane explains as signifying "a man of science or learning . . . a term more particularly given to a doctor of the law. European writers generally use the plural form of this appellation for the singular."[119] The plural form of "alim" is given by Lane as "Ulama," more commonly spelled "Ulema." Lane's note on this term relates to "The Story of Alee of Cairo" in the *Arabian Nights,* in which "the Kadee of the holy law" and all the Ulama are summoned to solve a problem.[120] In *Mardi* both Aleema and Alma may be con-

118. Ibid., p. 7.
119. *Arabian Nights,* 2, 634, n. 14.
120. Ibid., p. 630.

sidered as "Kadees of the holy law," for Aleema is a priest
and Alma a prophet, and both are venerated by their followers as divinely inspired teachers and guides.

Moreover, both names suggest the Arabic word for
knowledge, "'ilm," from which "Alim" and "Ulama" derive. It has been pointed out that in naming the figure of
Alma Melville probably bore in mind the Alma of Spenser's
Faerie Queene and Matthew Prior's *Alma, the Progress of
the Mind*.[121] But the etymological relationship of Aleema
and Alma—always a significant feature in Melville—seems
to link the characters in a way that expresses both an analogy and a contrast in the function of the heathen Polynesian
priest and the illustrious prophet who "came to redeem the
Mardians from their heathenish thrall."[122]

Melville's interest in the meaning of words also shows
itself in his coinages from the Hebrew. As has already been
noted, the name of the "sacred lake" Yammo in *Mardi* is
clearly a derivation from the Hebrew word for "sea" or
"lake," i.e. "yam."[123] The place name "Maramma" strikes
one as an equally obvious derivation. Maramma is the
"lofty" seat of the Mardian priesthood and deity. It is described as an island dominated by a "great central peak,"
and Melville continually reiterates the idea of "loftiness"
in its description.[124] The name has been plausibly associated with Dante's "pestilent fen" called "Maremma" in the
Inferno.[125] The linked analogy is enhanced, moreover, by
association with the Hebrew "Merom" (on high), which reflects Melville's idea of loftiness; the word occurs in Kitto's
Cyclopaedia of Biblical Literature, in connection with "the

121. Davis, p. 167, n. 3.
122. *Mardi, 2, 31.*
123. Ibid., chap. 7.
124. Ibid., chap. 1.
125. Davis, p. 150.

waters of Merom," or "the upper or highest lake of the Jordan."[126]

The Arabian tapestry of Melville's Polynesian romance is readily apparent to every reader in names like Babbalanja, Donjalolo, and Alla-Malolla. These name formations, on the model of the *Arabian Nights,* stress the Oriental coloring of *Mardi* like a decorative collection of Oriental pipes and daggers in a drawing room. That Melville was interested in the picturesqueness of Oriental words and settings may be taken for granted. But his absorption with significances is paramount in every detail of his work and is an integral part of his symbolic method. Inevitably, therefore, the Arabian character of *Mardi* is not only an intimation of "the part-&-parcel allegoricalness of the whole"[127] but seems to probe at its very axis.

FEDALLAH AND HIS REFLECTIONS

Among the books Melville obtained from Bentley in London in 1849 was a copy of William Beckford's *Vathek.* The influence of this romance on *Moby-Dick,* which was composed within the period immediately following its acquisition, may be traced in several parallels. Like the satanically obsessed captain of the *Pequod,* Vathek, "though well versed in the course of the heavens, no longer knew his situation on earth. He thundered even louder than the elements." Like Ahab, who turns a deaf ear to the pleadings of his chief mate, Starbuck, Vathek disregards the warnings of a wise old man who says to him: "Woe to the rash mortal who seeks to know that of which he should remain ignorant; and to undertake that which surpasseth his power!"

126. *Cyclopaedia of Biblical Literature* (Edinburgh, 1848), p. 577; see also *Illustrated Commentary on the Old and New Testaments* (London, 1840), *2, 19.* Cf. *Clarel, 1, 270,* where the geologist Margoth computes the fall of the Jordan from Merom's spring.

127. *Letters,* p. 146.

Melville describes the fascination of Ahab's glance—a characteristic of the Carlylean hero as Prophet—of which the three mates stood in mortal fear. "For did ye three but once take the full-forced shock," says Ahab of his eye, "then mine own electric thing, *that* had perhaps expired from out of me. Perchance, too, it would have dropped ye dead." Vathek's glance, too, had an exaggerated power: "When he was angry, one of his eyes became so terrible, that no person could bear to behold it, and the wretch upon whom it was fixed, instantly fell backward, and sometimes expired."[1]

In *Moby-Dick* the satanism of Ahab is underlined by a machinery of pagan rites which is centered on Fedallah, a fire-worshiping Parsee, and includes a mysterious Spirit Spout, first descried by Fedallah. Similarly, the khalif, by virtue of his birth the spiritual leader of Islam, abandons his faith and indulges in heretical fire worship. The Spirit Spout, a symbol of delusion, corresponds to the mysterious supernatural light which in *Vathek* lures its victim into the power of wickedness and catastrophe.[2] The climax of the tale is Vathek's doom in the subterranean Hall of Eblis, which was already lingering in Melville's mind when he was writing *White Jacket*[3] and which, in its note of silent horror, cast its reflections on the ending of *Moby-Dick*:

1. *Moby-Dick*, chap. 36. *Vathek* (Bentley's Standard Novels, No. 41), p. 1.
2. *Moby-Dick*, chap. 51. *Vathek*, p. 56.
3. *White Jacket*, chap. 73. "Eblis" (īblīs), probably a corruption of "diabolos," appears in the Koran in the story of creation (Sura 15). Byron explains that he took it from *Vathek* (notes to *The Giaour*). Cf. "Kaf the peak of Eblis" in "Look-Out Mountain," *Collected Poems*, p. 58. In Islamic tradition Kaf, a mythical mountain range surrounding the earth, forms the boundary between the visible and invisible worlds. The term found its way into *Vathek* from the *Arabian Nights;* cf. *Anastasius, 1,* note to chap. 12; also "L'Envoi," *Collected Poems*, p. 256.

A deathlike stillness reigned over the mountain and through the air; the moon dilated on a vast platform the shade of the lofty columns which reached from the terrace almost to the clouds; the gloomy watch-towers were veiled by no roof, and their capitals, of an architecture unknown in the records of the earth, served as an asylum for the birds of darkness, which, alarmed at the approach of such visitants, fled away croaking.[4]

The use of Islamic coloring in the creation of the most outlandish Oriental character in *Moby-Dick,* a Parsee with a Mohammedan name, suggests itself as a matter of course in the light of Melville's reading of *Vathek.* Vathek, like Ahab, in the delirium of his blind ambition "to fathom the decrees of the Most High," surrounds himself with all sorts of "subterranean" dervishes and mysterious figures each of whom had "some mummery peculiar to himself." Like Ahab's Fedallah, the khalif's evil spirit is a "malignant phantom" who appears to him in the shape of an Indian, "but from a region of India which is wholly unknown."[5] In the end this Indian turns out to be the Giaour, a "wicked Diva with his malignant grin" who conducts Vathek to his inevitable doom.[6] But, unlike Ahab's Parsee, he is utterly devilish. There is no trace of the tragic mysticism that suffuses "Fedallah," the essence of the "evil shadow" to whom Ahab surrenders his soul.

Here is how Melville describes Fedallah:

The figure . . . was tall and swart, with one white tooth evilly protruding from its steel-like lips. A rumpled Chinese jacket of black cotton funereally invested him, with wide black trowsers of the same dark stuff. But strangely crowning his ebonness was a glistening white

4. *Vathek,* p. 87.
5. Ibid., p. 12.
6. Ibid., p. 93.

plaited turban, the living hair braided and coiled round and round upon his head. Less swart in aspect, the companions of this figure were of that vivid, tiger-yellow complexion peculiar to some of the aboriginal natives of the Manillas;—a race notorious for a certain diabolism of subtilty, and by some honest white mariners supposed to be the paid spies and secret confidential agents on the water of the devil, their lord, whose counting-room they suppose to be elsewhere.[7]

In describing the physical appearance of Fedallah and the sinister trait of "subtilty" in his character, Melville, it has been shown, was probably indebted to the portrayals of Manila and Sulu natives in one of his favorite source-books: Charles Wilkes' six-volume *Narrative of the United States Exploring Expedition during the Years 1838–1842.*[8]

But the character has an unquestionably Arabic name, which, moreover, in its Arabic connotations is vibrant with hidden meaning. Its significance cannot be excluded in considering the mystic reflections of Melville's linked analogies.[9] Again we have to remind ourselves of Cassirer's statement about the mythmaking consciousness: "the name does not merely denote but actually *is* the essence of the object, . . . the potency of the real thing is contained in the name."

Where did Melville find the name Fedallah? The answer to this question is an important clue to the most openly Islamic figure in his works.

In the opinion of Henry A. Murray, "Fedallah" suggests "dev(il) Allah." In view of the "wicked Diva" in *Vathek*

7. *Moby-Dick,* chap. 48.

8. See David Jaffe, "Some Origins of *Moby-Dick:* New Finds in an Old Source," *American Literature, 29* (1957), 274–75.

9. Henry A. Murray, "In Nomine Diaboli," *Moby-Dick Centennial Essays,* ed. Tyrus Hillway and Luther S. Mansfield (Dallas, 1953), p. 11. See also my article, Dorothee Grdseloff, "On the Origin of Fedallah in *Moby-Dick,*" *American Literature, 28* (1955), 396–403.

who hails "from a region of India which is wholly unknown," the nature of Ahab's diabolic Parsee may be also
expressed in an association with "Deev" or "Dive." This
Zoroastrian term was generally known to Melville's contemporaries as a designation for evil spirits and the powers of
darkness, not only from Oriental romances like *Vathek* and
Anastasius but also from the *Literary World* and the *Knickerbocker Magazine*.[10] In Islamic imagery the dives were a
species of "jinn" or genii, a race of spirits which was supposed to pervade the universe and was an indispensable part
of the romantic machinery. Fedallah and his companions
easily lend themselves to this interpretation, for Ahab's five
dusky phantoms, in the traditional manner of Arabian jinn,
"seemed fresh formed out of air."[11]

The name and the major conception of Fedallah have
also been connected with an essay in the *Spectator* of 1714.[12]
This essay, by an unidentified author, is based on a Persian
tale called "Fadlallah and Zemroude" in which Fadlallah, a
virtuous king of Mosul, is betrayed by "a lively and entertaining" young dervish who flings his own soul into the
royal body while demonstrating to the king the secret of
transmigration. Melville's interest in the transmigration of
souls is suggested in *Mardi,* when the taciturn sailor Jarl is
described, in repose, as if "his intellects stepped out, and
left his body to itself."[13] The relation of Fedallah to Ahab is
obviously a problem of alter ego: "as if in the Parsee Ahab
saw his forethrown shadow, in Ahab the Parsee his abandoned substance."[14]

10. See *Anastasius, 1,* 145. *Literary World, 3* (1848), 124. *Knickerbocker, 20* (1842), 447.
11. *Moby-Dick,* chap. 47.
12. *Moby-Dick,* ed. Mansfield and Vincent, Explanatory Notes, p.
731.
13. *Mardi, 1,* 42.
14. *Moby-Dick,* chap. 130.

The editors of *Moby-Dick*, Luther Mansfield and Howard Vincent, suggest that the *Spectator* essay was Melville's
source for the character:

> Perhaps he [Melville] did not even consciously re-
> member the story, for to his own character clearly sug-
> gested by the wicked but unnamed dervish, he gave his
> approximation of the virtuous king's name. That he
> was using the Arabic form of the Persian original he
> probably did not know, and he must surely have been
> ignorant of the fact that the name meant "Generosity
> of God," and that under the Islamic dispensation, it
> would have been an impossible name for a Parsee.[15]

This theory is clearly untenable. There is no "Islamic dispensation" which makes it "impossible" for a Parsee to bear
an Islamic name. In Moslem law the fire-worshiping Zoro-
astrians were treated like Jews and Christians, "the people
of the Book," as distinguished from the heathen.[16] They
could if they wished bear Islamic names, as did many Jews
living in Moslem countries, and though Melville probably
hardly concerned himself with this fact, there is no historical
reason why he should have hesitated to give his Parsee an
Islamic name. Also, Melville's Fedallah is not "clearly" suggested by the wicked dervish in the Persian tale. Melville
makes it clear that Fedallah was old. He is a "white-turbaned
old man . . . with one white tooth evilly protruding."[17] The
dervish in the Persian tale of the *Spectator* is described as
young. Melville stresses Fedallah's hypnotic silence. The
dervish in the tale is "lively and entertaining."[18] Finally,

15. Ibid., Explanatory Notes, p. 732.
16. See A. S. Tritton, *The Caliphs and Their Non-Muslim Subjects*
(London, 1930), pp. 97 f. Magians were listed among the "dhimmis"
or "the people of protection" (p. 5).
17. *Moby-Dick*, chap. 48.
18. *Spectator*, No. 578, August 9, 1714.

the name Fedallah is not an "approximation" and is not "the Arabic form of the Persian original." "Fadlallah" in the Persian tale is not Persian but Arabic, for Arabic names were current in Persia after the Moslem conquest. If Melville had used that name it is hardly likely, in view of his great interest in meaning, that he would have been ignorant of the fact that the name meant "Generosity of God." Both Fadlallah and Fedallah are pure Arabic forms and represent two different names bearing two different meanings. Fadlallah is a common Arabic name meaning "the Bounty of God." Fedallah means "the Sacrifice [or Ransom] of God."

It is, of course, possible that Melville came across the name Fadlallah in the *Spectator* and perhaps also in sources relating to the story of Tamerlane, Ahab's lame prototype. A well-known Persian dervish of the fourteenth century, who invited "the accursed lame man" to adopt his doctrine and was slain by Tamerlane's son, was named Fadlallah. This Fadlallah was the founder of a secret order, the Hurufi, which concerned itself with the mystical meaning of letters, and considered himself an incarnation of the deity.[19]

However, the name that Melville used is not Fadlallah but Fedallah, which derives from a different root and seems a more plausible designation for the character than "the Bounty of God." The name is a compound made up of two elements: feda (*fidā'*), the Arabic word for "sacrifice" or "ransom," which in its Latinized form appears in the name of the famous Arab historian of the crusades, Abulfeda (Abu'l-Fidā), who was mentioned in the *Literary World*.[20] The second element, "Allah," is familiar in Arabic names. In its Latinized transliteration Fedallah has definite seman-

19. E. G. Browne, "Some Notes on the Literature and Doctrines of the Hurufi Sect," *Journal of the Royal Asiatic Society*, 3d ser. 8 (1898), 61–89.

20. *Literary World, 4* (1849), 111.

tic overtones which seem worth investigating. It suggests
the Arabic terms "fedai (*fidā'i*)" and "dai (*dā'i*)" which
aroused considerable attention in Melville's time. "Fedai"
means "the devoted one" or "he who offers up his life." It is
a term of great interest, for it was applied to the avenging
ministers or "destroying angels" of the "Old Man of the
Mountain," chief of the Persian Assassins who had been
described by the crusaders, Marco Polo, Samuel Purchas,
and other famous travelers to the Near East.[21]

"The chiefe or Grand Master of them being called The
Old Man," says *Purchas His Pilgrimes,* "was obeyed in
whatsoeuer hee commanded, were the attempt neuer so
dangerous. If he gaue to one or more of them a weapon, and
enioyned the killing of such an Enemie, Prince or priuate
man, they gladly vndertooke it, with the death of that
partie, or themselues in attempt. Both Saracens and Christians called them (the reason of the name vnknowne)
Assysines."[22]

The characteristics and terminology of the Assassins were
discussed at length by Melville's contemporaries, particularly as the meaning of the word "Assassin" became public
knowledge when, in the second decade of the century, it was
finally explained by the most famous Orientalist of the time,
the Frenchman Silvestre de Sacy (1758–1838), who showed
that the term derived from "Hashish," the Arabic word for
hemp.[23] The "Assassins" were simply "smokers of hemp"—
a secret order of Islamic mystics pledged to commit murder
in the service of Allah. They consumed hashish or hemp in

21. On the spell which the Old Man of the Mountain exercised on
Coleridge see Lowes, *The Road to Xanadu,* chap. 19, sec. 2, and notes.
22. Purchas, *11,* 207–8.
23. Silvestre de Sacy, "Mémoire sur la dynastie des Assassins, et sur
l'étymologie de leur nom," in *Mémoire de l'Institut Royal,* Classe
d'histoire et de littérature ancienne (Paris, 1818), *4,* 1–84.

order to induce a state of ecstatic tranquillity that would
bring them into communion with the divine.

"Dai" means "he who calls," or missionary. The term was
applied to propagandists of Islamic mysticism who headed
five orders of religious dignitaries. They were "men with a
profound knowledge of the human heart and of the methods whereby their peculiar doctrines might be best insin-
uated into minds of the most diverse character," says Professor Browne in his *Literary History of Persia*.[24]

Hurufi, Fedai, and Dai, then, are names connected with
various facets of a medieval Islamic movement that attracted
the attention of Western scholars throughout the nineteenth century. This movement was an amalgam of several
mystic Islamic sects, some perhaps of pre-Islamic Persian
origin, and is generally known as the Ismailiya or Ismailism.
Apart from the early accounts given by medieval historians
like William of Tyre and travelers like Marco Polo and
Purchas, the subdivisions of the movement were described
in eighteenth-century travel books, for example Niebuhr's
account of his journey to Arabia from which Hawthorne,
and probably Melville, drew information on the Bombay
Parsis.[25] The first authoritative account, however, appeared when de Sacy published his famous *mémoire* on the
dynasty of the Assassins and the etymology of their name in
1818. Melville undoubtedly knew of de Sacy, if only from
the *Literary World* and Carlyle's lecture on Mohammed.[26]
In any case, at a time when the characteristics of Islamic
mysticism were discussed far and wide, like the Dead Sea
Scrolls today, he could hardly help coming across them in
his diversified reading. His intense interest in dervishes and
mystics of all kinds was bound to acquaint him with the

24. *Literary History of Persia*, 2, 196.
25. *Travels through Arabia*, *1*, 184–90.
26. *Literary World*, *3* (1848), 27. Carlyle, Lecture II.

secretive character of the movement, its quasi-masonic or-
ganization, and the haze of mystery concealing both doctrines and personalities from the uninitiated.[27]

The Ismailiya received its name from the belief that the
series of Imams, the revealed prophets of Islam who followed Mohammed, would stop with the seventh Imam,
Ismāʿīl, the Arabic for Ishmael, to whom the religious texts
refer as "the hidden prophet."[28] The doctrine of the Ismailiya has many traits which conform with Indian beliefs.
The Ismaili mystics believe in metempsychosis and the incarnation of the divinity; they explain the appearance of
man by the need which the universal soul feels to attain
perfect knowledge—all motifs familiar in both *Mardi* and
Moby-Dick.

De Sacy's famous account dealt with the branch of the
Ismailiya best known in the Western world—the Assassins.
At the time of the first crusade, in the eleventh century, this
sect occupied a hill fortress in northern Persia. "Here, and
in similar bases established in Syria in the following century, the 'Old Man of the Mountain,' as the Grand Masters
of the sect were called, commanded bands of devoted and
fanatical followers, waging a campaign of terror and 'assassination' against the kings and princes of Islam in the name
of a mysterious hidden Imām."[29] His ministers of vengeance, the Fedais, were sent to all parts of the world on
missions of assassination as a religious duty. They were distinguished by the determination with which they exposed
their lives in order to destroy their victims, the voyages
which they undertook to achieve their purpose, and the

27. B. Lewis, *The Origins of Ismāʿīlism* (Cambridge, 1940), p. 2.

28. An Imam is originally a person who serves as a guide.

29. B. Lewis, *The Arabs in History* (London, 1958), p. 149. See also
by the same author "The Sources for the History of the Syrian Assassins," *Speculum*, 27 (1952), 475 f.

calmness with which they waited for the moment favorable for their design.[30]

In *Moby-Dick* all these qualities are characteristic of Fedallah, whose age, moreover, is highly suggestive of the Assassin "Old Man." Equally pertinent to Fedallah, who was smuggled aboard the *Pequod* away from the eyes of the crew, is the principle of concealment characteristic of Islamic mysticism. The Old Man of the Assassins did not publicly proclaim his mission.

The name and function of the Fedais were explained to Melville's contemporaries in such widely read books as Malcolm's *History of Persia:*

> The term Fedawee, which is now vulgarly understood to signify any warrior of extraordinary courage and ability, literally and properly means a person who gives, or is ready to give, his life as a ransom for his companions, or for their cause; and is here applied to a class of warriors who owed no allegiance to any sovereign unless to a chief of their own choice; the same class who are called, in our histories of the Crusades, "Assassins": which appellation the very learned orientalist De Sacy has, I think, rightly pronounced to be a corruption of "Hashshasheen," a name derived from their making frequent use of the intoxicating hemp, called "hasheesh."[31]

Also in the *Modern Egyptians* Lane describes the Fedais as using hemp "to make a formidable enemy or rival their prisoner . . . so that they were able to bind him at their leisure, and convey him whither they would."[32] In Lane's edition of the *Arabian Nights* a note "On the Use of Hemp

30. De Sacy, "Mémoire," pp. 55, 82 f. *Literary History of Persia,* 2, 209.

31. *History of Persia, 1,* 241, 295.

32. *Modern Egyptians,* 2, 161.

to induce Intoxication" defines the Assassins as "hemp-eaters, or persons who intoxicate themselves with hemp."[33]

Another reference to the properties of hemp is found in the *History and Present Conditions of the Barbary States* by the Right Reverend Michael Russell, whose work on *Polynesia* (1843) Melville elaborately cited in *Omoo*.[34] "The hashisha, or African hemp-plant, is very generally cultivated in the western parts of the Barbary States," says Russell, "not so much for its use in the manufacture of cordage, as for those qualities in which it resembles opium."[35]

In view of all this, it is hardly surprising that the "original" meaning of hemp seems to be suggested in *Moby-Dick*. The clue is in Fedallah's prophecy to Ahab: "Hemp only can kill thee."[36] If we take "hemp" in Fedallah's mysterious pronouncement to suggest its Arabic meaning, the interpretation of the prophecy acquires a new significance. For Fedallah is Fate's devoted "assassin" sent to "assassinate" Ahab, the heretic, who will be killed by the secret weapon which makes assassination possible—hashish, or hemp—i.e. intoxication beyond the reach of reason.

In describing Fedallah and his companions as "paid spies and secret confidential agents on the water of the devil, their lord," Melville may indeed have been prompted, on the literal level, by a reference in Charles Wilkes' *Narrative* concerning Sulu pirates who were equipped by princes who,

33. *Arabian Nights,* chap. 2, n. 46.

34. *Omoo,* chap. 48, n. 1: *"Polynesia: or an Historical Account of the Principal Islands of the South Sea.* By the Right Rev. M. Russell, LL.D. (Harper's Family Library Edition)."

35. *History of the Present Condition of the Barbary States* (New York, 1835), p. 327.

36. *Moby-Dick,* chap. 117; cf. chap. 60, "The Line": "Hemp is a dusky, dark fellow, a sort of Indian; but Manilla is as a golden-haired Circassian to behold."

in their turn, were receiving a stipend for the suppression of piracy.[37] It is hardly probable, however, that on the allegorical level he was totally unaware of the significance of the Assassin Fedais as spies and confidential agents of their chief, the Old Man of the Mountain, when so much was written about them. Moreover, one of Beckford's notes to *Vathek*, on the authority of Habesci's *State of the Ottoman Empire*, describes the mutes retained at Eastern courts as "the secret instruments" of the monarch's private vengeance "in carrying the fatal string."[38]

The "mute" and "motionless" face of Fedallah reflects the "fatalistic despair" of "unchanging Asiatic communities."[39] The secret instrument of the catastrophe which through him is wreaked upon Ahab is hemp, "cultivated," to repeat the Reverend Michael Russell, "not so much for its use in the manufacture of cordage as for those qualities in which it resembles opium"—the secret weapon which, through intoxication, leads the fanatical victim to his doom.

Fedallah is one of the most intricate "original" symbols in *Moby-Dick*, for behind the Islamic associations of a Polynesian creature stands the fire-worshiping Parsee. In his copy of Hope's *Anastasius*, which he acquired at the same time as *Vathek*, Melville marked a passage on the Yezidis, the Arab devil worshipers who were also visited and described by Layard.[40] "If you have never seen that sight, then suspend your decision about the propriety of devil-worship, and the expediency of conciliating the devil," he says in *Moby-Dick* to describe the diabolism of sharks.[41] To the

37. Jaffe, p. 275.
38. Beckford refers the reader to Elias Habesci's *The Present State of the Ottoman Empire*, London, 1784; cf. Melville's image of Turkish mutes bowstringing their victim in *Moby-Dick*, chap. 135.
39. *Moby-Dick*, chaps. 50, 118.
40. See above, p. 160.
41. *Moby-Dick*, chap. 64.

crew of the *Pequod,* Fedallah is the devil, and his fire worship and Ahab's devil worship are inextricably linked.[42]
None of the interpretations of the character—Polynesian,
Islamic, Zoroastrian or Yezidi—excludes the other. On the
contrary, their fusion reveals the accumulative technique
of Melville's characterization.

This fusion is found in the chapter entitled "The Candles" in which the fire symbolism of the book is concentrated. Ahab grasps the links of the lightning chain, places
his foot upon the kneeling Fedallah, and addresses the
"clear spirit of clear fire."[43] In this picture the satanism of
Ahab is expressed through the rites of fire worship and
Islamic mysticism. The lightning chain is clearly associated
with the chain of dervishes which, for example, is described
in *Vathek* and Buckingham's *Travels.*[44] The "last link" to
which Ahab "held fast" may even represent the "chain of
order" (Arabic: silsila, chain) which, in the apostolic succession of Islamic heads from the prophet Mohammed to
the present day, binds a dervish up to Allah himself. The
relationship of the individual dervish to the links of the
chain is through his teacher who introduces him into the
fraternity. The introduction is effected through a covenant
consisting of religious professions in close contact with the
teacher.[45] In this case the teacher is Fedallah, both fire-
worshiper and dervish: "Such an added gliding strangeness
began to invest the thin Fedallah now; such ceaseless shud-
derings shook him."[46]

42. Ibid., chap. 73.
43. Ibid., chap. 119.
44. *Vathek,* p. 99. Buckingham, *Travels, 1,* 275.
45. See D. B. Macdonald, "Derwish," *The Encyclopaedia of Islam,*
1, 950.
46. *Moby-Dick,* chap. 130. The character of Fedallah as a dervish is
reflected in the image of the lean Parsee in Melville's poem "The
Rose Farmer." See below, p. 259.

Melville obviously invested Fedallah with the characteristics of Moslem santons. In fact, the whole crew of the
Pequod evokes the image of a mystic sect in quest of divine
revelation. The nine gams of the *Pequod* suggest nine
stages of initiation; Fedallah and his four creatures, the
"five dusky phantoms," recall the five Ismaili orders headed
by the Dai, the missionary.

In de Sacy's account of the Ismailiya the members of the
sect were called "companions in a voyage," or simply *refiq*,
companions. This term applied to all excluding the "phantom" clergy and the assassins.[47] The position of Fedallah
and his "phantoms" is analogous among the *Pequod's* crew.
For they are segregated into a separate "distinct" unit which
fills the others with trepidation and awe.[48] Indeed, the word
"phantom" actually appears in de Sacy's description of the
spiritual ministers of the Ismailiya, and so does a classification in "superior" and "inferior" orders[49] which recalls
Melville's designation of "subordinate phantoms" for the
five "queer" mariners that were "hidden" aboard.

It is perhaps unlikely that Melville read de Sacy. But he
may well have browsed in other contemporary sources relating to the Ismailiya movement, like Hammer-Purgstall's
History of the Assassins, which appeared in an English
translation in 1835 and was available at the New York
Society Library.[50] At the end of his life there can be no
question that he was familiar with the Ismailiya, for the
"Ismailians," the Old Man of the Mountain, and the derivation of the name "Assassin" from hashish were discussed,

47. De Sacy, "Mémoire," pp. 82 f.
48. *Moby-Dick,* chap. 50.
49. See de Sacy, *Exposé de la religion des Druzes, 2,* 393, 401.
50. Hammer's *Geschichte der Assassinen aus morgenlaendischen
Quellen* originally appeared in 1818. The English translation was by
O. C. Wood. See *Alphabetical and Analytical Catalogue of the New
York Society Library,* p. 460.

like other aspects of Sufism, in Fitzgerald's preface to Omar Khayyam which Melville read and marked.[51]

It cannot be sufficiently stressed that Islam was a popular literary subject in the nineteenth century. The scholarly researches of de Sacy and Hammer-Purgstall received wide attention and were quoted by the most prominent men of letters, including Goethe and Emerson.[52] Melville's own interest in the various manifestations of Islam when he wrote *Moby-Dick* is attested by his markings in *Anastasius* where, for instance, he marked a whole passage dealing with the doctrine of the fanatical Puritan Wahabees.[53] Indeed, the "poor Wahabee" of "The Timoneer's Story" in *Clarel* reflects Fedallah's sinister influence. Like his prototype, he is "smuggled aboard" a vessel which is called *The Peace of God*.[54]

It is unlikely that Melville would have coined an Islamic name to express the "muffled mystery" of Fedallah in ignorance of its "hidden significances," particularly as the meaning of the elements which make up the name was a subject of extraordinary interest to his age. Fedallah would then be "the one who sacrifices himself for God." He would symbolize the "destroying angel" sent by God to bring about the "assassination" of Ahab, the heretic, not only in body, but through the deep damnation of his spirit and soul by the satanic intoxication of hatred and pride which possess the captain of the *Pequod* in his fanatical pursuit of the White Whale. Fedallah is as "mute" and "motionless" as eternity, the sun, moon, and stars, which are, in fact, called "assassins" by Stubb. In the accomplishment of his mission, Fedallah, the diabolic infidel mystic, offers up his life in

51. See Melville's copy of the *Rubaiyat* (Boston, 1878), pp. 6–7.
52. Goethe, *West-Oestlicher Divan, Noten und Abhandlungen.* Emerson, *Letters, 3,* 341; *4,* 531; *6,* 216. *Journals, 9,* 539.
53. Melville's copy of *Anastasius, 2,* 210–11.
54. *Clarel, 2,* 60–61.

"fatalistic despair." He thus becomes a true Islamic *fidā'i*, a being that sacrifices itself as a ransom for a cause—the submissive instrument of a higher will.

THE ATTAR-GUL AND THE ROSE

The rose symbolism in Melville's work, particularly in his poetry where it is most in evidence, is as important a feature of his art as the architectonic images which recur in the novels, stories, and poems. His preoccupation with grapes and roses is first noticeable in *Mardi*, but it is most marked in *Clarel*, in the story "Under the Rose," and the later poetry culminating in the posthumously published collection of poems which he had planned and entitled "A Rose or Two." The image of the blooming and fading rose is linked with the bacchic imagery and, particularly in the later poetry, with the attar-gul, the Persian name for the essence of the rose.

In *Mardi* the rose imagery is an integral part of the general flower symbolism which pervades the novel. Its relationship to Islamic sources and concepts has already been pointed out. This symbolism not only emanates from Hautia, the sensuous queen of the black-eyed damsels of Mardi's Moslem paradise, but is also centered around Yoomy, the poet, the interpreter of Hautia's flower messages and composer of a song to the "royal rose." Yoomy is an Oriental poet, "plumed and turbaned."[1] His name connects him with the Persian poet Jami. Yoomy's verses on the rose, sung while "picking the thorny roses culled from Hautia's gifts; and holding up their blighted cores,"[2] intensify the Persian atmosphere of Melville's "romance," for Yoomy's rose imagery presents us with the very genre of poetry which is commonly associated with the Persian poets.

1. *Mardi, 1, 312.*
2. Ibid.

The relationship of the grape imagery to Persian poetry is made abundantly clear in *Mardi*. The narrator, later Taji, finds "an aromatic cask of prime old Otard" on the abandoned ship *Parki,* and for a moment considers the advisability of mixing the wine with sea brine in order to prevent his companions from intoxication. In the end he decides to leave the wine undisturbed: "What: dilute the brine with the double distilled soul of the precious grape? Hafiz himself would have haunted me!"[3] The usual nineteenth-century designation of Hafiz as the "Anacreon of Persia" also appears in *Mardi*. Anacreon and Hafiz are coupled by Melville in the important chapter on "Dreams" which is a key to the multiplicity of Melville's symbolic expression.[4]

Melville had probably come across Jones' translation of "A Persian Song of Hafiz" by the time he was writing *Mardi*. A representative view in the first half of the nineteenth century described it as "one of those pieces that, by a nameless charm, fasten themselves on the memory."[5] There is a "Persian" tone in the couplet composed for Yoomy:

> Yoomy: Full round, full soft, her dewy arms,
> Sweet shelter from all Mardi's harms.[6]

Compare the opening lines of Hafiz:

> Hafiz: Sweet maid, if thou would'st charm my sight,
> And bid these arms thy neck unfold;
> That rosy cheek, that lily hand,
> Would give thy poet more delight
> Than all Bocara's vaunted gold,
> Than all the gems of Samarcand.[7]

3. Ibid., p. 123.
4. Ibid., 2, 54.
5. H. F. Cary, "Sir William Jones," in *Lives of English Poets* (London, 1846), p. 385.
6. *Mardi*, 2, 84; cf. *Clarel*, 2, 269.
7. Jones, *Works, 10,* 251.

Melville was aware of the Persian connotations of rose and wine imagery long before he read Saadi's *Gulistan* and Fitzgerald's *Omar Khayyam*. Yoomy's "Persian air" wafts its perfume on the story of "Jimmy Rose" (1855), where Jimmy's cheeks are compared to "Persian roses."[8] "The double distilled soul of the precious grape" to which the narrator refers in *Mardi*[9] seems to imply a knowledge of the double significance which was held to be contained in the Persian poets, i.e. the sensuous and the mystical connotations of their wine and rose imagery in the manner of the biblical Song of Songs.

Yoomy's reference to his enemies who accounted his poetic fancies as "lewd conceits"[10] recalls the accusations leveled against the sensuousness and ribaldry of Hafiz by the Moslem mystics, the Sufis. Hafiz, like most medieval Persian poets, was himself a professed Sufi. He belonged to the sect of Moslem ascetics and mystics whose creed advocated the contemplation of beauty as a guide to the essence of God and the veneration of wine as a vehicle for the manifestation of the divine spirit. In Sufi symbolism the relation between God and the soul was described in terms of earthly love, beauty, and intoxication. What had happened was that "the early Sufi poets had taken the current phraseology of the contemporary singers of Love and Wine, and by imparting a mystic signification to the terms thus adopted, they had constructed a species of symbolic language."[11] In the case of Hafiz, his "odes" were probably arranged with at least a view to Sufistic interpretation. At the same time it is "ridiculous" to suppose "that the glowing imagery, the gorgeous and often tender descriptions of natural beauties,

8. Leyda, *Complete Stories,* p. 249.
9. *Mardi, 1,* 123.
10. Ibid., *2,* 136.
11. Sir Denison Ross, "Note on Persian Poetry," *A Persian Anthology* (London, 1927), p. 47.

the fervent love passages, and the roystering drinking songs
were composed in cool blood or with deliberate ascetic
purpose."[12]

Melville's awareness of the mystic interpretations of this
type of poetry is apparent when one examines the chapter in
Mardi which describes the bacchanalian revels of Donjalolo's royal banquet: To Taji "the drinking of this wine
was as the singing of a mighty ode, or frenzied lyric to the
soul."[13] Wine is offered to Taji by Donjalolo as a mystical
essence: "drink deep . . . in this wine lurk the seeds of the
life everlasting . . . thou drinkest that which will enable thee
to stand up and speak out before mighty Oro himself."[14]
In *Clarel* Melville explicitly alludes to the "mystic burden"
attributed to "the Bonzes Hafiz' rhyme . . . / Which lauds
the grape of Shiraz."[15] There is also a whole poem on Hafiz,
attributed to Derwent, which expresses the symbolism of
the grape and the rose and clearly indicates its association
with Persian poetry in Melville's mind:

> To Hafiz in grape-arbour comes
> Didymus, with book he thumbs:
> My lord Hafiz, priest of bowers—
> Flowers in such world as ours?—
> Who is the god of all these flowers?—
> Signior Didymus, who knows?
> None the less I take repose—

12. See article on "Hafiz" in *Encyclopaedia Britannica, 11,* 69.

13. *Mardi, 1,* 299. The poems of Hafiz were commonly described as
"odes" in the nineteenth century. See S. Robinson, *Persian Poetry for
English Readers* (Glasgow, 1883), p. 385. Modern scholars generally
equate the "ghazal" with the sonnet (Arberry, *Fifty Poems of Hafiz,*
p. 1) and describe the "qasida" as an ode (see ed. Arberry, *Persian
Poems,* p. vi). The poems of Hafiz were designated as "odes" by Sir
William Jones.

14. *Mardi, 1,* 299.

15. *Clarel, 2,* 265–66.

> Believe, and worship here with wine
> In vaulted chapel of the vine
> Before the altar of the rose.[16]

The significance of the bacchic imagery is most pronounced in *Clarel*. It is the theme of five cantos in the second volume, of which four are part of the section "Mar Saba," and one of the final section, "Bethlehem." The second volume of *Clarel* was mainly written after the acquisition of Saadi's *Gulistan* in 1868, at a time in which Melville's interest in the Persian poets is clearly established. As is indicated by Melville himself, the second volume suggests the "Paradiso" following the hero's infernal experience of the Holy Land as the *terra damnata*.[17] The "ascent" leads through the desert convent Mar Saba to the city of hope, Bethlehem.

Mar Saba is not the entirely barren desert of faith that has been suggested.[18] The symbolic significance of the desert convent in the Judean wilderness is not completely identical with that of the Church of the Holy Sepulchre in the first volume. There the degradation of the holiest place in Christendom, which Clarel witnesses in Jerusalem, proclaims the absolute sterility and failure of religious faith. But the stark horrors of the petrified Judean landscape in which the desert convent is situated are humanized in scenes of revelry and boon companionship, and lastly even transcended in the vision of the Palm. This effect is achieved by what has been called "the interillumination of opposing values,"[19] a vital principle in Melville's symbolic technique, which resolves the barrenness of Mar Saba in the final epilogue of human feeling and hope.

16. Ibid., p. 66.
17. See reference to *Divine Comedy* in *Clarel*, 2, 123.
18. Baird, pp. 415–18.
19. Ibid., pp. 184–85.

In the transition from the *terra damnata* to Bethlehem,
the revelries Melville describes at Mar Saba have a crucial
function. Their meaning may be delineated on three principal planes: First, they are a variation on Melville's favorite
theme—the attempt of humanity to evade reality through
hedonism. In a literal and figurative sense the revels at Mar
Saba are a defense against the surrounding desert, i.e. the
reality of death. It is particularly significant that they center around two figures who represent the evasion of reality
in the easy complacency of institutionalized faith: the gay
Greek purveyor of the convent, the Lesbian, and the self-
satisfied Anglican clergyman, Derwent, who is the least
complex of the pilgrims. Second, as will be shown below,
the symbolism of the cantos expresses the striving of the
soul for union with the divine as practiced within the mystical orders of organized religion. Third, the revels, as an
expression of a feeling of brotherhood and love of man for
man, project the final resolution of despair and skepticism
in the Epilogue of Hope in *Clarel:*

> Then keep thy heart, though yet but ill-resigned—
> Clarel, thy heart, the issues there but mind;
> That like the crocus budding through the snow—
> That like a swimmer rising from the deep—
> That like a burning secret which doth go
> Even from the bosom that would hoard and keep;
> Emerge thou mayest from the last whelming sea,
> And prove that death but routs life into victory.[20]

One of the most interesting features in Melville's use of
the grape and rose imagery in *Clarel* is the distinction which
emerges between its purely sensuous connotations and its
sensuous-mystical significance. Pure physical sensuousness
is associated with the bacchanalia of Greek paganism, as is

20. *Clarel,* 2, 298.

seen in the canto "The Cypriote."[21] On the other hand,
"The Beaker," in which the revels at Mar Saba are described, centers on the religious significance of the imagery:

> A shady rock, and trickling too,
> Is good to meet in desert drear:
> Prithee now, the beading here—
> Beads of Saba, saintly dew:
> Quaff it, sweetheart, I and you:
> Quaff it, for thereby ye bless
> Beadsmen here in wilderness.
> Spite of sorrow, maugre sin,
> Bless their larder and laud their bin:
> Nor deem that here they vainly pine
> Who toil for heaven and till the vine.[22]

Throughout *Clarel* the grape and rose imagery group in
various combinations three pervasive Melvillean themes:
the organic interrelation of death and life, the mystical
search of the soul for the godhead, and the eternal brotherhood of man.

The complex implications of the bacchic imagery are
clearly visible in regard to Vine, one of the main characters
in *Clarel,* in whom Melville projected his image of Hawthorne as a man whose fullness and ripeness "runs the
gamut from physical sensuousness to spiritual sensibility."[23]
The formation of Vine may be traced in Melville's correspondence from the beginning of their relationship in 1850.
In a letter to Evert Duyckinck on February 12, 1851, Melville refers to Hawthorne's "Twice-Told Tales" as "an
earlier vintage from his vine."[24] In a later letter to Hawthorne, there is a facetious reference to a vision Melville

21. Ibid., p. 18.
22. Ibid., p. 53.
23. Bezanson, p. 180.
24. *Letters,* p. 121.

had of Hawthorne and himself sitting down in Paradise
with a bottle of champagne. He concludes that the summer
heat they then experienced was "indispensable to the nour-
ishment of the vine which is to bear the grapes that are to
give us the champagne hereafter."[25] Finally, the feeling of
fraternity between them is expressed in terms of boon companionship in the great letter of November 1851, in which
Melville replied to Hawthorne's praise of *Moby-Dick:*
"Whence come you, Hawthorne? By what right do you
drink from my flagon of life? . . . I feel that the Godhead is
broken up like the bread at the Supper, and that we are the
pieces. Hence this infinite fraternity of feeling."[26]

In the interpretation of the character of Vine it is significant that the metaphysical quality of the imagery connected
with his name is spiritual rather than mystic. Vine's syba-
rism is of the spirit, not of the soul. The song which Derwent induces him to sing at the Mar Saba revels lacks the
Persian connotations suggested by Derwent's hymn to
Hafiz.[27] Vine's song is associated with Florence. It expresses
the spiritual sensibility of the artist and moralist rather
than the passionate search of the soul.

The overtones of the grape and rose imagery connected
with Vine are biblical and Hellenic rather than Persian.
Melville's familiarity with the Bible made him aware of the
Hebraic connotation of "vine" as the symbol of peaceful
content and self-sufficiency.[28] The Hellenic aspect of the
symbolism as sensuous enjoyment is carried over into the
nature of the relationship that binds Clarel to Vine. In the
canto "Vine and Clarel" both are depicted lounging in a
luxuriously shady retreat on the bank of the river Jordan.
Both have been drinking wine, and Clarel is filled with a

25. Ibid., p. 128.
26. Ibid., p. 142.
27. *Clarel*, 2, 66.
28. See Micah 4:4; 1 Kings 4:25.

"thrill of personal longing" for Vine's love and esteem, but is rejected.[29] The psychological significance of this scene for Melville's relationship to Hawthorne is striking. But its direct impact on the meaning of *Clarel* lies in the expansion of the feeling of fraternity which binds Clarel to Vine to include the whole company of pilgrims at the revels of Mar Saba. The mystical properties of Saba's "saintly dew" unite East and West, American, Greek, and Oriental, Christian and Moslem in an all-embracing vision of human brotherhood.

The five cantos in *Clarel* whose meaning centers on the grape and rose imagery are "The Cypriote," "The Beaker," "Song and Recitative," "The Revel Closed," and "The Prodigal," all of them in the second volume entitled "Mar Saba and Bethlehem." The theme of this volume, Clarel's "paradiso," is struck at the very beginning:

> There shall the Tree wheron He hung,
> The olive wood, leaf out again—
> Again leaf out, and endless reign
> Type of the peace that buds from sinless pain?[30]

The final resolution of what Auden has called Melville's "terror"[31] is, of course, reached in *Billy Budd,* when Billy "ascending, took the full rose of the dawn." In *Clarel* the great debate is still on. But the second volume represents an emergence from the doom of Jerusalem and the Wilderness —the *Terra Damnata.* It depicts the dialectical progress toward the final resolution in terms of a symbolic tension between the imagery of the Judean desert and the Persian imagery of roses and wine. On their way to Mar Saba the pilgrims sit down

29. *Clarel, 1,* 284.
30. Ibid., *2, 3.*
31. "Herman Melville," *Collected Poetry of W. H. Auden* (New York, 1945), pp. 146–47.

> In lifted waste, on ashy ground
> Like Job's pale group, without a sound.[32]

Suddenly they hear the song of the Cypriote, a "hymn of
Aristippus" on wine and roses.[33] The Cypriote, an incarnation of youth and beauty, is returning from a pilgrimage to
Mar Saba. His voice is heard as he descends from a rock on
his mule. He had gone to Mar Saba at the request of his
mother to bring an offering of "three flagons good for holy
wine" to Saint Saba's shrine. When the pilgrims meet him,
he is on his way to dip his mother's shroud in the waters of
the Jordan. The significance of this Greek custom, which
Rolfe explains, is directly related to the Hellenic connotations of the grape and rose imagery which characterizes the
Cypriote. Its essence is expressed in his final song as he goes
down singing toward "Death's Sea":

> With a rose in thy mouth
> Through the world lightly veer:
> Rose in the mouth
> Makes a rose of the year!

> With the Prince of the South
> O'er the Styx bravely steer:
> Rose in the mouth
> And a wreath on the bier![34]

In "The Cypriote," the rose and wine imagery depicts
one of the two alternative conditions of hedonism in the
face of evil which Melville defined in *Moby-Dick:* "that
mortal man who hath more of joy than sorrow in him, that

32. *Clarel*, 2, 14.

33. The creation of this character may have been inspired by a
"singular young man" who presented Melville with a flower in Florence and "talked like one to whom the world was delightful" (Horsford, *Journal*, pp. 219–20).

34. *Clarel*, 2, 19.

mortal man cannot be true—not true, or undeveloped."[35]
The canto shows the state of innocence of the Hellenic
pagan which is due to immaturity. The symbolical and
structural antithesis to "The Cypriote" is "The Prodigal,"
in the section called "Bethlehem," the last of the bacchic
cantos in *Clarel*. There the clinging to grapes and roses
symbolizes the obstinate refusal to face reality which is due
to moral and spiritual cowardice—the Prodigal is a Jew who
hides his Judaism.

The Prodigal, a commercial traveler from Lyons, is full
of a self-conscious and somewhat desperate joie de vivre.
Significantly, he is encountered in Bethlehem when Clarel's
probings into the nature of reality achieve a new and final
impetus. He is depicted as sharing a cell with Clarel at a
Bethlehem convent, where he arrives singing at nightfall,
a chance visitor from Jerusalem. He is irritated at Clarel's
earnestness

> to know how the most drear
> Solemnity of Judah's glade
> Affect might such a mind.[36]

He shies away from Clarel's musings on the history and
destiny of "dead Judea." But it is "as in despair" that he
insists on dwelling on the beauty of wine, women, and song:

> Well, me for one, dame Judah here
> Don't much depress: she's not austere—
> Nature has lodged her in good zone—
> The true wine-zone of Noah. . . .[37]

To illustrate his point he refers to the emblem of grapes
depicted on "the ducat of the Maccabees" and the Judean

35. *Moby-Dick*, chap. 94.
36. *Clarel*, 2, 261.
37. Ibid., p. 264.

Temple—an image which Melville drew from Stanley.[38]
He describes "the spies from Eshcol, full of glee" tripping
back to camp, with clusters of grapes swung from a pole on
their shoulders.[39] Finally, he mentions the grape and rose
imagery of Solomon's Song and of Hafiz of Shiraz.

The Prodigal tenaciously refuses to see a special mystery
in "the Hebrews and their lot" which so preoccupies Clarel.
After all, "the Parsees are an odd tribe too."[40] To conclude
what to him is an uncomfortable conversation, he bursts
into song about the damsels of Shushan, symbolically identified with the Hebrew "shoshanah," a rose.[41] Later, Clarel
learns from a Russian pilgrim that the Prodigal is a Jew who
hides his Judaism.[42] In other words, he is a man whose
hedonistic philosophy is an act of cowardice and, fun-
damentally, of despair.

The function of the grape and rose imagery in this canto
is to define the Prodigal as an antithesis to Clarel. The
symbolical and structural tension between the hedonism of
innocence ("The Cypriote") and the corrupt hedonism resulting from fear of spiritual awareness ("The Prodigal") is
caught and drawn to a climax in three intervening bacchic
cantos which describe the revels at Mar Saba: "The Beaker,"
"Song and Recitative," and "The Revel Closed." The crucial symbolic act at the convent in the Judean wilderness is
the ritualistic meal of bread and wine in which the pilgrims

38. *Sinai and Palestine*, p. 163.
39. *Clarel, 2,* 265.
40. Ibid., p. 268.
41. Melville played on the "original" meaning of Eshcol and Shushan. "Eshkol," in Hebrew, is a cluster of grapes. "Shoshanah," actually a "lily," was mistakenly connected with the name of the city of
Shushan (Susa, an Elamite name) in Kitto's *Cyclopaedia of Biblical
Literature* (1857), 2, 763.
42. *Clarel, 2,* 276.

participate.[43] They are thus initiated into the mysteries of Mar Saba.

After the meal is finished and the monks have left, the pilgrims are joined by the Purveyor, the monastery's *oeko-nomos,* a Greek from Lesbos; the Arnaut, a Moslem warrior temporarily resident at Mar Saba as a military escort for pilgrims; and the Spahi, a former soldier in the Turkish cavalry and the leader of the Bethlehem Arabs who escort Clarel and his companions on their journey. The two Moslems and Derwent, Rolfe, and Clarel are "ranged at the board for family feast" around "one flask of stature tall" filled with Saba wine which a monk has deposited before them. Rolfe is seated next to "the not-of-Sharon Rose," i.e. Clarel, the searcher who refuses to accept the grape and rose philosophy at its face value. Vine and Mortmain, the melancholy Swedish pilgrim, sit apart, each on his own, watching the "Bacchic throng." The company, all "brethren" whom the wine draws "closer in comradeship," are served by the Purveyor who goes from one to the other pouring the wine and singing a song which describes the interrelation of death and life as symbolized on Moslem and Hebrew tombstones:

> The mufti in park suburban
> Lies under a stone,
> Surmounted serene by a turban
> Magnific—a marble one!

> A rabbi in Prague they muster
> In mound evermore
> Looking up at his monument's cluster—
> A cluster of grapes of Noah![44]

43. Ibid., pp. 47–54.
44. Ibid., p. 54.

The Hebraic implications of the grape imagery in this instance stem from Stanley's discussion of the "symbol of Judah" in *Sinai and Palestine,* where it is stated that "the grapes of Judah still mark the tombstones of the Hebrew race in the oldest of their European cemeteries, at Prague."[45]

The Lesbian, too, sings the theme song of the canto in which the religious connotations of the wine imagery are made explicit: the "saintly dew" of Saba is identified with rosary beads and the monks tilling the wine are "beadsmen" who "toil for heaven" in the wilderness.[46] Later, it is the Lesbian who shows Derwent "that blessed tree," the Palm of Saint Saba, the landmark of spiritual life in the surrounding desert and the central symbol of hope.

The symbolic value of the Palm in *Clarel* is analogous to that of the doubloon in *Moby-Dick.* It is contemplated by different characters with a different vision. Derwent, the clergyman, is the first of the pilgrims to be confronted with the Palm, but unlike the lay pilgrims who contemplate the Palm on their own, he is guided to it by the Lesbian. The Purveyor's function as a spiritual guide is made abundantly clear in the comparison between Virgil and Dante which Derwent makes as he follows the Purveyor "up" from the valley of Kidron on their sight-seeing tour.[47] The Lesbian is thus both the one who serves the pilgrims with wine and the guide to the "ascending path."

The exact equivalent of this double function is found in the image of the saqi, or cupbearer, in Persian poetry. In Sufi symbolism, the "cupbearer," like the Purveyor, represents the shammas ad-dair, i.e. the guardian of the convent, who offers the loving cup of wine to the elect who long for mystic union with the deity. The Sufi "cupbearer" or

45. Stanley, p. 163.
46. *Clarel,* 2, 53.
47. Ibid., p. 123.

"wine shop" is the spiritual instructor, the "giver of the goblet of celestial aspiration"[48] who offers "wine" (spiritual knowledge) to the "reveler," i.e. the one who aspires to a mystical grasp of the divine essence. Wine, which was forbidden by Koranic law, represents the esoteric knowledge of the Sufi elect who are permitted to transcend legalistic conventions in order to achieve "intoxication"—a state of religious ecstasy.

The Sufi connotations of the imagery used by the Persian poets were discussed in detail in two American works: *The Poetry of the East* by William Rounseville Alger—whose later work on *The Solitude of Nature and Man* (1867) Melville owned—a collection of Persian poetry from a German anthology of Oriental mystics which was "laid on the shrine of American Literature" in 1856;[49] and a book on *The Dervishes, or Oriental Spiritualism* by John P. Brown, of the American Legation at Constantinople, published in Philadelphia in 1868: "These Soffees . . . give an imaginary signification to outward forms," writes Brown. "For instance, when, like Hafiz, they mention wine, they mean a knowledge of God, which, extensively considered, is the love of God. The wine-shop, with them, means the *murshid* . . . [spiritual director], for his heart is said to be the depository of the love of God; the wine-cup . . . signifies the words which flow from the murshid's mouth respecting divine knowledge and which, heard by the sālik (the Dervish, or one who pursues the true path) intoxicates his soul, and divests his mind (of passions), giving him pure

48. See Lucy Garnett, *Mysticism and Magic in Turkey* (London, 1912), p. 45.

49. See W. R. Alger's preface in *Poetry of the East* (Boston, 1856), pp. v–vii. The section on Sufism is based on Tholuck's German Anthology from the Oriental Mystics (F. A. G. Tholuck, *Bluethensammlung aus der morgenlaendischen Mystik,* Berlin, 1825). For Melville's annotated copy of Alger's *Solitudes* see Leyda, *Log,* p. 720.

spiritual delight."[50] Melville's interest in dervishes, as has
already been pointed out, was of long standing. It is attested
not only in *Mardi* and *Moby-Dick* but in the *Journal* of his
Near Eastern trip and the repeated references to santons
and fakirs in *Clarel*.[51] It is most likely that he did some
reading on the subject while he was writing *Clarel*, in which
case he was bound to acquire a knowledge of Sufi terminology. The complete identity in the functions of the Lesbian and the "saqi" is undeniable. The Lesbian "purveys"
wine to the pilgrims:

> . . . in the act of singing
> Near and more near one cup he's bringing.
>
> . . . .
>
> The Lesbian who had Derwent served,
>   Officiated for them all;
> And as from man to man he swerved,
>   Grotesque a bit of song let fall.[52]

He does not drink himself but "flourishes" his wine cup
"for sign," which, in the mystical language of Sufism, would
refer to the divine knowledge that flows from the cupbearer's mouth. Finally, on the morning after the revels,
he "offered straight" to be a "guide."[53]

The Lesbian's Epicurean appearance and manner, and
his particular association with Derwent, the complacent
Anglican clergyman, express the satirical vein which pervades the cantos on the Mar Saba revels and which is directed at the complacency of institutionalized religious
faith. The Lesbian flourished his wine cup "though it
lacked the wine." In other words, he himself does not have

50. Brown, *The Dervishes*, p. 366.
51. Horsford, *Journal*, pp. 89, 169–70. *Clarel*, *1*, 36, 205; *2*, 131, 134,
266.
52. *Clarel*, *2*, 54.
53. Ibid., pp. 66, 121.

the knowledge to which he pretends. His close association
with Derwent resembles the connection between the "wine-
shop" and the dervish in Sufi symbolism as described by
Brown. The wine-shop's words "respecting divine knowledge" are heard by the dervish and give him "pure spiritual
delight."[54] The analogy is sufficiently striking to make one
wonder if Melville had come across the nineteenth-century
interpretation of the word "dervish" as "one who pursues
the true path,"[55] and intended it as an ironic overtone in
the name of Derwent, the professional seeker after the divine. It is only Derwent, the representative of institutionalized religion among the pilgrims, who listens to the Purveyor and follows his guidance. The lay members of the
company—Vine, Mortmain, Rolfe, and Clarel—do not
need a guide to explore Mar Saba. They see the Palm for
themselves, each from his own point of vantage. To all of
them "Derwent, and his good gossip cosy, / The man of Lesbos, light and rosy" are "viewless and quite inaudible."[56]

On one level of meaning the cantos on the revels represent an indictment of the futile attempts of organized religion to grasp the essence of the godhead through mystical
sects and fraternities. But the grape and rose symbolism
through which these mystic gropings manifest themselves
also serves to define an inevitable stage in the pilgrims'
progress toward Bethlehem by revealing the significance of
Mar Saba as an experience *beyond* the formal terms of the
three great religions, Judaism, Christianity, and Islam. In
spite of himself, Clarel, too, participates in the pilgrims'
revels and directs his step to the Palm, the emblem of hope,
and Bethlehem, the city of hope. The final victory which

54. Brown, *The Dervishes*, p. 366.
55. The word is commonly explained as derived from the Persian
and meaning "mendicant," but its real etymology is unknown. See
article on "Derwish" in *Encyclopaedia of Islam*, *1*, 949–50.
56. *Clarel*, 2, 128.

he achieves essentially springs from the sense of brotherhood experienced at the "family feast" of Mar Saba—a
feeling of kinship with all mankind.

The influence of Persian imagery persists in the series
of rose poems which was first arranged by Melville under
the title "A Rose or Two" in February 1890; this work
was subsequently rearranged in August 1891, with a dedication to his wife, as "Weeds and Wildings Chiefly: with a
Rose or Two." The series contains eleven poems, variations
on the theme of roses which "had become something of a
passion with Melville."[57] As he said himself in the poems,
he "came unto his roses late."[58] The opening poem is a
hymn of "Amoroso" to his "Rosamond." But there is a
serious symbolism in the apparent lightheartedness of the
verses which associates these poems with the rose symbolism
of *Mardi, Clarel,* and "Under the Rose." Much of the symbolism is purely Christian, as in "The New Rosicrucians"
and "Rosary Beads." But the longest of the poems in the
series, "The Rose Farmer," originally entitled "The Roses
of Damascus," is an allegorical poem in a Persian frame, like
"Under the Rose." It evidently relates to Melville's reading
of Saadi's *Gulistan,* although it seems to have been directly
inspired by the following lines in *Vane's Story,* a "self-tor-
turing" poem by James Thomson which Melville received
from James Billson in November 1884:

> Oh, what can Saadi have to do
> With penitence? and what can you?
> Are Shiraz roses wreathed in rue?[59]

57. Leon Howard, *Herman Melville* (Berkeley, 1951), pp. 316–17.
58. "The Rose Farmer," *Collected Poems,* pp. 303, 306.
59. *Vane's Story, Weddah and Om-El-Bonain, and Other Poems*
(London, 1881), p. 22.

The theme of "The Rose Farmer" is the antithesis between the rose and its attar, the attar-gul or the essence of
the rose. The narrator relates how he received the bequest
of a rose farm from an Eastern "grandee" and could not
decide how to use the roses. Should he make "heaps of
posies" or distill "some few crystal drops of Attar"? The
"grandee" in the poem is obviously a replica of the Azem
in "Under the Rose."[60] The implied image of the deity is
intensified by a reference to a "turbaned urn" that was
"reared" for the grandee "whose shadow has decreased,"
and a "chowder" which was prepared "for his feast . . .
against his Rhamadan."[61] On the surface the allusion is
simply to two well-known Moslem institutions, the turbaned tombs that Melville observed in Moslem cemeteries[62] and the fast of Ramadan that plays so important a
role in the relationship of Queequeg and Ishmael. It is
clear, however, that the reference to the "dying" Moslem
grandee hides a vicarious onslaught on a deity propitiated
by shrines, fasts, and sacrificial offerings. The "turbaned
urn" is a tomb, but at the same time a Moslem shrine and
a domed house of worship; "his Rhamadan" and the food
prepared for "his feast" convey the homage of the worshiper, but also the senseless decrees of the deity in its own
behalf. The dilemma which faces the receiver of the grandee's bequest, i.e. man—the narrator of the poem—is what
to make of it. The choice between the rose and its attar is
the perpetual conflict between the enjoyment of life and
the quest for the meaning of life.

60. Cf. *Vane's Story*, p. 21:
> As well a weevil might determine
> To grow a farmer hating vermin;
> The *I am that I am* of God
> Defines no less a worm or clod.

61. "The Rose Farmer," *Collected Poems,* p. 304.

62. Horsford, *Journal,* p. 72. *Clarel,* 2, 54.

The imagery and symbolism of "The Rose Farmer" present an analogy with the image of Saadi as it emerges from Melville's reading of the "Rose-Garden" and that of Zardi in "Rammon." Melville read Saadi's *Gulistan* while composing *Clarel,* at a time of intense preoccupation with the problem of the "rose" and its "attar." Similarly, in the poem, the narrator, while meditating on the dilemma presented by the grandee's bequest, "chanced" upon a Persian

> gentleman-rose-farmer
> On knees beside his garden-gate
> Telling his beads. . . .[63]

Saadi of Shiraz, as Melville knew, was venerated as a pious Sufi and Moslem saint. The last sixty or seventy years of his extremely long life were spent in a hermit's cell in religious devotion.[64] The preface to the *Gulistan,* like all Moslem books, opens with a long invocation to the glory of Allah. There Saadi describes himself as enticed by a friend to quit a state of religious abstraction and retirement.[65] The pious composer of the "Rose-Garden" would therefore, as a matter of course, suggest the image of the "Rose Farmer," practicing his devotions beside the "garden gate." In the poem, the rose farmer's beads are golden coins strung upon a wire of silver:

> And every time a coin he told
> His brow he raised, and eyes he rolled
> Devout in grateful orison.

It has already been pointed out that Melville's view of Saadi, as it emerges from his markings in the *Gulistan,*

63. "The Rose Farmer," *Collected Poems,* p. 305.
64. "An Essay on the Life and Genius of Sheik Saadi" by James Ross was appended to the American edition of the *Gulistan* to which Emerson wrote a preface.
65. Melville's copy of the *Gulistan,* p. xiv.

greatly differed from that of Emerson, who idealized Saadi as a mystic visionary. Melville's judgment as reflected in his notations approaches the view of modern scholarship, which holds that worldly wisdom rather than mysticism is Saadi's chief characteristic. Similarly, Melville's rose farmer operates on the principles of worldly wisdom in the guise of piety. He is astonished that the narrator comes with his question, "touching the Roses and the Attar" so late in life. He is amazed that the narrator—"an older man than I"—is still occupied with the search for the meaning of existence. For answer he directs his questioner's attention to a "Parsee yonder . . . lean as a rake with his distilling."[66] The lean Parsee, a reflection of Fedallah, corresponds to the image of the wretched dervish in the *Gulistan* who has renounced the world to serve truth.[67] The quest for "attar" leads to poverty, misery, loneliness, and, finally, annihilation. In addition, the searcher for absolute truth commits an unpardonable sin, like the mystics whom Fitzgerald's Omar despised. He is the Blue Beard of the flowers:

> To get a mummified quintessence
> He scimetars the living rose!

On the other hand, there is always a market for roses and those who cultivate them are blessed by the heavens and flourish.

> But Attar, why it comes so dear
> 'Tis far from popular, that's clear.
>
> . . . .
>
> But now, Sir, for your urgent matter.
> Every way—for wise employment,
> Repute and profit, health, enjoyment,
> I am for roses—*sink* the Attar!

66. "The Rose Farmer," *Collected Poems*, p. 307.
67. *Gulistan*, chap. 2.

The narrator turns away with a reflection which may well
be regarded as Melville's comment on Saadi's philosophy in
the *Gulistan:*

> . . . this prosperous Persian
> Who, verily, seemed in life rewarded
> For sapient prudence not amiss,
> Nor transcendental essence hoarded
> In hope of quintessential bliss;
> No, never with painstaking throes
> Essays to crystallize the rose.[68]

The symbolism of Melville's grape and rose imagery
ranges beyond the connotations of Persian poetry. It en-
compasses classical antiquity, the Bible, Christian ritual,
and the field of art, e.g. the sensuous seventeenth-century
paintings of the Dutchman Jan Steen in the poem entitled
"At the Hostelry." But the Persian element in this pattern
of "linked analogies" is sufficiently distinct to throw new
light on their interpretation. Melville's indebtedness to
Islamic concepts is a sparkling drop of attar in his multi-
colored rose.

68. "The Rose Farmer," *Collected Poems,* pp. 307, 309.

7. The Journey to Terra Damnata

Melville's departure for Europe and the Levant on October 11, 1856, was prompted by personal reasons. It was undertaken on the urging of family and friends and with the financial help of Judge Lemuel Shaw, Melville's father-in-law, in order to recuperate his failing health and to restore his spirits from a mood of profound depression. His decreasing reputation as an author, after the failure of *Pierre* (1852), the constant struggle against debt and ill health, overwork on *The Confidence-Man*, which he left behind for publication—all these had brought on a state of physical and mental exhaustion which made it imperative to undertake a voyage as a way of "driving off the spleen and regulating the circulation." But though Melville embarked in the spirit of his own Ishmael, his voyage to the Near East was not extraordinary in itself. On the contrary, it was part of a well defined cultural pattern. "In many respects the trip that Melville made did not differ remarkably from those made by thousands of his contemporaries, English and American, clerical and lay," writes the editor of his *Journal*. There are hundreds of accounts written by travelers to the Holy Land, Egypt, Turkey, and Syria during the middle decades of the nineteenth century, and most of them record activities like those Melville engaged in.[1]

In Melville's own circle, George William Curtis and Bayard Taylor had made literary capital out of their visit

1. Horsford, *Journal*, "Introduction," p. 10.

to the Near East. Curtis had traveled in Egypt and Syria in 1849, and his *Nile Notes of a Howadji* (1851) and *The Howadji in Syria* (1852) achieved wide popularity.[2] These books were based on letters sent to the *New York Tribune,* with which Curtis was connected at the time. Bayard Taylor, who "embodied the height of romantic literary success" among the New York literati,[3] left New York in August 1851 for a tour of the Near and Far East. On his return he gave innumerable lectures to lyceum audiences and enjoyed a popularity which prompted Melville to remark that "as some augur predicted the misfortunes of Charles I from the infelicity of his countenance so Taylor's prosperity 'borne up by the Gods' was written in his face."[4] Among Taylor's numerous publications *The Lands of the Saracen* (1855) described his experiences in Palestine, Syria, Asia Minor, Sicily, and Spain. He also published *Poems from the Orient* (1854) and a *Cyclopaedia of Modern Travel* (1856), and, in 1865, was active in a travelers' club to which "from his pinnacle," he invited Melville, then "at the bottom" of his literary reputation.

Melville's Near Eastern tour thus turned him into a qualified member of a literary group whose travels in Syria and Palestine were as much a sign of the times as the European exile of the American expatriates half a century later.

Melville had first contemplated a trip to the Near East in 1849, on his second voyage to Europe. He and a traveling companion, Franklin Taylor, a cousin of Bayard Taylor, had "sketched a plan for going down the Danube from

2. See *The Athenaeum, 24* (1851), 344: " 'Nile Notes' is not a book of travel. There is not a line in it copied from the guide book—not a word compiled from previous writers."

3. Leyda, *Log,* p. xxxiii.

4. Extract from Evert Duyckinck's diary, entry for October 1, 1856, in Leyda, *Log,* p. 523.

Vienna to Constantinople; thence to Athens on the steamer, to Beyrouth & Jerusalem—Alexandria & the Pyramids. From what I learn, I have no doubt this can be done at a comparatively trifling expense. . . . I am full (just now) of this glorious *Eastern* jaunt. Think of it! Jerusalem & the Pyramids—Constantinople, the Aegean, & old Athens!"[5] When Melville finally did make this journey, exactly seven years later, he was a "drastically different man." Hawthorne observed, when he saw him at Liverpool that "he did not anticipate much pleasure in his rambles, for that the spirit of adventure is gone out of him."[6]

It may be argued that Melville's morbid state of mind determined his bleak vision of Egypt and Palestine and that the Near East would not have affected him so, had he made the journey in the buoyant and enthusiastic mood of 1849. But actually there is no reason to suppose that his impressions would have been different, though the degree of his disillusionment might have been less tragically intense. Even writers less profound and less troubled by religious doubt than Melville, who went on the journey in the romantic mood of "raised expectations," had to admit that all was not well with the Holy Land. Alexander William Kinglake, the author of *Eothen,* whom Melville had met in London in 1849, stated in his preface: "My narrative . . . conveys . . . not those impressions which *ought to have been* produced upon any 'well constituted mind,' but those which were really and truly received at the time. . . . I ought, for instance, to have felt as strongly in Judea, as in Galilee, but it was not so in fact; the religious sentiment . . . which had heated my brain in the Sanctuary of Nazareth was rudely chilled at the foot of Zion, by disenchanting scenes."[7] Cur-

5. Metcalf, *Journal,* pp. 9–10.

6. Extract from Hawthorne's Journal, entry for November 17, 1856, in Leyda, *Log,* p. 53.

7. *Eothen* (New York, 1846), pp. vii–viii.

tis, Melville's friend and editor, mocked at the indiscrim-
inating enthusiasm of such travelers as "poet Harriet Martineau" and "the other poetical Howadji." For himself he
had this to say of Jerusalem: "But going up to Jerusalem as
to the holiest city of the purest faith, you are disappointed
by what you see of that faith there, as you would be upon
approaching a banquet of wit and beauty, to find a festival
of idiots and the insane."⁸ The English traveler Eliot Warburton, author of *The Crescent and the Cross*, whose dragoman Melville met in Beirut, was overwhelmed by feelings
of religious awe at the sight of Jerusalem in its bleak land-
scape.⁹ But William Bartlett, equally moved by religious
feeling, wrote that "there was nothing grand or striking
in the vision—a line of dull walls, a group of massive towers, a few dark olives, rising from a dead and sterile plain,
were all that met the eye; yet, enough that this was Jerusalem—the Holy City."¹⁰ The most famous literary traveler of the time, William Makepeace Thackeray, who visited the Near East in 1844 and whom Melville met at
Duyckinck's in the winter of 1855–56, found the landscape
around Jerusalem "*frightful . . .* unspeakably ghastly and
desolate." On approaching "this awful place" he was overcome with a "feeling of devout terror."¹¹

Melville reached Palestine from Liverpool, sailing most
of the way aboard the English steamer *Egyptian,* by way
of Gibraltar, Algiers, Malta, Greece, Turkey, and Egypt.
He spent eighteen days in the Holy Land, departing for
Beirut on January 24, 1857, and returning to Europe via
Cyprus. Most of his time on the return journey was spent

8. *The Howadji in Syria* (New York, 1852), p. 190.

9. *The Crescent and the Cross* (New York, 1845), pp. 60, 106.

10. *Walks about Jerusalem,* p. 14.

11. On Melville's meeting with Thackeray see A. F. Sanborn,
Reminiscences of Richard Lathers (New York, 1907), p. 51; and
Eastern Sketches (London, 1846), p. 400.

in Italy where he arrived on February 18. On April 14 he left for Switzerland, visited Germany, Holland, and England, and arrived back in New York on May 19, 1857.

Melville approached Jerusalem on January 7, 1857, by the usual route from Jaffa via Ramleh through the hills of Judea: "Withered & desert country. Breakfasted by ruined mosque—Cave. Hot & wearisome ride over the arid hills. Got to Jerusalem about 2 P.M. Put up at Mediterranean hotel. Kept by a German converted Jew."[12] There is not a single comment on his first sight of the city, and this silence, tense with disappointment and dramatic in its matter-of-fact transition to the details of the hotel in which he put up, projects, at the outset, his tragic vision of the Holy Land as the "terra damnata."

The average Christian traveler accepted the barrenness of nineteenth-century Palestine, particularly bleak in the rainy season when Melville saw it, as the fulfillment of the prophetic curse. But to Melville the "unleavened nakedness of desolation" was the result not of the curse but of the "embrace" of the deity. The entries in the *Journal* cry out against a god that crushes his creatures to pieces whenever they attempt to grasp his essence: "Is the desolation of the land the result of the fatal embrace of the Deity? Hapless are the favourites of Heaven."[13] Throughout the passages on Palestine the words barren, black, funereal, arid, mouldy, stony, ghastly, terrible, diabolical, hammer Melville's terror-stricken image of Judea into the imagination until, in the region of the convent Mar Saba, it arises in its petrified, horrible whiteness as the incarnation of evil and death: "Whitish mildew pervading whole tracts of landscape-bleached-leprosy-encrustation of curses-old cheese-bones of rocks—crunched, knawed & mumbled—mere refuse & rub-

12. Horsford, *Journal*, p. 125.
13. Ibid., p. 154.

bish of creation— . . . all Judea seems to have been accumulations of this rubbish."[14]

From Jerusalem, itself indistinguishable from the arid rock when viewed at a distance, the landscape becomes more "diabolical" as it approaches the Dead Sea. That part of Judea is the waste land of body and spirit where "nought grows but wiry, prickly bush . . . the horrible cactus." The bitterness of the Dead Sea waters and the stony sterility of Judea symbolize the essence of the "terra damnata"—where man was stoned to death:

> smarting bitter of the water,—carried the bitter in my mouth all day—bitterness of life—thought of all bitter things—Bitter is it to be poor & bitter, to be reviled, & Oh bitter are these waters of Death, thought I. . . . Judea is one accumulation of stones—Stony mountains & stony plains; stony torrents & stony roads; stony walls & stony fields, stony houses & stony tombs; stony eyes & stony hearts. Before you, & behind you are stones. Stones to right & stones to left.[15]

The feeling of doom was unredeemed by the "red poppies" of the Plain of Sharon which Melville noted after "a delightful ride" and the "lovely landscape" viewed from the hill on which Jaffa is situated. In Jaffa, Melville had the "genuine, old Jonah feeling"—he wanted to escape: "No country will more quickly dissipate romantic expectations than Palestine—particularly Jerusalem. To some the disappointment is heart sickening. . . . In the emptiness of the lifeless antiquity of Jerusalem the emigrant Jews are like flies that have taken up their abode in a skull."[16]

14. Ibid., p. 137.
15. Ibid., pp. 136, 152.
16. Ibid., p. 154.

Melville's preoccupation with the "original" inhabitants of this "terrible" land, the Jews, is evident both in the *Journal* and *Clarel*. Like other travelers, he had come in contact with English and American missionaries in Palestine who considered "that the time for the prophetic return of the Jews to Judea is at hand, and therefore the way must be prepared for them by Christians, both in setting them right in their faith and their farming."[17] At the time that Melville visited Palestine the Jewish population numbered about 9,000, mostly elderly people from Poland who had come to die in the Holy Land and lived there in abject poverty and precarious conditions, on funds sent to them from Europe. The American missionaries whom Melville met in Jaffa—Mr. and Mrs. Charles Saunders from Rhode Island, Mrs. C. Minor from Philadelphia, and Mr. and Mrs. Walter Dickson from Boston—had come to Palestine in the wake of a religious movement which swept England and America in the 1840's and '50's. They aimed at "facilitating prophecy" by rehabilitating the Holy Land and restoring "God's ancient people" to their ancient soil through conversion to Christianity and the establishment of agricultural schools.

In 1839 a "Mission of Inquiry to the Jews," consisting of four members, among them Dr. Alexander Keith, to whom Melville refers in *Clarel*,[18] was sent to the Near East by the Scottish Church with the object "to see the real condition and character of God's ancient people, and to observe whatever might contribute to interest others in their cause."[19] In Palestine this mission met Sir Moses Montefiore, an Anglo-Jewish financier and philanthropist, and a "devout

17. Ibid., p. 158.
18. *Clarel, 1,* 295.
19. *Narrative of a Mission of Inquiry to the Jews from the Church of Scotland in 1839* (Philadelphia), preface, p. v.

believer in the literal restoration."[20] Sir Moses was on his
second visit to Palestine in an effort to improve the lot of
the Palestinian Jews. In his *Journal* Melville refers to this
meeting, speaking of Montefiore in a somewhat ironical
vein. But the point which interested him most was the
project of employing Jews in agriculture, of which he took
a dim view.

Melville arrived in Palestine one year after Sir Moses
Montefiore's third visit, in 1855, on which "this Croesus
. . . bought a large tract on the hill of Gihon & walled it
in for hospital grounds."[21] He also planned the almshouses
outside the walls of Jerusalem, bequeathed by another
"Croesus"—the American Judah Touro of New Orleans.
Montefiore did not undertake any elaborate agricultural
projects but was determined "to devote the funds in his
hands to reproductive enterprise" and to improve the condition of the Jews of Palestine by "agricultural and indus-
trial labour." This resolution was carried out in spite of
considerable opposition and the claim on the part of the
beneficiaries "that it was no part of their duty to work or
to learn to earn their living, and . . . that their task in life
was sufficiently fulfilled by prayer and religious exercise."[22]
If this was their reaction to Sir Moses Montefiore's efforts,
it may well be imagined that, as Melville states, "not a single
Jew was converted either to Christianity or Agriculture"
by the missionaries.[23] As might be expected, Melville had
no patience with "their preposterous Jew mania" and their
"Quixotism":

> The idea of making farmers of the Jews is vain. In the
> first place, Judea is a desert with few exceptions. In the

20. Lucien Wolf, *Sir Moses Montefiore* (New York, 1885), p. 106.
21. Horsford, *Journal*, p. 160.
22. Wolf, pp. 58, 150.
23. Horsford, *Journal*, p. 157.

second place, the Jews hate farming. All who cultivate the soil in Palestine are Arabs. The Jews dare not live outside walled towns or villages for fear of the malicious persecution of the Arabs & Turks. —Besides, the number of Jews in Palestine is comparatively small. And how are the hosts of them scattered in other lands to be brought here? Only by a miracle.[24]

The interest of these remarks does not only lie in their relation to subsequent developments by which Jewish farmers in Palestine transformed the nature of the landscape and brought about the re-establishment of Israel. Melville, himself a Pittsfield farmer, who recorded the quality of the soil and crops in the Nile Delta,[25] seems to have felt a particular dislike for a people whom he considered incapable of cultivating the soil.

This animus is strongly felt in *Clarel,* where it is personified in the character of Margoth, the Jewish geologist whom Bezanson has called "the most devastating portrait in *Clarel.*"[26] Margoth is a scoffer; for him all spiritual values have been replaced by science. He represents those scientists in nineteenth-century America who "were so enamoured of their facts and hypotheses that they claimed too much. They seemed to take pleasure in the destruction of that which was old. They inclined towards a materialistic explanation of all phenomena to the exclusion of spiritual reality altogether."[27] To Margoth Jerusalem was an anachronism:

24. Ibid., pp. 160–61.
25. Ibid., p. 121.
26. Bezanson, pp. 270–71.
27. Henry K. Rowe, *History of Religion in the United States* (New York, 1924), p. 134; cf. W. Braswell, *Melville's Religious Thought* (Durham, 1943), p. 111.

> Stale is she!
> Lay flat the walls, let in the air
> That folk no more may sicken there!
> Wake up the dead; and let there be
> Rails, Wires, from Olivet to the sea,
> With station in Gethsemane.[28]

The enterprising spirit that the geologist brings to the Holy Land depicts the commercialism and materialism of the United States following the Civil War. But Melville embodied it in a Jew:

> One can't forbear
> Thinking that Margoth is—a *Jew*.[29]

Melville's distaste for all that Margoth represents is evident in the circumstances in which the geologist is encountered. He is first seen standing by the Dung Gate in the south wall of Jerusalem "by dust-heaps of rubbish in a lonely scene." Then he is espied in the wilderness of the Dead Sea:

> . . . the Jew . . .
> Coasting inquisitive the shore
> And frequent stooping.[30]

It is clear that in Melville's symbolical scheme of values the Jew was an outcast in accordance with the cultural pattern of Christianity. Though Melville, in the poem, disclaims any attempt at "satire" of the Jews as a whole "in picturing Margoth, fallen son of Judah," the awkwardness of this disclaimer has been noted.[31] The simple fact is that Melville, like most Christians reared in a religious atmosphere, had ambivalent and complex feelings about the Jews

28. *Clarel, 1,* 250.
29. Ibid., p. 257.
30. Ibid., p. 309.
31. Bezanson, p. 276, n. 80.

which he tried to externalize in the poem. His intense pre-occupation with the character and destiny of the "Hebrews" is attested in the space he devoted to "the Jewish question" in *Clarel*. There is the usual admiration for ancient Juda-ism, triumphant over the heathen, and simultaneously the distrust of the contemporary Jew. Yet the dislike of the mod-ern Jew also carried over to the biblical Jews, for they were responsible for the desolation of the Holy Land, "Jewry's inexhausted shore of barrenness." Even before Jeremiah's curse, they had imported bleakness from Egypt:

> That bondman from his doom
> By Nile, and subsequent distress,
> With punishment in wilderness,
> Methinks he brought an added gloom
> To Nature here.[32]

The modern Jew, praised in the figures of Heine, Moses Mendelssohn, and particularly the mystic "visionary" Spi-noza whom Melville admired, emerges, on the whole, as an ignoble figure, yet is given the benefit of an explanation:

> Priests make a goblin of the Jew
>
> .   .   .   .
>
> .   .   .   Society
> Is not quite catholic, you know,
> Retains some prejudices yet—
> Likes not the singular. . . .[33]

In the *Journal*, Melville recorded his impression of the Roman Ghetto: "Tragic looking place enough."[34]

The most dignified Jewish figure in *Clarel* is Abdon, the "Black Jew" of Cochin who has come "from Ind to Zion"

---

32. *Clarel, 1,* 122; *2, 30.*
33. Ibid., *2,* 276.
34. Horsford, *Journal,* p. 194.

to die.[35] Nathan, the father of Ruth, the heroine, is modeled on Warder Cresson of Philadelphia: "An American turned Jew—divorced from (former) wife—married a Jewess &c.— Sad."[36] Nathan's Zionist obsession to which he sacrifices himself and his family is meant to characterize the zeal of a convert rather than Jewish fanaticism. However, the origin of his determination to cultivate the land in Palestine is his love of

> A Jewess who about him threw
> Else than Nerea's amorous net
> And dubious wile. 'Twas Miriam's race
>
> . . . .
>
> Still as she dwelt on Zion's story
> He felt the glamour, caught the gleam;
> All things but these seemed transitory—
> Love, and his love's Jerusalem.[37]

Actually Agar, Nathan's wife and the mother of Ruth, is a passively tragic figure when we see her in the poem in Clarel's company. She represents the failure of an ideal: "The waste of Judah made her lorn."[38]

The problem of the contemporary Jew living outside Palestine in a world that refuses to accept him is personified in the figure of the Prodigal, the gay commercial traveler from Lyons who hides his ancestry, shuns Clarel's probings into the reasons of "Judah's mournful sway," feels that the Jews were "misconceived," and is finally identified as a Jew by a Russian pilgrim. Melville's elaboration of this episode has been described as "rather curious psychologically and not entirely clear."[39] There is, however, no lack of clarity,

35. *Clarel, 1,* 11.
36. Horsford, *Journal,* p. 143.
37. *Clarel, 1,* 75.
38. Ibid., p. 106.
39. Bezanson, p. 276. See *Clarel,* 2, 260–69, 275.

if we consider the peculiar symbolical significance of the episode which has already been pointed out. On the surface, the Prodigal represents the sensuous abandon to the joy of life associated with the Song of Songs and the Persian poets. "You of the West, What devil has your hearts possessed, You can't enjoy?" he says to Clarel.[40] But his gaiety and unconcern can only be maintained by a refusal to recognize the "mystic burden" underlying "Solomon's Song" and the poetry of Hafiz, and by a rejection of his true heritage which is "Judah's mournful sway." Clarel's effort to penetrate and understand the repressed and hidden Judaism of the Prodigal is another symbolic manifestation of the mystical probings at the axis of reality of Melville's heroes. The prodigal Jew, like those in *Moby-Dick* who "worm-like . . . would craven crawl to land" rather than "perish in that howling infinite" of the highest truth, tries to evade the issue by denying his heritage, but to Clarel, who "dives," the symbolical aspect of Judea and the lot of its "original" people, the Hebrews, are crucial questions which concern the destiny of man and the nature of God. In a sense, the rejected Judaism of the Prodigal is related to Melville's symbolic concepts of the pyramid, the tomb, and the chimney, whose mysterious core the average man fears to face. The Prodigal's secret rejection of Judaism represents the predicament of all humanity—the failure to pursue the mystery "in bold quest thereof" for fear of being destroyed. Like Stubb, the mate in *Moby-Dick,* and the gay Neapolitans of whom Melville writes in his *Journal,* the Prodigal in his seemingly "invulnerable jollity of indifference" rides on the brink of an abyss and whistles in the dark.

Islam was the only religion that Melville was able to view with comparative detachment. The architectural beauty of monuments, mosques, kiosks, and fountains exhilarated

40. *Clarel,* 2, 264.

him at Constantinople: "One is amazed to see such delicate & fairylike structures out of doors. One would think the elements would visit them too rudely; that they would melt away like castle of confectionary."[41]

The great mosques of Istanbul which Melville visited, named after famous sultans, Ahmed, Suleiman, Bayezid, conveyed the true spirit of religion. Their minarets were "lighthouses" and their interiors like "a marble marquee" derived from "the tent." The custom of taking off one's shoes on entering was "more sensible than taking off hat. Muddy shoes; but never muddy heads."[42] Melville was impressed with the practical foresight of Islam in viewing a closed-off gallery in the Pigeon Mosque which served as a storage room and safe-deposit vault for the baggage of worshipers. The "goods laid up in a mosque" were later associated with a similar custom in the Jewish Temple, reported in Maccabees, and the counting house of Rothschild which he saw in Frankfurt.[43] As may be expected, he was even more forcibly struck by the irony of Byzantine churches which had been turned into mosques upon the Turkish conquest of Constantinople, particularly St. Sophia, which, in the beauty of its dome, he thought, surpassed even St. Peter's in Rome: "Moslems in St. Sophia: transverse." Another "significance" peculiar to St. Sophia was that the church looked "as partly underground, as if you saw but the superstructure of some immense temple, yet to be disinterred. You step *down* to enter. . . . The worshipping—head prostration."[44]

The Moslem city, with its crowds, its robbers, its wild dogs, its cemeteries, fabulous palaces, and labyrinth of streets in which he feared assassination, all the "union of

41. Horsford, *Journal*, p. 94.
42. Ibid., p. 83.
43. Ibid., p. 264.
44. Ibid., pp. 102, 210.

picturesque and poverty-stricken," presented both physi-
cally and symbolically a unified view in which minarets and
cypress trees were the most conspicuous objects. The cypress
seemed "a green minaret & blends with the stone ones.
Minaret [perhaps] derived from cypress shape. The intermingling of the dark tree with the bright spire expressive of
the intermingling of life & death." Viewed from one of the
two bridges across the Golden Horn on the way to Pera,
"the great mosques are shown to be built most judiciously
on the domed hills of the city. Fine effect. Seems a spread-
ing, still further, of the tent."45

The full significance of Melville's vision of the Moslem
City is brought home in a later record of his visit to Jericho
when, "sitting at door of tent looking at mountains of
Moab," he described the tent as "the charmed circle, keep-
ing off the curse."46 Islamic Constantinople, it seems, had
kept off the curse of Jerusalem which, in the Journal, made
itself progressively felt as Melville advanced through Egypt
to Palestine.

In Melville's Journal, the impact of Islam in Cairo is
overshadowed by the "eternal sorrows" of the pyramids of
ancient Egypt which, in Melville's view, had created the
"ghastly theology" of biblical Judaism. The mosques and
minarets of Cairo were affected by the "dust of ages," like
pharaonic monuments: "Minarets unlike those of Constantinople which gleam like lighthouses,—but of an ashy
color, and wonderfully venerable." There were also
mosques emblematic of "the dirty rites of religion." In the
lonelier parts of the city he saw "ruined mosques, domes
knocked in like stoven boats. Others, upper part empty &
desolate with broken rafters & dismantled windows; (rubbish) below." Cairo was "a grand masquerade of mortality,"
evil in its essence. There Nature fed on man: "Crookedness

45. Ibid., pp. 90, 94.
46. Ibid., p. 135.

of the streets—multitudes of blind men—worst city in the
world for them. Flies on eyes at noon. Nature feeding on
man . . . splendor & squalor, gloom & gaity. . . . —Too much
light & no defence against it." Yet the rottenness was suffused by a climate which he experienced as the reign of
spring upon earth: "Soft luxurious splendor of mornings.
Dewy. Paradise melted & poured into the air. Soft intoxication; no wonder these people never drink wine. Wondered
at the men in hotel drinking it here."[47]

Melville spent only one day in Cairo, which included a
visit to the Citadel, the Pyramids, and the Cairo suburbs.
But the number and vividness of his observations on Cairo
street scenes, the camels, donkeys, beggars, the appearance
of women, the noise, confusion, and picturesqueness of the
whole, evoke a panorama of the "dust coloured city" as an
oasis of animated life on the desert road to Jerusalem.

Islam, like other religions, failed to arrive at the "ultimate
truth," but it taught its followers to submit, to compromise
with reality in its doctrine of resignation, tolerance, liberality, and serenity. It is these qualities which struck Melville
in the Islamic countries of the Near East and which he recorded both in the *Journal* and in *Clarel*. The Moslem virtue of resignation was demonstrated aboard the *Egyptian*
in a thick fog in December 1856. In Salonica Turkish deck
passengers and their harems boarded the boat for Constantinople: "Very thick, & damp & raw. Very miserable for the
Turks & their harems; particularly when they were doused
out by the deck-washing. Some sick & came below to the fire;
off with their 'ashmacks'. . . . Old Turk . . . I said to him
'This is very bad' he answered 'God's will is good,' & smoked
his pipe in cheerful resignation."[48] The same serenity,
associated with the pipe, Melville's "original" symbol of
peace—which in *Moby-Dick* is thrown away by Ahab—is

47. Ibid., pp. 115, 116, 120.
48. Ibid., p. 76.

observed in Cairo: "Turk on donkey, resting his pipe vertically before him on pommel. Grave & tranquil."[49]

Yet there was considerable skepticism among the Moslem upper classes, as Melville learned from a Turkish envoy on board a French steamer on the way to Leghorn: "Turkish flag hoisted in honor of Turk envoy to Sardinia. Talked with him. His views of Mahometism & Upper classes of Turkey indulge philosophical opinions upon religion &c."[50] Melville was impressed with what he saw of Moslem morality: "Harem (sacred) on board steam boats. Lattice division. Ladies pale, straight noses, regular features, fine busts. Look like nuns in their plain dress, but with a roundness of bust not belonging to that character. Perfect decorum between sexes. No ogling. No pertness. No looking for admiration. No Cyprians. No drunkards. Saw not a single one, though liquor is sold."[51]

When, on his return, he used his traveling experiences as material for lectures, he compared the honesty of the infidels with the dishonesty of Christians—a point also made in *Clarel*. Like Gibbon, he contrasted the liberality of the Khalif Omar with the barbarism of the crusaders;[52] the question of Turkish moral superiority is the theme of the canto "Of Pope and Turk" in *Clarel*. The crimes and tyranny of Moslem rulers are considered as "wrongdoing chiefly personal," as the Koran respects neither place nor person. In the manner of modern admirers of Islam, Melville played with the idea that the economic and social backwardness of the Moslem world was a sign of spirituality

49. Ibid., p. 116; cf. p. 163.

50. Ibid., p. 215.

51. Ibid., p. 103.

52. *Clarel, 1,* 124. Cf. Melville's lecture "Traveling: Its Pleasures, Pains, and Profits" in Merton Sealts, *Melville as Lecturer* (Cambridge, Mass., 1957), pp. 183–84. See also the anecdote of the French merchant and his Christian and Moslem creditors, in *Clarel, 2, 203.*

in contrast to the "worldliness" and "materialism" of the West. But this interpretation, too, presented the pervasive irony:

> Are Turks our betters? Very strange
> Heaven's favour does not choicely range
> Upon the Islam people good.[53]

Moslems, like Jews and Christians, were inhabitants of a terra damnata.

But the greatest shock in the Bible Lands was Christianity, as meaningless as the "rank lies of Islam's herd" which Melville dutifully noted in *Clarel*.[54] Melville's outcry against Jehovah in Egypt was turned into revulsion by the "sickening cheat" of Christianity as he saw it in Jerusalem. There he tried to offer himself up as "a passive subject . . . in pursuance of my object, the saturation of my mind with the atmosphere of Jerusalem." Ironically he often experienced the feelings of Margoth, his detested Jewish scientist in *Clarel*. He remarked on "the insalubriousness of so small a city pent in by lofty walls obstructing ventilation, postponing the morning & hasting the unwholesome twilight," and described the Church of the Holy Sepulchre as "the thronged news-room & theological exchange of Jerusalem."

As we have seen, the Holy City was commonly a disillusionment to travelers of the time. To Melville, the Church of the Holy Sepulchre, with its "battered dome," was a "confused & half-ruinous pile" which smelled "like a deadhouse." The anointing-stone of Christ "veined with streaks of a mouldy red looks like a butcher's slab." The door of the church is "like that of a jail." The summing up is devastating: "All is glitter & nothing is gold. A sickening cheat. The countenances of the poorest & most ignorant pilgrims

53. *Clarel*, 2, 203–5.
54. Ibid., 1, 29.

would seem tacitly to confess it as well as your own." The presence of the Turkish guards in the Church of the Holy Sepulchre and the talk of the guides on the Via Dolorosa heighten the sense of profound irony: " 'Here is the stone Christ leaned against, & here is the English Hotel.' 'Yonder is the arch where Christ was shown to the people, & just by that open window is sold the best coffee in Jerusalem.' "

The Islamic character of Palestine under Turkish occupation intensified Melville's despair at the decadence of Christianity and the sterility of biblical Judaism, which lay behind it. He repeatedly recorded the irony of seeing Islam triumphant over Christianity in the Holy Land: "Wearily climbing the Via Dolorosa one noon I heard the muezzin calling to prayers from the minaret of Omar. He does the same from that of Mt. Olivet."[55] The experience of seeing a Moslem in the Bethlehem hills pray with his *back* to Jerusalem was so striking that he later elaborated it in *Clarel*.[56] The indifference of nature to the spiritual probings of humanity was evident in the Holy City: "The mind can not but be sadly & suggestively affected with the indifference of Nature & Man to all that makes the spot sacred to the Christian. Weeds grow upon Mount Zion; side by side in impartial equality appear the shadows of church & mosque, and on Olivet every morning the sun indifferently ascends over the Chapel of the Ascension." The secret conviction that Christianity, too, is a myth reveals itself in an observation on the return journey at the sight of Cyprus: "From these waters rose Venus from the foam. Found it as hard to realize such a thing as to realize on Mt. Olivet that from there Christ arose."[57]

Yet Melville was convinced of the "finality" of Christ's

55. Horsford, *Journal*, pp. 145–51.
56. Ibid., p. 139. *Clarel*, 2, 195–96.
57. Horsford, *Journal*, pp. 141–42, 164.

message as a religion. To him this "finality" was symbolized in the Golden Gate. The Roman or Byzantine structure, "one of the most interesting things in Jerusalem," was supposed to occupy the position of the eastern gate of the Jewish Temple and was identified by Christian tradition with the Beautiful Gate in the Acts of the Apostles. As Melville noted, it was associated with Christ as the gateway through which he had passed on his way to Bethany and the Mount of Olives and through which he made his way into Jerusalem at Passover. The gate, situated in the east wall of the old Temple grounds on the site of the Mosque of Omar, was opened by the crusaders twice a year, but was subsequently walled up by the Turks because of the tradition, which Melville records, that Jerusalem would be taken through this gate by a Christian conqueror who would enter on a Friday.[58] To Melville the walling up of the Golden Gate seemed "expressive of the finality of Christianity, as if this was the last religion of the world,—no other, possible."[59] Thus the failure of "the last religion of the world" signified the failure of all religion.

The *Journal* and *Clarel*, like all of Melville's works, reveal Melville's lifelong persistence in a search for what Hawthorne called "a definite belief." This persistence colors the *Journal* as a record of travel, so that the scenery and people that are described have, as they do in *Clarel*, the symbolical significance of the doubloon, the riveted gold coin in *Moby-Dick*. They are "set apart and sanctified to one awe-striking end": the attempt to define the human condition and the nature of the godhead. The vision probing

58. The tradition is reported in various guidebooks, e.g. *Three Weeks in Palestine and Lebanon* (Boston, 1836), p. 56. On Melville's use of guidebooks see Horsford, *Journal*, p. 10, n. 13. Murray's *Handbook for Travellers in Syria and Palestine* was not published till 1858.
59. Horsford, *Journal*, p. 145.

the mystery of the universe envelops the most factual record of things seen, e.g. Constantinople:

> Up early; went out; saw cemeteries, where they
> dumped garbage. . . . No plan to streets. . . . Perfect
> labyrinth. Narrow. Close, shut in. If one could but get
> up aloft, it would be easy to see one's way out. . . . saw
> a woman over a new grave— . . . . Called to the dead,
> put her head down as close to it as possible as if calling
> down a hatchway or cellar; besought— 'Why dont you
> speak to me? My God!— It is I!— Ah, speak— but one
> word!'—All deaf.—So much for consolation.—[60]

It is Melville's quality of relating everything which he did
and saw to "everything that lies beyond human ken," which
distinguishes the *Journal* and *Clarel* from other writings,
both in prose and poetry, which recorded similar journeys
and noted identical scenes, e.g. the picturesqueness of
Oriental life in the bazaars of Constantinople and Cairo,
the architectural beauty of Moslem fountains and mosques,
the lattice-work in the windows of harems, or the sharp line
of desert and verdure in Egypt. To Melville this line was
"plainer than that between good and evil."

Yet there was also a crossing. When Melville, on Tuesday,
December 16, 1856, took the steamer up the Bosporus, the
strait which not only separates but unites West and East, it
was, like all his voyages, a profoundly symbolical action:
"Magnificent! The whole scene one pomp of art and nature.
Europe and Asia here show their best." "The Continents"
is a poem inspired by this crossing from Asia to Europe in
which both worlds are encompassed in one oceanic vision
of beauty. It was written when Melville remembered "Fruit
of Travel of Long Ago." Like *Billy Budd,* it was published
posthumously, when the immortal yearnings of Melville's

---

60. Ibid., pp. 79, 89.

spirit had bridged the gulf between the unknown and the
known:

> From bright Stamboul Death crosses o'er;
> Beneath the cypress evermore
> His camp he pitches by the shore
> Of Asia old.
>
> Requiting this unsocial mood
> Stamboul's inmyrtled multitude
> Bless Allah and the sherbert good
> And Europe hold.
>
> Even so the cleaving Bosphorus parts
> Life and Death. —Dissembling hearts!
> Over the gulf the yearning starts
> To meet—infold!

Bibliography

Because the aim of this bibliography is to acquaint the reader with the less familiar materials in the preceding study, it does not include either the standard editions of Melville's works or critical studies of him. Many are cited in the notes. They are well known to every specialist in the field; others are referred to the comprehensive check list in Milton R. Stern, *The Fine Hammered Steel of Herman Melville* (Urbana, 1957), and to the *Melville Bibliography 1952–1957*, compiled by the Bibliographical Committee of the Melville Society, multilithed by the Providence Public Library, 1959. The most important volume of Melville scholarship to have appeared since the *Bibliography* is *The Letters of Herman Melville* ed. Merrell R. Davis and William H. Gilman, New Haven, 1960. Two recent additions to Melville criticism are Merlin Bowen, *The Long Encounter*, Chicago, 1960; and Richard Harter Fogle, Melville's *Shorter Tales*, Norman, 1960.

First editions of Melville's individual works, both English and American, have been consulted in the Berg Collection and the Rare Book Room of the New York Public Library. So have the Melville Papers at the Houghton Library, Harvard; the Duyckinck Papers at the New York Public Library; and, for Melville's early years, the "Records" of the Young Men's Association of Albany at the Harmanus Bleecker Library, Albany, and the "Charging-Book" of the Albany Library at the New York State Library, Albany.

Most of the books which have survived from Melville's own library are now in the possession of the Houghton Library, Harvard University; the New York Public Library (Gansevoort-Lansing and Osborne Collections); and the Yale University Library (Yale Collection of American Literature). These and

other books owned and borrowed by Melville, essential to any
study of the man and his work, are listed in Merton Sealts' invaluable compilation: "Melville's Reading: A Check-List of
Books Owned and Borrowed," *Harvard Library Bulletin*, 2
(1948), 141–63, 378–92; *3* (1949), 119–30, 268–77, 407–21; *4*
(1950), 98–109; *6* (1952), 239–47. The annotations and markings
which occur in several of these books have been many times
carefully examined for their characteristics and significances,
in particular by William Braswell, "Melville as a Critic of
Emerson," *American Literature, 9* (1937), 317–34; and W. E.
Bezanson, "Melville's Reading of Arnold's Poetry," *PMLA, 69*
(1954), 367. Certain books surviving from Melville's library are
of special importance to this investigation because they deal
directly with the Near East. These are here listed in the order
of their acquisition by Melville as recorded in Jay Leyda's
indispensable *The Melville Log*, 2 vols. New York, 1951.

Hope, Thomas, *Anastasius; or Memoirs of a Greek,* 2 vols.
London, 1836. Acquired in 1849.

Sa'di, *The Gûlistân, or Rose-Garden. By Musle-Huddeen Shaik
Sâdy, of Sheeraz. Translated from the Original. By Francis
Gladwin. A New Edition,* London, 1822. Acquired in 1868.

Bartlett, William Henry, *Forty Days in the Desert, on the Track
of the Israelites; or, A Journal from Cairo, by Wady Feiran,
to Mount Sinai and Petra,* 5th ed. New York, Scribner, n.d.
Acquired in 1870.

———*The Nile-Boat; or, Glimpses of the Land of Egypt,* 5th
ed. New York, Scribner, n.d. Acquired in 1870.

Stanley, Arthur Penrhyn, *Sinai and Palestine in Connection
with Their History,* New York, 1863. Acquired in 1870.

Bartlett, William Henry, *Walks about the City and Environs of
Jerusalem*. London, Virtue, n.d. Acquired in 1870.

Omar Khayyām, *Rubáiyát of Omar Khayyám, the Astronomer-
Poet of Persia. Rendered into English Verse. First American
from the Third London Edition,* Boston, 1878. Acquired
around 1886.

Omar Khayyām, *Rubáiyát of Omar Khayyám, the Astronomer-
Poet of Persia. Rendered into English Verse by Edward Fitz-*

gerald, with an Accompaniment of Drawings by Elihu Vedder, Boston, Houghton, Mifflin [1886]. Acquired around its date of publication, 1886.

With the exception of *Anastasius,* the books in the above list date from the second half of Melville's life and are of direct importance to the study of *Clarel* and the rose imagery in Melville's poetry and later prose pieces.

Among the books which Melville is known to have owned, though the original copy has not survived, the most important source of Near Eastern fact and romance is William Beckford's *Vathek: An Arabian Tale, with Notes, Critical and Expository,* Standard Novels, 41, London, Bentley, 1834. *Vathek* was acquired in 1849 together with *Anastasius.* The two books were in Melville's possession before he wrote *Moby-Dick,* and details concerning them are recorded in his *Journal of a Visit to London and the Continent, 1849–1850,* ed. Eleanor Melville Metcalf, Cambridge, Mass., 1948. (For an introduction to Beckford and Beckfordism, a special field, see the brilliant and humorous essay by Sacheverell Sitwell, *Beckford and Beckfordism,* London, Duckworth, 1936. Full-length studies are Lewis Melville, *The Life and Letters of William Beckford of Fonthill,* London, 1910, and, more recently, H. A. N. Brockman, *The Caliph of Fonthill,* London, 1956.) Other books owned or borrowed by Melville which deal with the Near East, contain Near Eastern material, or are by authors whose preoccupation with the Near East had literary repercussions, are listed below. The editions Melville is known to have used are starred:

ENCYCLOPEDIAS

Bayle, Pierre, *An Historical and Critical Dictionary,* 4 vols. London, 1710.
*Chambers, Ephraim, *Cyclopaedia: or, An Universal Dictionary of Arts and Sciences,* 2 vols. London, 1728.

TRAVEL BOOKS

Gobat, Samuel, *Journal of Three Years' Residence in Abyssinia,* New York, 1850.

*Macgregor, John, *The Rob Roy on the Jordan, Nile, Red Sea, and Gennesareth, &c. A Canoe Cruise in Palestine and Egypt, and the Waters of Damascus,* New York, 1870.

*Palmer, Edward Henry, *The Desert of the Exodus; Journeys on Foot in the Wilderness of the Forty Years' Wanderings; Undertaken in Connection with the Ordnance Survey of Sinai and the Palestine Exploration Fund. With Maps and Numerous Illustrations from Photographs and Drawings Taken on the Spot by the Sinai Survey Expedition and C. F. Tyrwhitt Drake,* New York, 1872.

Sailing Directions for the Mediterranean, Part IV, the Levant, London, James Imray and Son, n.d.

Sandys, George, *A Relation of a Journey Begun An:Dom: 1610,* London, 1627.

*Thomson, William McClure, *The Land and the Book; or, Biblical Illustrations Drawn from the Manners and Customs, the Scenes and Scenery of the Holy Land,* 2 vols. New York, 1859.

HISTORY

Gibbon, Edward, *The History of the Decline and Fall of the Roman Empire,* 6 vols. Dublin, 1788–89.

Herodotus, Translated from the Greek, with Notes by the Rev. William Beloe, 4 vols. Philadelphia, 1814.

POETRY AND LETTERS

*Alger, William Rounseville, *The Solitudes of Nature and of Man; or the Loneliness of Human Life,* Boston, 1867. (Alger is the author of an "Introduction to Oriental Poetry" prefaced to an anthology which he edited, entitled *The Poetry of the East,* Boston, 1856.)

*Arnold, Sir Edwin, *The Poems: Containing The Light of Asia; Pearls of the Faith, or Islam's Rosary; and The Indian Song of Songs,* New York, Hurst [1879].

*Arnold, Matthew, *Poems,* Boston, 1856.

Carlyle, Thomas, *On Heroes, Hero-Worship, and the Heroic in History. Six Lectures,* New York, 1841.

*Fitzgerald, Edward, *Polonius: A Collection of Wise Saws and Modern Instances,* London, 1852.

*———*Works,* 2 vols. New York and Boston, 1887.

The London Carcanet. Containing Select Passages from the Most Distinguished Writers. From the Second Edition, New York, 1831. (The *Carcanet* contains poems by Byron, Moore, and Scott, whose romantic Orientalism and its effect on Melville are examined in William H. Gilman, *Melville's Early Life and 'Redburn,'* New York, 1951.)

*Thomson, James, *Vane's Story, Weddah and Om-el-Bonain, and Other Poems,* London, 1881.

*———*A Voice from the Nile, and Other Poems,* London, 1884.

Of special importance are the writings of the two Western prophets of romantic Orientalism: Byron and Moore. The following works of the two poets are listed by Sealts in his check list:

Byron, George Gordon Noel, *The Complete Works,* Paris, Galignani, 1842.

———*The Bride of Abydos.*

———*Don Juan,* 2 vols. London, Murray, 1837.

———*Dramas,* 2 vols. London, Murray, 1837.

———*Miscellanies,* 3 vols. London, Murray, 1837.

———*Tales,* 2 vols. London, Murray, 1837.

———*The Poetical Works,* 10 vols. Boston, Little, Brown [1851?].

Moore, Thomas, *Life of Lord Byron: With His Letters and Journals,* 6 vols. Boston, Little, Brown [1851?].

———*The Poetical Works ... Collected by Himself ... With a Memoir ... ,* 6 vols. Boston, Little, Brown, 1856 [1854?].

Unfortunately, there is only one full-length study, and this unpublished, on Byron and Byronism in Melville: Edward Fiess, "Byron and Byronism in the Mind and Art of Herman Melville," doctoral dissertation, Yale University, 1951.

To a student of Oriental romance and its impact on the romantics two short studies written at the beginning of the present century are still indispensable guides: Martha Pike Conant, *The Oriental Tale in England in the Eighteenth Century.* New

York, 1908; and Marie E. de Meester, *Oriental Influences in the English Literature of the Nineteenth Century.* Heidelberg, 1915. Highly important for a knowledge of the scholarly sources from which romantic writers drew their Oriental material is the classic work of the German Orientalist H. H. Schaeder, *Goethes Erlebnis des Ostens,* Leipzig, 1938.

The concrete evidence of Melville's reading has to be considered within the framework of the whole scope of contemporary writing on the Near East. The range is best defined by library catalogues and periodical publications:

CATALOGUES

A Catalogue of Books in the Albany Library. July 1828, Albany, 1828.
A Catalogue of Books in the Library of the Young Men's Association of the City of Albany, Albany, 1837.
Alphabetical and Analytical Catalogue of the New York Society Library, New York, 1850.

PERIODICALS

The American Quarterly Review, 22 vols. Philadelphia, 1827–37.
The American Review, a whig journal, devoted to politics and literature, 16 vols. New York, 1845–52.
Arcturus. A Journal of Books and Opinion, 3 vols. in 2, New York, 1841–42.
Blackwood's Magazine, Vols. 1–61, Edinburgh, 1817–47.
The Broadway Journal, 2 vols. New York, 1845–46.
The Dial. A Magazine for literature, philosophy, and religion, 4 vols. Boston, 1840–44.
The Edinburgh Review, Vols. 32–150, American edition, Boston, 1819–79.
The Foreign Quarterly Review, 37 vols. London, 1827–46.
Harper's Magazine. Vols. 1–70, New York, 1850–85.
The Knickerbocker, or New York Monthly Magazine, 66 vols. New York, 1833–65.
The Literary World, 13 vols. New York, 1847–53.

The Monthly Anthology and Boston Review, 10 vols. Boston, 1803–11.

The North American Review, Vols. 1–126, New York, 1815–80.

The Penny Magazine of the Society for Useful Knowledge, London, 1834.

Putnam's Monthly Magazine, 16 vols. New York, 1853–70.

The Quarterly Review, Vols. 1–155, London, 1809–83.

Sartain's Magazine, Vol. 5, Philadelphia, July–December 1849.

The United States Democratic Review, 42 vols. Washington and New York, 1837–59.

The virtually inexhaustible reservoir from which nineteenth-century writers in Europe and America drew their knowledge of the Near East consisted of encyclopedias, travel books, histories, biographies, translations of Oriental literature, and innumerable publications by scholars and literati of all kinds. In its influence the entire output ranks second to the great classic of all times: *The Arabian Nights.* By the middle of the nineteenth century one famous translation of this had become not only the bible of Oriental romance but a handbook on the manners and customs of the Near East: Edward William Lane, *The Thousand and One Nights, Commonly Called, in England, The Arabian Nights' Entertainments. A New Translation from the Arabic, with Copious Notes. Illustrated by Many Hundred Engravings of Wood, from Original Designs by William Harvey,* 3 vols. London, Charles Knight, 1841. Three earlier nineteenth-century editions are of special interest because of their popularity in America:

Arabian Nights' Entertainments: Consisting of a collection of stories, told by the Sultaness of the Indies . . . containing a better account of the customs, manners, and religion of the eastern nations . . . than hitherto published: Translated into French from the Arabian mss. by Mr. Gallard and now into English, from the Paris edition, New York, E. Duyckinck, 1815.

The Arabian Nights' Entertainments, carefully revised, and occasionally corrected, from the Arabic. To which is added, a selection of new originals. Also, an introduction and notes,

*illustrative of the religion, manners, and customs of the Ma-
hummedans. By Jonathan Scott*, 6 vols. Philadelphia, 1826.
The Arabian Nights' Entertainments. Complete in one volume,
Philadelphia, 1831.

The reader may find it rewarding to turn to the monumental
bibliography of the *Arabian Nights* in the nineteenth century
in Victor Charles Chauvin, *Bibliographie des ouvrages arabes
ou relatif aux Arabes, publiés dans l'Europe chrétienne de 1810
à 1885*, 4 vols. Liége, 1892–98. More manageable and recent is
the useful publication of the Institut Français de Damas: Nikita
Elisséeff, *Thèmes et motifs des Mille et Une Nuits. Essai de
Classification*, Beyrouth, 1949. The "Editor's Introduction" in
The Portable *Arabian Nights,* ed. Joseph Campbell, New York,
Viking, 1952, is short, well documented, and popular. Other
background material consulted for this study is listed in the
following groups. The names of authors mentioned by Melville
or definitely connected with him are marked with an asterisk.

GENERAL WORKS OF REFERENCE

Anthon, Charles, *A Classical Dictionary,* New York, 1845.
Brockelmann, Carl, *History of the Islamic Peoples,* trans. Joel
    Carmichael and Moshe Perlmann, New York, 1947.
Browne, Edward G., *A Literary History of Persia,* 4 vols. Cam-
    bridge, 1928.
Dictionary of American Biography, ed. Allen Johnson et al.,
    20 vols. New York, 1928–37.
Dictionary of National Biography, 63 vols. New York, 1885–
    1900.
*Dictionary of the Religious Ceremonies of the Eastern Na-
    tions,* Calcutta, 1787.
Encyclopaedia of Islam, 4 vols. Leyden, London, 1913–36.
Hastings, James, *Dictionary of the Bible,* New York, 1902.
Herbelot de Molainville, Barthélemy, *Bibliothèque Orientale,*
    4 vols. La Haye, 1777–79.
Kitto, John, *Cyclopaedia of Biblical Literature,* Edinburgh,
    1848.
The Legacy of Egypt, ed. S. R. K. Glanville, Oxford, 1942.

The Legacy of Islam, ed. Sir Thomas Arnold and Alfred Guillaume, Oxford, 1931.

The Legacy of Persia, ed. Arthur J. Arberry, Oxford, 1953.

Literary History of the United States, ed. Robert E. Spiller, Willard Thorp, Thomas H. Johnson, and Henry Seidel Canby, 3 vols. New York, 1948.

———— *Bibliography Supplement,* ed. Richard M. Ludwig, New York, 1960.

Nicholson, R. A., *A Literary History of the Arabs,* Cambridge, 1956.

Universal History, An, from the Earliest Account of Time to the Present, Compiled from Original Authors; and Illustrated with Maps, etc. 23 vols. Dublin, 1744–65.

TRAVEL BOOKS

Atkins, Sarah, *Fruits of Enterprise Exhibited in the Travels of Belzoni in Egypt and Nubia, Interspersed with the Observations of a Mother to Her Children,* Boston, 1824.

*Belzoni, Giovanni Battista, *Narrative of the Operations and Recent Discoveries within the Pyramids, Temples, Tombs, and Excavations, in Egypt and Nubia, and of a Journey to the Coast of the Red Sea, in Search of the Ancient Berenice, and Another to the Oasis of Jupiter Ammon,* London, 1821.

*Bruce, James, *An Interesting Narrative of Travels into Abyssinia to Discover the Source of the Nile,* Boston, 1798.

*Bry, Johann Theodor de, *Collectiones Peregrinationum in Indiam Orientalem et Indiam Occidentalem,* 3 vols. Frankfurt, 1590–1602.

Buckingham, J. S., *Travels in Assyria, Media, and Persia,* 2 vols. London, 1830.

*Burckhardt, John Lewis, *Notes on the Bedouins and Wahabys,* London, 1830.

————*Travels in Arabia,* London, 1829.

————*Travels in Nubia,* London, 1819.

————*Travels in Syria and the Holy Land,* London, 1822.

*Chateaubriand, F. A. R. de, *Travels in Greece, Palestine, Egypt, and Barbary, during the years 1806 and 1807,* Trans-

lated from the French by Frederic Shoberl, Philadelphia, 1813.

Clarke, E. D., *Travels in Various Countries of Europe, Asia and Africa*, 11 vols. London, 1816–24.

De Forest, J. W., *Oriental Acquaintance*, New York, 1856.

Denon, Dominique Vivant, *Travels in Upper and Lower Egypt, during the campaigns of General Bonaparte in That Country, and Published under His Immediate Patronage, Translated from the French by A. Aikin*, 2 vols. New York, 1803.

Fryer, John, *A New Account of East-India and Persia, Being Nine Years of Travels, Begun in 1672 and Finished 1681*, London, 1698.

A Handbook for Travellers in Syria and Palestine, 2 vols. London, J. Murray, 1858.

Hanway, Jonas, *Journal of Travels*, 4 vols. London, 1753.

*Harris, John, *A Compleat Collection of Voyages and Travels*, 2 vols. London, 1705.

*Herbert, Thomas, *Travels in Persia: 1627–1629*, ed. Sir William Foster, New York, 1929.

Ibn Haukal, *The Oriental Geography of Ebn Haukal*, trans. Sir William Ouseley, London, 1800.

*Kinglake, A. W., *Eothen, or Traces of Travel brought Home from the East*, New York, 1846.

*Lamartine, A. de, *A Pilgrimage to the Holy Land*, 2 vols. Philadelphia, 1835.

*Langsdorff, G. H. von, *Voyages and Travels in Various Parts of the World*, 2 vols. London, 1814.

*Layard, Sir Austen Henry, *Nineveh and Its Remains, with an Account of a Visit to the Chaldaean Christians of Kurdistan, and the Yezidis, or Devil-Worshippers, and an Enquiry into the Manners and Arts of the Ancient Assyrians*, New York, 1849.

*Leo Africanus, *A Geographical Historie of Africa, Written in Arabicke and Italian by John Leo a More . . . Translated and Collected by John Pory*, London, 1600.

Loftus, W. K., *Travels and Researches in Chaldaea and Susiana*, London, 1857.

*Martineau, Harriet, *Eastern Life,* Philadelphia, 1848.

Morier, James, *A Journey through Persia,* Philadelphia, 1816.

New Voyages and Travels, Consisting of Originals, Translations and Abridgements, 8 vols. London, 1814–22.

Niebuhr, Carsten, *Travels through Arabia and Other Countries in the East,* trans. Robert Heron, 2 vols. Edinburgh, 1792.

*Park, Mungo, *Travels in the Interior Districts of Africa: Performed under the Direction and Patronage of the African Association in the Years 1795, 1796, and 1797,* London, 1800.

Polo, Marco, *The Travels of Marco Polo. Greatly Amended and Enlarged . . . With Copious Notes . . . by Hugh Murray,* New York, 1845. Harper's Family Library, No. 173.

*Purchas, Samuel, *Hakluytus Posthumus, or Purchas His Pilgrimes,* 20 vols. Glasgow, 1905–07.

———*Pvrchas his Pilgrimage, or Relations of the World and the Religions Observed in all Ages and Places Discouered, from the Creation vnto This Present, in Foure Partes,* London, 1613.

Roberts, David, *The Holy Land, Syria, Idumea, Arabia, Egypt and Nubia, from Drawings Made on the Spot,* 3 vols. London, 1842.

*Russell, Michael, *History of the Present Condition of the Barbary States,* New York, 1835.

Sherley, Sir Anthony, *Travels into Persia,* London, 1613.

Slade, Adolphus, *Travels in Turkey, Greece, &c.,* 2 vols. Philadelphia, 1833.

Stephens, John Lloyd, *Incidents of Travel in Egypt, Arabia Petraea, and the Holy Land,* 2 vols. New York, 1837.

———*Incidents of Travel in Greece, Turkey, Russia and Poland,* 2 vols. New York, 1838.

*Taylor, Bayard, *Cyclopaedia of Modern Travel,* Cincinnati, 1856.

———*The Lands of the Saracen,* New York, 1859.

*Thackeray, W. M., *Eastern Sketches: A Journey from Cornhill to Cairo,* London, 1846.

*Thevenot, Jean de, *The Travels of Monsieur de Thevenot into the Levant. In Three Parts,* 3 vols. London, 1687.

*Volney, C. F. de, *Travels through Syria and Egypt*, 2 vols. London, 1788.
*Warburton, Eliot, *The Crescent and the Cross*, New York, 1845.

HISTORIES

Cantemir, Demetrius, *A History of the Growth and Decay of the Othman Empire*, trans. N. Tindal, London, 1756.
Dale, Thomas Aquila, *Campaigns of Osman Sultans, from the German of Joseph von Hammer*, London, 1835.
Fraser, James B., *Historical and Descriptive Account of Persia*, New York, 1841.
———*Mesopotamia and Assyria*, New York, 1845.
Gooch, G. P., *History and Historians in the Nineteenth Century*, London, 1955.
Habesci, Elias, *State of the Ottoman Empire*, London, 1784.
Hammer, Joseph von, *Geschichte des Osmanischen Reiches*, 10 vols. Pest, 1827–35.
———*Histoire de l'Empire Ottoman, depuis son origine jusqu'à nos jours*, 3 vols. Paris, 1844.
Hilprecht, V., *Explorations in Bible Lands during the 19th Century*, Philadelphia, 1903.
The History of Timur-Bec. Known by the Name of Tamerlain the Great, Written in Persian by Cherefeddin Ali, Translated into French by the Late Monsieur Petis de la Croix, Now Faithfully Render'd into English, London, 1723.
Knolles, Richard, *The Turkish History*, 3 vols. London, 1687–1700.
Lewis, Bernard, *The Arabs in History*, London, 1958.
Malcolm, Sir John, *The History of Persia*, 2 vols. London, 1829.
Mignot, Vincent, *History of the Turkish Empire*, from the French by A. Hawkins, 4 vols. Exeter, 1787.
Morgan, John, *A Complete History of Algiers*, London, 1731.
Ockley, Simon, *History of the Saracens, comprising the Lives of Mohammed and his Successors*, London, 1847.
Pliny's Natural History, in Thirty-Seven Books, Translated

by Ph. Holland, with Critical and Explanatory Notes, 2
vols. London, 1847–48.
*Strabo, *Geography,* trans. Horace Leonard Jones, 8 vols. Lon-
don, 1917–32.
Tott, François, Baron de, *Memoires of the Baron de Tott, on
the Turks and the Tartars,* 2 vols. London, 1785.
Tritton, A. S., *The Caliphs and Their Non-Muslim Subjects,*
London, 1930.

BIOGRAPHIES

Arberry, Arthur J., *Asiatic Jones,* London, New York, 1946.
Beattie, William, *Brief Memoir of the late William Henry
Bartlett,* London, 1855.
Beston, Henry, *The Book of Gallant Vagabonds,* New York,
1925. See especially chapters on Belzoni and James Bruce.
Boulainvilliers, Henri de, *The Life of Mahomet,* trans. from
the French, London, 1731.
Bush, George, *The Life of Mohammed,* New York, 1830.
Cary, H. F., *Lives of English Poets,* London, 1846.
Ceram, C. W. [Kurt W. Marek], *Gods, Graves, and Scholars,*
trans. from the German by E. B. Garside, New York, 1953.
See especially chapter on Belzoni.
Davis, Richard Beale, *George Sandys, Poet-Adventurer,* Lon-
don, 1955.
*De Quincey, Thomas, *Autobiographic Sketches,* Boston, 1853.
Ellis, S. M., *The Solitary Horseman, or the Life and Adven-
tures of G. P. R. James,* Kensington, 1927.
*Goethe, Johann Wolfgang von, *The Auto-Biography of Goe-
the. Truth and Poetry: From My Own Life,* trans. Rev. A.
J. W. Morrison, 2 vols. London, Bohn, 1848–49.
*Hawthorne, Julian, *Nathaniel Hawthorne and His Wife,* 2
vols. Boston, 1844.
*Haydon, Benjamin Robert, *Life of Benjamin Robert Haydon,
Historical Painter, from His Autobiography and Journals,*
ed. T. Taylor, London, 1853.
Hewitt, R. M. "Harmonious Jones," in *Reginald Mainwaring
Hewitt (1887–1948). A Selection from His Literary Remains,*
ed. Vivian de Sola Pinto, Oxford, 1955.

*Irving, Washington, *Mahomet and His Successors*, 2 vols. New York, 1849–50.

Lamb, Harold, *Tamerlane: The Earth Shaker*, New York, 1928.

*Layard, Sir Arthur Henry, *Autobiography and Letters*, 2 vols. London, 1903.

Lives of Eminent Persons, London, Library of Useful Knowledge, 1833.

Merriman, R. B., *Suleiman the Magnificent*, Cambridge, Mass., 1944.

Otter, William, *The Life and Remains of the Rev. Edward Daniel Clarke*, London, 1824.

Sanborn, Alvan F., ed., *Reminiscences of Richard Lathers*, New York, 1907.

Sparks, Jared, *The Life of John Ledyard*, Cambridge, 1828.

Wolf, Lucien, *Sir Moses Montefiore. A Centennial Biography, with Selections from Letters and Journals*, New York, 1885.

RELIGION AND THOUGHT

Arberry, Arthur J., *Sufism: An Account of the Mystics of Islam*, New York, 1950.

*Bacon, Francis, *The Essays, and a Discourse of the Wisdom of the Ancients*, London, 1696.

Brown, John P., *The Dervishes: or Oriental Spiritualism*, Philadelphia, 1868.

——*The Darvishes*, London, 1927.

Browne, Edward G., "Some Notes on the Literature and Doctrines of the Hurufi Sect," *Journal of the Royal Asiatic Society, 61–89*, January 1898.

De Sacy, Silvestre, *Exposé de la religion des Druzes*, 2 vols. Paris, 1838.

——"Mémoire sur la dynastie des Assassins et sur l'étymologie de leur nom," *Mémoire de l'institut Royal*, Classe d'histoire et de littérature ancienne, *4* (1818), 1–84.

Dunbar, Flanders, *Symbolism in Medieval Thought*, New Haven, 1929.

Eliade, Mircea, *The Myth of the Eternal Return*, trans. from the French by Willard R. Trask, New York, 1954.

Garnett, Lucy M. J., *Mysticism and Magic in Turkey*, London, 1912.

Gibb, H. A. R., *Mohammedanism: An Historical Survey*, New York, 1954.

Hammer, Joseph von, *Die Geschichte der Assassinen, aus morgenlaendischen Quellen*, Stuttgart and Tübingen, 1818.

———*The History of the Assassins*, London, 1835.

Horowitz, Josef, *Koranische Untersuchungen*, Berlin and Leipzig, 1926.

*Hume, David, *Essays and Treatises on Several Subjects*, 4 vols. London, 1770.

Hyde, Thomas, *Veterum Persarum et Parthorum et Medorum Religionis Historia*, Oxford, 1760.

Illustrated Commentary on the Old and New Testaments, from the Best and Most Authentic Sources, London, 1840.

Jackson, A. V. W., *Zoroaster*, London, 1899.

*Jones, Sir William, *Institutes of Hindu Law or The Ordinances of Menu, Verbally Translated from the Original, with a Preface, by Sir William Jones*, London, 1825.

Keightley, Thomas, *The Fairy Mythology*, 2 vols. London, 1833.

Lane, Edward William, *An Account of the Modern Egyptians*, 2 vols. London, 1842.

Lewis, Bernard, *The Origins of Ismā'īlism*, Cambridge, 1940.

———"The Sources for the History of the Syrian Assassins," *Speculum*, 27 (1952), 475–89.

Maurice, Thomas, *Indian Antiquities*, 2 vols. London, 1800.

Narrative of a Mission of Inquiry to the Jews from the Church of Scotland in 1839, ed. A. A. Bonar and R. M. M'Cheyne, Philadelphia, 1842.

*Plutarch, *The Philosophy, Commonly Called, The Morals*, trans. Philemon Holland, London, 1657.

———*Plutarch's Morals, trans. from the Greek by Several Hands. Cor. and Rev. by William W. Goodwin . . . With an Introduction by Ralph Waldo Emerson . . .* , 5 vols. Boston, 1870.

Prideaux, Humphrey, *The True Nature of Imposture Fully Display'd in the Life of Mahomet*, London, 1697.

Rowe, Henry K., *The History of Religion in the United States,* New York, 1924.

Sale, George, *The Koran,* translated from the original Arabic, with Explanatory Notes, to which is prefixed *A Preliminary Discourse,* 2 vols. London, 1825.

Spence, Lewis, *Myths and Legends of Ancient Egypt,* London, 1922.

A Summary View of the Millenial Church, or United Society of Believers, Commonly Called Shakers, Albany, 1848.

Timur the Great, *Institutes, First Transl. into Persian by Abu Taulib Alhusseini; and Thence into English, with Marginal Notes,* by Major Davy, Oxford, 1783.

*Tucker, Abraham, *An Abridgement of the Light of Nature Pursued,* London, 1807.

POETRY AND LETTERS

'Antar: A Bedoueen Romance, trans. from the Arabic by Terrick Hamilton, 4 vols. London, 1819.

Arberry, Arthur J., *Fifty Poems of Hafiz,* Cambridge, 1947.

——*Omar Khayyām. A New Version Based upon Recent Discoveries,* New Haven, 1952.

——*Persian Poems. An Anthology of Verse Translations,* London, 1954.

——*The Romance of the Rubáiyát,* London, 1955.

*Arnold, Matthew, *Essays in Criticism,* Boston, 1865.

The Asiatic Miscellany, Consisting of Translations, Imitations, Fugitive Pieces, Original Productions, and Extracts from Curious Publications, ed. W. Chambers and Sir W. Jones, Calcutta and London, 1792.

Asin, Miguel, *Islam and the Divine Comedy,* London, 1926.

*Carlyle, Thomas, *Sartor Resartus,* New York, 1844.

Costello, Louisa Stuart, *The Rose Garden of Persia,* London, 1845.

*Curtis, George William, *The Howadji in Syria,* New York, 1852.

——*Nile Notes of a Howadji,* New York, 1856.

Dante, *Dantis Alighierii Epistolae,* ed. Arnaldo Monti, Milan, 1921.

———*The Letters of Dante*, trans. and ed. Paget Toynbee, Oxford, 1920.

Davidson, Lucretia Maria, *Amir Khan and Other Poems, with a Biographical Sketch by Samuel F. B. Morse*, New York, 1829.

*De Quincey, Thomas, *Confessions of an English Opium-Eater*, Boston, 1841.

Disraeli, Benjamin, *Tancred: or The New Crusade*, 3 vols. London, 1847–50.

*D'Israeli, Isaac, *Romances*, London, 1799.

Du Vigneau, Sieurde Joanots, *Le Secretaire Turc, contenant l'art d'exprimer ses pensées sans se voir, sans se parler & sans s'écrire*, Paris, 1688.

*Emerson, Ralph Waldo, *Complete Works*, ed. Edward Waldo Emerson, Centenary Edition, 12 vols. Boston, 1903–04.

———*Journals*, ed. Edward Waldo Emerson and Waldo Emerson Forbes, 10 vols. Boston, Houghton, Mifflin, 1909–14.

———*Letters*, ed. Ralph L. Rusk, 6 vols. New York, 1939.

Firdausi, *The Poems of Firdosi*, trans. by Joseph Champion, Calcutta, 1785.

———*The Shah-Namah of Firdausi. The Book of the Persian Kings, Described by J. V. S. Wilkinson*, London, 1931.

Fuller, S. M., *Conversations with Goethe in the Last Years of his Life, Translated from the German of Eckermann*, Boston, 1839.

Fundgruben des Orients, Mines d'orient, ed. Joseph von Hammer-Purgstall, 6 vols. Vienna, 1809–18.

Garnett, Richard, *Essays of an Ex-Librarian*, New York, 1901.

Gladwin, Francis, *Ayeen Akbery, or the Institutes of the Emperor Akber*, trans. from the original Persian by Francis Gladwin, 2 vols. London, 1800.

*Goethe, Johann Wolfgang von, *West-Oestlicher Divan*, Akademie der Wissenschaften in Berlin, 3 vols. ed. Ernst Grumach, Berlin, 1952.

———*West-Eastern Divan*, in twelve books, trans. Edward Dowden, London, 1914.

Hammer, Joseph von, *Geschichte der schoenen Redekuenste Persiens, mit einer Bluethenlese aus zweihundert persischen Dichtern*, Vienna, 1818.

*Hawthorne, Nathaniel, *Complete Writings,* 22 vols. Boston and New York, 1900.

*Irving, Washington, *The Alhambra,* Philadelphia, 1832.

———*Biography and Poetical Remains of the late Margaret Miller Davidson,* Philadelphia, 1841.

*Jones, Sir William, *Works, with the Author's Life by Lord Teignmouth,* 13 vols. London, 1807.

*La Motte-Fouqué, Friedrich Heinrich Karl de, *Undine, and Sintram and His Companions,* New York, 1845.

Lowes, John Livingston, *The Road to Xanadu,* New York, 1959.

*Mayo, W. S., *Kaloolah, or Journeyings to the Djebel Kumri: An Autobiography of Jonathan Romer,* New York, 1850.

Montagu, Lady Mary Wortley, *Letters and Works,* 3 vols. London, 1837.

Morier, James, *Ayesha: The Maid of Kars,* Paris, 1834.

The Oriental Collections, ed. Sir William Ouseley, 2 vols. London, 1797–99.

Ouseley, Sir William, *Persian Miscellanies,* London, 1795.

*Poe, Edgar Allan, *The Works of the Late Edgar Allan Poe, with a Memoir by Rufus Wilmot Griswold and Notices of His Life and Genius by N. P. Willis and J. R. Lowell,* New York, 1859.

Richardson, John, *A Dissertation on the Languages, Literature, and Manners of Eastern Nations,* Oxford, 1778.

Robinson, Samuel, *Persian Poetry for English Readers,* Glasgow, 1883.

Ross, Sir Denison, *A Persian Anthology,* trans. from the Persian by E. G. Browne, London, 1927.

Scott, Jonathan, *Bahar-Danush; or, Garden of Knowledge. Transl. from the Persic of Einaiut Oollah,* 3 vols. Shrewsbury, 1799.

*Scott, Sir Walter, *Works,* 5 vols. Edinburgh, 1806.

Smiles, Samuel, *A Publisher and His Friends. Memoir and Correspondence of the Late John Murray,* 2 vols. London, 1891.

*Smith, Albert, *A Month at Constantinople,* New York, 1852.

*Southey, Robert, *Thalaba, the Destroyer,* 2 vols. London, 1814.

Tholuck, F. A. G., *Bluethensammlung aus der morgenlaen-dischen Mystik, nebst einer Einleitung ueber Mystik ueber-haupt und morgenlaendische insbesondere,* Berlin, 1825.
*Thoreau, Henry D., *Journal,* ed. B. Torrey and F. H. Allen, Boston, 1949.
Voltaire, *Oeuvres complètes,* ed. L. E. D. Moland, 52 vols. Paris, 1877–85.

MISCELLANEOUS

Bell, Millicent, "Hawthorne's 'Fire-Worship': Interpretation and Source," *American Literature, 24* (March, 1952), 30–39.
Bodkin, Maud, *Archetypal Patterns in Poetry,* New York, 1958.
Bonwick, James, *Pyramid Facts and Fancies,* London, 1877.
Brooks, Van Wyck, *New England: Indian Summer,* New York, 1940.
Cassirer, Ernst, *Freiheit und Form,* Berlin, 1918.
Comptes rendus hebdomadaires des séances de l'Academie des Sciences, Paris, Bachelier, 1845.
Curtis, James, *A Dissertation upon Odd Numbers, Particularly No. 7 and No. 9,* London, 1909.
Dieckmann, L., "The Metaphor of Hieroglyphics in German Romanticism," *Comparative Literature, 7* (Fall 1955), 306–312.
Gallery of Antiquities, Selected from the British Museum by F. Arundale.
Hope, Thomas, *Household Furniture and Interior Decoration,* London, 1807.
Lancaster, Clay, "The Egyptian Hall and Mrs. Trollope's Bazaar," *Magazine of Art, 43* (1950), 94–99.
Lewis, R. W. B., *The American Adam,* Chicago, 1955.
Miller, Perry, *The Raven and the Whale,* New York, 1956.
Prideaux, W. F., *Notes for a Bibliography of Edward Fitz-gerald,* London, 1901.
Tauchnitz, Bernhard, *The Harvest. Being the Record of One Hundred Years of Publishing, 1837–1937,* Leipzig, 1937.
A Treatise upon the Law of Copyright, London, 1902.
Turner, Arlin, *Hawthorne as Editor,* Baton Rouge, University of Louisiana, 1941.

Williams, Stanley T., and Mary Allen Edge, *A Bibliography of the Writings of Washington Irving,* New York, 1936.

Finally, there is the central question of bibliographical material on the subject of Near Eastern influences in American literature. This is an area which has not yet come into its own. The short bibliography in the *Literary History of the United States* (ed. Robert E. Spiller et al.) is concerned with nineteenth-century Americans who traveled to the Near East. Significantly, there is no additional material in the "Bibliography Supplement" (ed. Richard M. Ludwig) of 1960. Arthur E. Christy's *The Asian Legacy and American Life* (New York, 1942) is a collection of essays by various specialists and is modeled on the British "Legacy" series (see above, p. 291). It is a convenient and useful general survey of the entire field, indicating Asian influences in music, art, agriculture, literature, religion, and thought. The only full-length study of a major American writer's use of the Orient is Frederic Ives Carpenter's *Emerson and Asia* (Cambridge, 1930), which was succeeded by Christy's *The Orient in American Transcendentalism. A Study of Emerson, Thoreau, and Alcott,* New York, 1932. K. W. Cameron's edition of Emerson's poem *Indian Superstition* is prefaced by *A Dissertation on Emerson's Orientalism at Harvard,* Hanover, N.H., 1954. These books cover the entire area of the Near East, the Far East, and the South East and are valuable pioneer efforts.

James Baird's *Ishmael* (Baltimore, 1958) is in a class by itself, not only because it is primarily concerned with Melville's psychological experience of Oceania but also because of its complex Jungian approach. An important scholarly contribution within a limited, narrow scope of the type which is essential to any progress in the field are the articles by J. D. Yohannan, "Emerson's Translations of Persian Poetry from German Sources" and "The Influence of Persian Poetry Upon Emerson's Work," both in *American Literature, 14* (1943), 407–20; and *15* (1943), 25–41. A series of similar, systematic investigations of detail in major and minor American writers is a still unfulfilled preliminary requirement to a much-needed study of Near Eastern patterns in American Literature.

Index

Abelard, Peter, 196
Abulfeda, Abu'l-Fidā (Arab historian), 229
Abyssinia (Ethiopia), 49–51, 137
Adams, Henry Brooks, 15
Aegean Sea, 263
Africa, 18, 43, 46, 49, 151, 168. *See also* Algiers; Barbary; Berbers; Egypt; Ethiopia; Libya; Morocco; Nubia; Red Sea
Ahmazd, Hormazd (highest Zoroastrian god), 159–60
Ahmed III, Sultan of Turkey, 274
Ahriman (Zoroastrian god), 160
Akbar the Great (Jalāl-ad-Dīn Muhammad), 14
Al-. *See under second element of name*
Albania, 58
Albany Academy, 209 n.
Albany Library, 26, 42, 123
Albany Young Men's Association, 27, 32, 42, 43, 58, 123
Alcott, Amos Bronson, 13
Alexander the Great, 133
Alexandria, Egypt, 53, 131, 263. *See also* Ramleh
Alger, William Rounseville, 253
Algiers, 43, 264. *See also* Africa; Barbary
Amenhotep III, King of Egypt, 137
America. *See* Central America; Lima; New England; New York; Palenque; Yucatan
"American Magazine of Useful and Entertaining Knowledge," 52

American Quarterly Review, 44, 92
American Review, 22–24, 157, 163
Ammon. *See* Jupiter Ammon
Anacreon (Greek lyric poet), 221, 240
Andersen, Hans Christian, 40
Anquetil-Duperron, Abraham Hyacinthe, 157, 159 n.
Antar ('Antarah ibn-Shaddād al-'Absi), 171
Anthon, Charles, 206
Appolinopolis, temple of, in Edfu, 129 n.
Arabi, Mohijeddin al-, 218
Arabia, Arabian, 4, 158, 181; travelers in, and travelogues on, 16, 52, 58, 65, 75, 88, 172; romances, 17–18, 56–57, 192, 194–97, 208, 219, 223, see also *Arabian Nights*, Romance; elements in HM and others, 41, 51, 171, 213, 214, 216, 235; language and terms, 44, 81, 83, 84, 85, 110, 193, 197, 204, 221, 222, 226, 228–30; natives mentioned, 84, 125, 127, 150, 251, 269. *See also* Bedouins; Et Tih; Hedjaz; Holy Land; Islam; Mecca; Medina; Petra; Red Sea; Sinai
Arabia Petraea, 75
Arabian Nights: and HM, general discussion of, 26–41; influence of, as literary type, 18, 42, 57, 189, 192, 214; contemporary articles on, 24, 194, 196, 210; names and information from, 113, 170, 187, 194, 199, 204, 206, 208, 214, 215, 221, 223, 224 n. *See also* Arabia; Romance